PSYCHOLOGY FOR PERFORMING ARTISTS

BUTTERFLIES AND BOUQUETS

PSYCHOLOGY FOR PERFORMING ARTISTS

BUTTERFLIES AND BOUQUETS

Glenn D. Wilson

Jessica Kingsley Publishers
London and Bristol, Pennsylvania

First published in the United Kingdom in 1994 by
Jessica Kingsley Publishers Ltd
116 Pentonville Road
London N1 9JB
and
1900 Frost Road
Bristol
Pennsylvania

Library of Congress Cataloguing-in-Publication Data
Wilson, Glenn, D. (Glenn Daniel)
Psychology for performing artists: butterflies and bouquets /
Glenn Wilson.
p. cm.
Includes bibliographical references and index
ISBN 1-85302-166-0 (pbk.)
1. Acting--Psychological aspects. I. Title
PN2071.P78W56 1994
792'.028'019--dc20

British Library Cataloguing in Publication Data
Wilson, Glenn D.
Psychology for Performing Artists:
Butterflies and Bouquets
I. Title
152.4

ISBN 1-85302-166-0

Printed and Bound in Great Britain by
Biddles Ltd., Guildford and King's Lynn

CONTENTS

PREFACE

Modern psychology has much to offer performing artists in terms of under-standing themselves and optimizing their art. It can explain the instinctual origins of the impulse to act and make music. It can examine the two-way relationship between performer and audience including social processes such as identification, charisma, idolization and group facilitation. It can describe the way in which emotions are transmitted to an audience by non-verbal processes such as posture and facial expression. It can test theories about the nature of humour and the power of music to influence our emotions. It can tell us what kind of people are attracted to performing and why, and the particular stresses that they are subject to. It can offer suggestions as to how stage fright can be managed and optimum performance achieved.

At the same time, the study of theatre is of great value to psychologists because it is a vital part of life. Essentially human preoccupations and conflicts are played out on stage and in films, not just for entertainment, but also for self-discovery, catharsis and impetus to social change. The power of theatre to influence individual and social behaviour has never been doubted by those who advocate sexual or political censorship of the entertainment media.

Psychology, then, as 'the science of behaviour and experience' and theatre as 'a mirror to life' each has a lot to offer the other. Psychology is analytic where theatre is holistic, but a great deal can be learned about a structure by taking it apart and putting it back together again. Laurence Olivier once remarked, after an exceptionally applauded performance of King Lear, 'I know it was great, but I don't know how I did it, so I don't know if I'll be able to do it again'. It is hoped that readers of this book will be less likely to find themselves in this condition of (albeit enviable) uncertainty.

This book has evolved out of courses taught at Stanford University, San Francisco State University and the University of Nevada, Reno. It replaces my first textbook on the topic, *The Psychology of Performing Arts*, published by Croom-Helm in 1985, but it is more than an updated revision. In the nine years since I compiled that book, the field has not only burgeoned, but has developed in integrity. The 'snake bites its tail' a great deal more than previously, with work in the different areas overlapping and interlocking to form a coherent branch of psychology, where previously there was just a disjointed collection of studies at the interface of psychology and the performing arts. The niche has well and truly consolidated over the last decade and it is my hope that this book will further its appeal within psychology and theatre arts departments around the world.

I should make clear that no attempt is made to undercut the training provided by drama and music teachers. The psychological perspective provided herein is intended to complement a traditional theatre arts training, not rival or supplant it. Psychologists will never be in a position to take over the training of performers from the specialists and experienced practitioners. As comedian Ken Dodd once said, 'The trouble with Freud is he never played the Glasgow Empire first house'. Nevertheless, I believe that the science of psychology does have something to add, and can clarify or give a new aspect to knowledge gained from direct experience.

In line with my own background and interest, classical drama, music and opera are concentrated upon, with most of the examples being drawn from these areas. Readers whose primary interest is in popular music, dance, mime, acrobatics, juggling, conjuring or other types of performance may find less of specific interest to themselves. However, most of the general principles, for example those relating to movement and gesture, the use of space on stage, attention-getting devices, communication with an audience, and coping with performance anxiety, will be seen to have application to performance of all kinds.

Many of my students were graduate psychologists and talented performers who contributed ideas to this book through term papers and classroom discussion. In this respect I would particularly like to thank Cheryl Bartley, Ruth Glasgow, Andi Cartier, Craig Dale, Daniel Petersen, Catherine Watt, Jerry Le Clair, Lucinda Scott-Smith and James Kuthy. I also benefited from discussions with professional actors and musicians, especially Andrew Downie, David Coussell and Carol Wells. Finally, I wish to thank Dr Paul Insel who initiated the idea for this course and persuaded Stanford University to experiment with it, and Professors Robert Solso, Jerry Ginsburg and Neal Ferguson who sponsored it at the University of Nevada, Reno.

Glenn D. Wilson

CHAPTER 1

THEATRE AND HUMAN EXPRESSION

Aspects of the theatrical experience form an important part of the lives of most people. Not everybody goes to see a Shakespearean play at Stratford-upon-Avon, an opera at the Metropolitan, or attends an orchestral concert in Vienna. But nearly everyone will have seen an adventure film like *Star Wars*, watched a 'soap' or police drama on television, been entertained by a comedian at a nightclub, a clown at the circus or a magician at a party, or listened to a politician making an election speech. What, if anything, do all of these experiences have in common?

At first sight the differences may seem more significant than the similarities. But they are all forms of entertainment. One person or group of people (the performers) are doing something that they hope will engage the interest and imagination of others (the audience). Supposing they succeed in this aim, what is it they have contributed to their audience or to society?

This chapter is concerned with the effects that theatre (in its broad definition) has upon individuals and society, for better or worse. Is it simply that we enjoy it, and if so why? Are there some deeper benefits that we seek and sometimes achieve, for example emotional catharsis, education or ennoblement? Is our enjoyment of theatre dependent on the author's ability to parade his or her conflicts and preoccupations in a way that connects with our own? In other words, is relevance the key to engagement of our interest? Can we be harmed by the entertainment to which we are exposed (e.g. depraved and corrupted), and if so, what are the conditions under which this is likely to occur? These are some of the questions addressed here.

EXCITEMENT

One of the most obvious functions of theatre in all its various forms is that of providing stimulation in a world that all too often threatens to bore us to tears. Humans are curious animals, with a certain lust for novelty and experience, if only to keep our huge brains ticking over and occupied. We have evolved an elaborate problem-solving mechanism in our cerebral cortex (more advanced than anything IBM is yet able to offer) and we retain from earlier phases of evolution a 'flight-fight' emergency system in the mid-brain which is geared for dealing with life-threatening situations such as the sudden appearance of a sabre-toothed tiger. Both of these facilities we have a need to exercise, just as a domestic dog likes to retrieve sticks.

Since there are few tigers stalking the streets of Clapham, and our daily routine often involves monotonous, repetitive tasks, we create our own monsters and diversions to keep ourselves intrigued and feeling alive. Theatrical entertainment is one of the ways in which we do this. A striking thing about many forms of entertainment, whether it be Wagner's *Ring Cycle* or heavy metal rock, *Macbeth* or *Indiana Jones,* is the apparent intention of the creator to produce an experience that will stimulate the senses and the emotions – something with 'impact'.

Of course, we do not always want greater excitement. If we are feeling stressed we may instead choose some entertainment that will relax us (soft music or a gentle comedy). And there are individual differences in the tendency towards sensation-seeking. Some people characteristically have a need for change and excitement in all aspects of their life (e.g. holidays, sex, work and entertainment) while others prefer a quiet, stable, familiar life style. People who score high on a scale of 'psychoticism' (characterised as impulsive, nonconforming and unempathic individuals) are drawn to graphically violent horror films and are uninterested in light comedy and romance (Weaver 1991). Sensation-seekers are also inclined to be 'grazers' and 'zappers' as regards their use of a TV remote control, finding it more difficult to settle on any particular channel (Schierman and Rowland 1985). Personality differences of this kind appear to be constitutional and can be traced to the prevalence of certain brain chemicals or 'neurotransmitters' such as monoamine oxidase (Zuckerman 1991).

Much of our behaviour is concerned with adjusting arousal to some optimal level. Entertainment can be used for 'kicks' in much the same way as 'white knuckle rides' at funfairs, gambling or fast motorcycle racing, but equally, it can be used for relaxation.

VICARIOUS EXPERIENCE

A particular form of excitement or escape from monotony that theatre and films often provide is that of indulging our pleasurable fantasies. That which is missing in our humdrum everyday life may be provided indirectly by way of the fantasies that are evoked in entertainment. For many women this is romance, or perhaps even seduction by a powerful man who happens to be available and motivated to pursue a long-term relationship. The typically male fantasy of triumph over competitors, enemies and attractive young women is obvious in films such as *Rambo* and the James Bond series. As a broad generalisation, it is still largely the case that women are preoccupied with social relationships and bonding, hence their enjoyment of soaps and romantic comedies, while men are more concerned with achievement and dominance, which is why they prefer to watch westerns, sport and documentaries (Austin 1985). Of course, there is plenty of overlap between the sexes, and many other fantasies that entertainment may engage but, generally speaking, plays and films are successful to the extent that they lock into the salient needs, fears and desires of the audience.

Sometimes the relevance of a theme to human fantasy is not immediately obvious and requires deeper analysis. For example, it is often asked what is the special appeal of horror stories such as *Dracula*, which have appealed over many generations and which seem to have a special fascination for women. It may be explained by recent theories developed by ethologists that for evolutionary reasons (dating right back to the reptilian era) male sexuality depends upon dominance while female arousal can be facilitated by fear and submission (Medicus and Hopf 1990). Hence many women gain a sexual tingle from being frightened, however much they may protest that they don't enjoy the experience. In addition, the *Dracula* myth is a barely disguised seduction metaphor. A tall, dark, handsome stranger of few words (but those intoned in a deep voice) makes a sudden appearance and with overwhelming authority proceeds to penetrate a vulnerable part of the body of a buxom young woman, draws blood and lays claim to her soulful devotion thereafter. This is like Jane Austen with the added frisson of fear. One does not need intensive training in psychoanalysis to appreciate the significance of themes such as this.

Another favourite character in horror movies, *Frankenstein*, impinges upon human psychology in more various ways. Sometimes the story is concerned with our fears of being destroyed by runaway technology, or the tendency of science to depersonalise people and turn them into mindless automatons (sometimes called 'future shock'). At other times our sympathy is evoked for an innocent, misunderstood and victimised monster (cf. *The Elephant Man*, *Beauty and the Beast* and *Phantom of the Opera*). The psychological significance of recurrent themes and characters is discussed further in Chapter 2.

Not all fantasies are concerned with providing gratification or wish-fulfilment. Some are more broadly exploratory and have a kind of 'educational' function (Wilson 1978). Apart from fantasizing about the things we most desire, we often think about the things we most dread, in order that we might better prepare ourselves to meet the contingency. This is a more likely explanation for the frequency with which we dream of much-feared events such as rape and death, and the popularity of disaster movies such as *Earthquake* and *The Towering Inferno*. The same applies to many classic tragedies and operas. Observing other people in desperate situations and seeing how they make out gives us an opportunity to rehearse our own emotional reactions and behavioural strategies so that we may cope better if something similar should befall us.

CATHARSIS

The gaining of ascendancy over horror, and especially traumas from our own past, is the essence of what has been called 'catharsis'. This is derived from a Greek word meaning 'purification' and it refers to a release of tension that is supposed to follow from the powerful unleashing of pent-up emotions, induced by theatre (especially tragic drama and opera). A similar idea was taken up by the psycho-analysts Breuer and Freud when they developed their couch therapy using the techniques of hypnosis, free association and dream analysis. Their concern was to relieve neurosis through 'abreaction', the release, and hence removal, of the crippling emotion associated with unpleasant childhood experiences which have been repressed into the unconscious mind.

Psychodrama, which will be discussed in greater detail in Chapter 12, com-bines elements of the Greek theatre and psychoanalytic traditions in a form of group psychotherapy based on dramatic improvisation of troubling life situations. Another procedure that was fashionable in the 1970s was called 'primal scream' therapy, the idea being that simply yelling and screaming as loudly as possible would somehow get frustration out of the system.

What exactly is released by powerful, emotional experience, and whether or not any benefit is gained, is controversial in psychological theory. Some psycho-logists think that emotions such as aggression, fear and sexual arousal are 'drives' which are reduced in the course of their expression. If so, the best way to cope with strong emotions might be to become aware of them and confront them. However, the mere experience of the emotion is probably not sufficient for it to be released. Some kind of consummation or resolution is usually necessary for drive reduction. Experiencing hunger does not diminish it; only eating will.

Although the original Greek concept of catharsis described the effects of tragedy on an audience, scientific work on the topic has been concerned mainly with the question of whether viewing violence (in films or on TV) leads to a reduction or an increase in real-life aggression. Early evidence indicated that fictional portrayals of violence could produce a discharge of aggressive feelings (Feshbach 1961). Since then, the greater weight of evidence has supported the argument that violence in the media increases aggressive behaviour in society through *imitation* and *desensitisation* (Eysenck and Nias 1978). Repeated exposure to fictional violence leads us to view aggression as normal and reduces our fear of its consequences, thus weakening resistance to acting aggressively.

It is important to make the distinction between an emotion and the type of behaviour that emotion gives rise to. Video 'nasties' such as *Driller Killer*, may liberate aggressive behaviour in certain people without necessarily making them more angry. As social learning theorists such as Bandura (1973) point out, the viewer may model his subsequent behaviour on what he has seen in the film because it gives him a new idea for something to do, or allows him to think of it as normative and less anti-social. In other words, manifest aggressive behaviour may be increased in individuals and society without any increase in anger or other emotions.

One of the most interesting studies relevant to the possible cathartic effects of witnessing violence made use of real historical events. Phillips (1980) studied the archives of Victorian England to examine connections between executions and the subsequent murder rate. He found that well-publicised executions, such as that of the notorious Dr Crippen, produced a striking deterrent effect for a week or so immediately afterwards. However, there was then an *increase* in murders above the norm, returning to base level about six weeks later. This study, which has renewed relevance with the return of public executions to American television, suggests that the horror of witnessing an execution causes a temporary inhibition of murderous tendencies in society which is offset by a later 'catching up' phase. Thus the idea that simply seeing somebody killed is cathartic in the sense of eliminating the urge to kill further is not supported, and the hoped-for deterrence effect is short-lived.

INDIVIDUAL DIFFERENCES

Both kinds of effect (decreases and increases of aggression) following the representation of violence may be possible depending on the individuals concerned and the precise circumstances. Gunter (1980) argues that catharsis of aggression occurs only for audience members who are skilled and creative in the use of imagination. He discusses evidence that 'the practised daydreamer can turn to fantasy activity to work out or resolve anger-arousing problem situations, whereas the inexperienced daydreamer is more limited to the direct behavioural expression of aggression'. He goes on to argue that the cathartic fantasy does not itself have to be violent (e.g. imagining hitting the boss after being refused a raise) as Freudian theory might suppose; it may involve pleasant, distracting themes such as dating and getting good grades at college. What matters is the individual's imaginative skill, not the thematic context of the fantasy. Since creativity relates to intelligence, this might explain a finding of Feshbach and Singer's (1971) that catharsis occurred only for middle-class boys given a diet of violent TV programmes, whereas working-class boys showed no reduction in the tendency to real aggression. Gunter suggests that the middle-class boys may have been better able to invent satisfying mental scenarios, where the working-class boys needed a direct physical outlet for the aggressive impulses aroused by the TV films.

Sex differences in catharsis have also been observed. In a study by Hokanson (1970), the blood pressure of subjects was monitored as they were made angry by deliberately cantankerous behaviour on the part of the experimenter's accomplices. In the case of men, their blood pressure returned to normal faster if they had been open in expressing their anger. However, the blood pressure of women returned to normal more quickly if they had been friendly to the experimenter's stooge rather than aggressive. Perhaps outwardly hostile behaviour is a more natural consummation of anger for men than it is for women, who have more civilised ways of dealing with aggressive feelings.

A similar sex difference appears as a consequence of viewing violence on TV and in films. Aggressive behaviour in the viewer is sometimes increased as a result of seeing violent movies, but the effect is most striking in young boys (Eysenck and Nias 1978). Little girls seem relatively immune. Some supposed that this would change with the advent of aggressive heroines such as The Bionic Woman, Charlie's Angels and Cagney and Lacey, but the fashion for such female models was fairly short-lived. Today's heroines have largely reverted to 'mother-earth' figures such as Roseanne and Oprah Winfrey.

INTEGRAL CONSUMMATION

An important factor determining whether emotional arousal increases or decreases related subsequent activities is that of whether or not any internal resolution of that arousal is available. There is evidence that the immediate expression of aggression reduces the likelihood of later hostile acts. Providing the opportunity for an angered person to 'act out' his or her hostility on the spot, reduces the need for subsequent displays of anger, even though the total aggressive output remains much the same (Deux and Wrightsman 1984). Apparently, aggressive acts reduce hostile fantasies and feelings, but the reverse does not hold; arousing the emotion does not reduce the likelihood of the act – on the contrary, it usually increases it unless some form of gratification can be achieved in fantasy or imagination.

If catharsis occurs when an emotion is consummated rather than just aroused, it is important to consider whether a film or dramatic performance provides *within itself* a resolution of the passions it evokes. Is justice arrived at by the time the film ends or the curtain comes down, or is the viewer left with a sense of deep frustration? A film that is frequently cited as one that is likely to provoke violence in susceptible people is *Straw Dogs,* in which Dustin Hoffman plays the part of a meek, introverted, American mathematician who seeks solitude for his work in a remote cottage in Cornwall. However, the locals turn out to be hostile, and he is harassed to breaking point. After his wife has been raped, an attempt is made to storm his house, and he proceeds to eliminate the intruders one by one with a variety of ingenious devices. The bulk of the film is devoted to arousing his anger (and vicariously that of the viewer) while the climax consists of the unmitigated discharge of his wholly justified rage. Such a pattern is not uncommon in violent films (e.g. Westerns and 'vigilante' movies) as well as classical plays (Macbeth gets his come-uppance after slaughtering Macduff's children). It is reasonable to hypothesise that without such release of hostility the audience would be more disposed to violence as they left the theatre. Unfortunately, relevant experiments, such as comparing the aggressiveness of audiences who have watched the whole of *Straw Dogs* with that of audiences who have watched only the first (anger-induction) half, do not seem to have been done, so much of the research that purports to examine the catharsis hypothesis fails to take account of what may be the most important variable.

With respect to sex, the position is also complicated. In the short term at least, erotica increases our sex drive, making us more liable to masturbate or have intercourse (Brown *et al.* 1976). Yet convicted sex criminals such as serial rapists and paedophiles do not appear to have had excessive exposure to pornography, either in general or specific to the nature of their crime. On the contrary, they are more likely to have been protected from it while young and thus perhaps missed out on a kind of inoculation which could have conferred immunity to psychologically damaging effects later on in life (Goldstein *et al.* 1971; Cook *et al.* 1971). As we shall see, however, there are ways in which certain forms of pornography may increase the likelihood that 'normal' men will engage in 'date rape'.

Perhaps the biggest difference between aggression and sex is that the sex drive can never be resolved vicariously. Whereas it may be possible to have someone else fight your battles or take revenge on your behalf, you cannot deputize somebody else to have your sex for you. Satisfaction can only be achieved by doing it yourself (for reasons that will readily be appreciated by anyone acquainted with sociobiology). Because of this characteristic of libido it is very difficult for a film or play to provide us with sexual release. Erotica and pornography can be effective in arousing sexual needs, but watching somebody else have an orgasm on the screen does little to discharge the excitement of the viewer. This being the case, the only sense in which catharsis could occur is for the sequence of being 'turned on' by pornography and consummating this arousal by intercourse or masturbation soon afterwards to lead to a reduction of sexual desire for the following day or so.

The emotion of fear could be resolved to some extent if everything turns out all right after all (the danger passes, or the monster is slaughtered). Fear and pity were central to the emotions evoked by Greek tragedies, but it is notable that these plays seldom arrived at a happy ending such that this could account for any catharsis that might occur. The possibility that some catharsis consists of a reduction of fear by affiliative bonding among audience members will be discussed in Chapter 3.

AUDIENCE AWARENESS

Scheff (1976, 1979) has offered a psychoanalytic hypothesis concerning the manner in which emotional arousal produced by watching a drama can be 'cathartic' even in the absence of a happy ending. Scheff says that when an audience watches a play that arouses their emotions, the reason they are aroused is because the action of the play touches upon situations that have occurred in their own lives in the past and therefore evokes emotional memories. In other words, drama does not create new emotional distress but revives old distress under relatively safe conditions. Scheff suggests that catharsis will occur provided two conditions are met: (1) there is sufficient identification with the characters and recognition of the situation for previously unresolved emotions to be rearoused, and (2) there is sufficient awareness that the current situation is really safe (i.e., that it is only a play and not for real).

Scheff introduces the concept of 'balance of attention', suggesting that the ideal is for audience attention to be absorbed roughly evenly between the distress restimulated by the play and the 'safe present' (awareness that one is sitting in a theatre watching actors engaged in fictional portrayals). In these circumstances, Scheff supposes that the emotional traumas of the past can be discharged to some extent. If no emotional disturbance is induced the play fails, but if the audience is too caught up in the restimulated distress they will be overwhelmed (as they were in the original situation) and no therapeutic benefit will be obtained. The similarity of this theory to one concerned with the mechanism of humour (Chapter 7) will be apparent.

As with many psychoanalytic hypotheses, this one is hard to test, however plausible it sounds. The best support that Scheff could offer was to cite clinical reports to the effect that patients often show striking improvement following abreaction, and that abreaction only seems to occur when the therapeutic situation is perceived by the patient as non-threatening. We shall return to this issue of therapeutic 'distancing' of drama in Chapter 12.

Of course, as Scheff notes, the cathartic benefits of drama are likely to be as much social as individual. If the content of a drama touches upon shared tensions in a community then collective discharge will, it is hoped, occur. That is, there will be an overall reduction in tensions within society and a renewal of social bonds between members of the audience.

THE ROLE OF THE MESSAGE

Whatever the content of a play or film (violence, horror, explicit sex, etc.) another aspect that almost certainly helps to determine its effect upon us, for good or ill, is the message or 'moral' it conveys. Many, if not all, dramatic works are trying to communicate some idea or attitude, to teach us a lesson or convince us in some way. *Macbeth*, for example, might be thought to contain a warning about the dangerous effects of runaway ambition; *Othello*, the perils of jealousy. More obviously, a film like *One Flew Over the Cuckoo's Nest* is concerned to point out the possible misuse of psychiatry as social control of awkward behaviour rather than medical treatment. The effect that these works have upon an audience will depend upon how successful they are in modifying our outlook; that is, how well they function as propaganda on the part of the author (always remembering that attempts to persuade can sometimes backfire and cause us to harden our attitudes in the opposite direction).

Even something that is superficially just entertainment may also convey a message. Cartoons such as *Popeye* and *Tom and Jerry*, which, incidentally, have been widely criticised as violent in content, may indirectly teach the moral that 'bullies will get their just desserts', or that 'might is not right, and will not prevail'. Thus, whenever the potential harm of a play or film is considered, its potential benefit should also be taken into account.

Of course, not all 'morals' are to the social good. Certain films, like the *Rambo* series, might be thought to justify outgroup hostility. Many people felt disquiet when the President of the United States (Ronald Reagan) quoted Clint Eastwood's famous phase, 'Go ahead – make my day' in a context of international confrontation.

While some people deplore pornography because they feel threatened by explicit sexuality, feminists are more particularly concerned with the implicit message that it may impart, in other words, the way in which it might modify attitudes, and hence behaviour, towards women. Masterson (1984) reviews evidence that certain types of pornography may increase the likelihood that susceptible males will rape by reinforcing the perception of women as sex objects, or worse still, or will eventually enjoy sadistic, coercive sex and get optimal satisfaction that way.

The lyrics of many modern pop songs are sexually provocative and hostile. Rap, in particular, is often blatantly racist and anti-police. When in 1992 a 19-year-old Texan driving a stolen car shot dead a policeman who stopped him, his plea for leniency was based on the claim that he was unduly influenced by the music he was listening to at the time. The lyrics of the record, sold commercially, included:

> 'Cops on my tail, so I bail till I dodge them/Remember Rodney King/And I bust his punk ass/Now I got a murder case... /What the fuck would you do?/Drop them or let them drop you?/I choose droppin' the cop.'

> (2 pac Amuru Shakur)

The distributors, Time-Warner, justified themselves by claiming 'an obligation to ensure the voices of the powerless, the disenfranchised and those at the margins are heard' (*Sunday Times*, 24th October 1992).

There is also concern that we may be corrupted by *subliminal* messages, those that are below the threshold of conscious perception. In the US the producers of pop records have sometimes been charged with implanting, within pop songs, hidden messages such as 'get the gun and try it' that have driven teenagers to suicide or anti-social behaviour. One reason for this kind of prosecution is that a freedom of expression clause in the US constitution protects explicit rock lyrics, whereas messages directed at the subconscious mind may not be so immune. These cases have so far been dismissed because they failed to prove the existence of the purported subliminal incitements, let alone their effectiveness.

Research evidence concerning the effect of subliminal persuasion is mixed. Most experts believe that stimuli that are truly below threshold or otherwise outside the bounds of *possible* perception cannot influence our behaviour, whereas those that are outside of present awareness, but which could be appreciated *if attended to*, may well affect us. This of course applies to advertisements which are all around us and which we may think we can ignore. Even though we do not register them consciously, because our attention is directed elsewhere, we are nevertheless influenced by them, and sometimes all the more so because our defences are down.

CENSORSHIP

There is no doubt that, while we may gain benefits from the theatrical experience, certain dangers have to be considered as well. The unleashing of hitherto restrained instincts and passions might endanger the performer himself (in whom psychosis might be precipitated), members of the audience (who may be morally corrupted), members of the public (e.g. victims of rape or violence outside the theatre) or society at large (e.g. political destabilisation). In all of these instances it might be supposed that the greatest danger would ensue when the performance aroused powerful emotions, such as anger or frustration, without providing any outlet or reassurance.

The concern is not new. Television is under particular attack in the modern world but music hall and melodrama were regarded as corrupting in Victorian days. In the 18th century *The Beggars' Opera* by John Gay was held to be responsible for an increase in highway robbery because the highwayman MacHeath was depicted as a hero.

The operas of Wagner have a long history of being suspected of harmful consequences, even by Wagner himself. Not only was he grandiose and exploitative to the point of psychopathy, but he feared that the expression of his mind and feelings through his works might threaten the sanity of others. In a letter to his enamorata, Mathilde Wesendonk he wrote:

> 'Child, this *Tristan* is turning into something fearful. This last act!!! I'm afraid the opera will be forbidden – unless the whole thing is turned into a parody by bad production – only mediocre performances can save me. Completely good ones are bound to drive people mad. I can't imagine what else could happen.'

> (Magee, 1969, p.77)

This might have seemed nonsense had not the tenor who sang Tristan in the first performance died shortly afterwards in a 'delirium of Wagner worship' (Magee 1969). Wagner held his work responsible, although of course it could have been sheer coincidence. Similar fates have befallen several other well-known singers of their time, including two more Tristans and a Brunhilde. Intense identification with a role sometimes seems on the face of it to have proved fatal, as, for example, when the American baritone Leonard Warren actually died almost on cue at the end of a performance of *The Force of Destiny*.

Those who denounce Wagner's music as inherently evil make a plausible case for its social destructiveness. As Magee (1969) says, 'It speaks with almost overpowering eloquence of incest wishes, unrestrained eroticism, of hatred and malice, the whole dark side of life'. In a sense it is hostile to society and therefore might have special appeal to unstable and paranoid people. Hitler loved it, and there are some who believe that it provided impetus for the Nazi movement and its atrocities. To this day, the works of Wagner are effectively banned in Israel, and some individual people admit fear of what excessive exposure to Wagner might unleash in them.

It is hard to evaluate the validity of these fears. We should avoid reading too much into the occasional death of a performer on stage; people have heart attacks in many different situations – about as often while asleep in bed as when jogging or making love. Likewise, unstable and psychotic people can take their cue from virtually any source – a Blake poem, a Hogarth etching, the Bible, or a full moon. It would be impossible to protect such people from all the possible triggers to violent or insane behaviour, therefore we should hesitate to blame a work of art for the anti-social act that might appear to have been inspired by it.

This argument has not prevented authorities in all parts of the world, and throughout history, from taking it upon themselves to decide what the masses should and should not be allowed to see at the theatre and in films. Sometimes, as in modern European society, it is mostly sex and violence that is subject to control, but historically censorship has often been politically or religiously motivated.

Molière's *Tartuffe*, which is a satire on religious hypocrisy, lasted one night in 1667 before being banned in France, and the Archbishop of Paris threatened with excommunication anyone who so much as read it in private. There has been very little change in attitude since then; as recently as 1967, Catholics were forbidden by Church authorities to attend a Los Angeles production.

The Beaumarchais play upon which Mozart's *The Marriage of Figaro* is based was banned because of its anti-aristocratic content, and the opera only just passed the censors because the non-vernacular language and musical jollity were thought sufficient to deflect and obscure the political message. Even so, some historians regard this opera as instrumental in sparking off the French revolution, and hence a series of upheavals throughout the Continent.

Verdi was always in trouble with the Italian censors because his operas dealt with tyranny, which the authorities somehow managed to identify with themselves. Characters had to be changed (e.g. the playboy Duke Of Mantua in *Rigoletto* was demoted from a king) and locations were made more remote (e.g. Sweden became New England in *A Masked Ball*). Puccini's *Tosca* is another opera that depicts a corrupt aristocracy and has a revolutionary theme and was thus threatened with censorship.

Psychologists sometimes get up in court and say that books and films have no power to harm anyone. This is almost certainly not true. Any work of art that provides intense emotional experience is bound to carry with it an element of risk. Therefore, it is really a case of weighing pros and cons. Does the 'cathartic' or other value of the work outweigh the danger that people will be adversely affected? This is not an easy matter to answer.

There is also the question of who decides what is right for whom? Concern for the integrity of individuals is often a poor mask for political motivation. Those in authority wish to preserve the *status quo,* and so fear 'revolutionary' art. Fortunately, democratic societies have the opportunity for change by non-violent means built into them, so there is less need to fear the revolutionary passions inspired by theatre or any art form.

There is particular concern today that pop music and the 'culture' which surrounds it, may be responsible for a breakdown in sexual and other morality among the young. While this might seem irrefutable to the older generation, a possible alternative is that pop music *reflects* a general increase in permissiveness and ill-mannered behaviour rather than causing it. Insofar as it is possible to untangle causal priorities among social movements and artistic expression, the latter interpretation seems to fit the facts better. Moore, Skipper and Willis (1979) conducted a content analysis of the performance style, lyrics and personal life of pop musicians over the last three decades and compared these with sexual mores prevailing at the time. Their conclusion was that rock music represents societal standards more obviously than it initiates change in them.

It appears that pop idols are chosen by their fans in much the same way that society chooses its political leaders – largely by a process of consensus. Because the pop music of any time is used by young people to express their rebellion against the older generation, it is easy for older people to arrive at the belief that it is the prime cause of moral decay. This would explain the perennial demands for censorship of pop songs, as well as the eventual failure to suppress the perceived evil.

EXPOSURE OF THE AUTHOR

Literary analysts have long recognised that any work of fiction, and perhaps especially drama, reveals something of the psychology of its author. This is the principle upon which projective tests of personality such as the Rorschach Inkblots are supposed to work and is the theory behind the diagnostic use of patients' poems and paintings. The more people are thrown onto their own resources in producing a work of art, the more they must draw upon their personal experiences, needs and preoccupations.

A playwright writing dialogue for Napoleon has to imagine himself into the mind of his character just as the paranoid schizophrenic may imagine that he *is* Napoleon. The latter may throw himself into the part more intensely and may be unable to distinguish fantasy from reality; otherwise, the main difference between them is in relevance to large numbers of people and the skill with which they document their experiences and fantasies (Esslin 1976).

When a playwright enters the mind of his various characters in turn he must use imagination based on aspects of his own experience. In creating Macbeth, Shakespeare might draw upon the ruthless and ambitious side of his own personality and in writing lines for Lady Macduff he may examine his own gentle and loving feelings. He might also base characters on other people that he knows well or has closely observed, but plays, like novels, frequently have autobiographical content.

Some writers fear that what they create is so idiosyncratic that the public might think them mad or perverted. When he wrote his first play *The Bald Primadonna*, Ionesco hesitated to have it staged because he doubted that it would appeal to anyone else. He was both delighted and relieved to discover that audiences found it funny, thus apparently understanding the secret fantasies that he feared might have stemmed from a private madness.

A tendency towards neurosis or psychosis can contribute to the creative process. Many eminent composers were manic-depressives who were particularly productive during the manic phase of their illness, or whose works showed mood swings that paralleled the condition of the writer (Frosch 1987; O'Shea 1990). Playwrights may also draw upon their own mental disturbances to generate interesting material for their works. Jamison (1989) found that no less than 63 per cent of dramatists had received treatment for psychological disorders, mostly depression. Poets seemed to be even more deeply disturbed; about half of them had been treated for manic-depressive illnesses with drugs such as lithium or anti-depressants, had ECT (shock therapy) or spent time in hospital. It may not be necessary to be mad to be creative, but apparently it sometimes helps. Indeed, genetic analyses using the twin-comparison technique confirm the link between creativity and psychosis.

Plays may appeal to an audience, or be interpreted, at different levels of meaning (Esslin 1976). First is the level of *concrete reality*, in which attention is focused on what the characters are actually doing and saying. For example, a slapstick comedian may be struggling with a recalcitrant motor car, or a prince investigating his dad's suspicious death and trying to raise the courage to kill the likely murderer. This is the simplest form of appreciation, but it may be quite sufficient for the enjoyment of an entertainment.

Second is the level of *poetic metaphor*, where broader allegorical associations are evoked, such as the idea of man and machine being natural enemies, or the general moral dilemma of whether revenge is a justifiable motive for taking the life of another person. Most significant works of drama lend themselves readily to the consideration of wider social and philosophical issues such as this and the intelligent audience spends much of its time following the work at this meta-level rather than the concrete level.

The third level of analysis, which concerns mainly the literary critic and the dynamic psychologist, is that of speculation concerning *the author's fantasy life*. This is the question of whether aspects of the author's psychology are partial determinants of the themes about which he writes and the way that his characters respond to the situations in which they find themselves. Does the author feel insecure in the context of rapidly advancing technology, such that his own car makes him feel inadequate? Did he suffer as a child because his father was usurped by another man that his mother insisted he call 'uncle'? These are possibilities, and it is interesting to reflect upon them, though it should be recognised that verification will not always be possible.

Interactions among these levels have been used by dramatists throughout history to add psychological depth to their works. In ancient Greek tragedy the 'chorus' was a commentator who highlighted the broad truths of which the actual events were examples. Medieval morality plays had characters who personified general principles but who would also be recognised by the audience as particular people in the community. The same is true of the Gilbert and Sullivan operettas, which could be enjoyed either as pure nonsense or biting social satire. Sir Joseph Porter, who appears in *HMS Pinafore* as the First Lord of the Admiralty who had never been to sea, was modelled on W.H. Smith, the well-known bookseller, who fitted this description in the day. Similarly, the books of Dr Seuss and the cartoons of Walt Disney may be enjoyed by children at the concrete level, but there is usually a deeper moral which is apparent to adults and which may be absorbed at some level of awareness by children.

The allegorical significance of a play depends partly upon the perceptions and prime concerns of the audience. The *avant garde* play *Waiting for Godot* deals explicitly with disappointed expectations but is variously interpreted according to the political climate prevailing in the country in which it is seen. Anglo-Americans usually interpret it religiously, but landless Algerian peasants are reported to have seen Godot as the oft-promised but never delivered land reform, while Poles saw it in terms of the national independence so long denied them. The play itself simply evokes an emotion, while the audience themselves provide the context.

Much the same is true of Wagner's *Ring Cycle*. Ambiguity is deliberately introduced to widen its appeal. Directors who specify the scenes, characters and era too precisely demonstrate their ability to perceive one possible solution to the work, but in so doing they restrict the scope of the audience's imagination. There is a danger that the director's specific interpretation will obstruct the process by which the writer has set out to stimulate the subconscious of the audience in looser and more personal ways.

There is nothing to stop an audience or critic from seeing more in a play than the author had intended or was conscious of at the time of writing. By the same token, there is nothing to say that they are wrong in doing so. Hamlet's hypothesised Oedipus complex (Bynum and Neve 1986) may have been a part of Shakespeare's insight into human nature that was deliberately incorporated into his character, or it may have been part of Shakespeare's own psyche that crept unwittingly in. Alternatively, the Oedipus complex may exist only in the Freudian imagination of the critic who observes it. It is difficult to know and probably not very important so long as the work is so powerfully evocative of so many thoughts and feelings, to so many people, over such a long time.

OBSESSIONS OF COMPOSERS AND WRITERS

Looking at the works of the greatest operatic writers, it is possible to see in them certain recurrent themes that appear to betray personal preoccupations. This could hold true even of composers who did not write their own lyrics, since they were usually very influential in choosing their subjects.

Father/daughter scenes appear with great frequency in the operas of Verdi. Typically, they love each other very deeply but the father loses his daughter in some tragic manner. This is probably related to the fact that Verdi's young wife and two of his children died within a period of two years towards the beginning of his career. At the time he was trying to write a comic opera, which not surprisingly failed, and for a while he felt he would never be able to write again. Then followed his great tragedies, many of which (*Luisa Miller, Rigoletto, La Traviata, Simon Boccanegra*) featured the theme of parental loss. Apparently, Verdi's personal tragedy had equipped him to write with particular power and insight on this subject.

Puccini's speciality was in subjecting frail and attractive heroines to slow torture and destruction at the hands of evil or misguided people. This does not necessarily mean he was inclined toward sadistic fantasies. More likely, he found he had hit upon a winning formula – a most emotive subject about which he could write effectively. Perhaps, as a youth, he was particularly taken by Verdi's *La Traviata* (as any sensitive person of his day would reasonably have been) and this remained his model throughout life. *La Rondine*, one of his least performed operas, is almost a remake of *La Traviata*, and may have suffered because of that, but many of his favourite operas contain echoes of Verdi's masterpiece.

Benjamin Britten did much the same to young men as Puccini did to beautiful women – subjected them (operatically) to cruel, inhuman treatment. His homosexual orientation was probably relevant here, together with the feelings of being misunderstood and isolated which resulted from this, and which apparently led to self-imposed exile first in America and then in Aldeburgh, a remote part of the Suffolk coast.

Mozart wrote about sexual infidelity with such insight and enthusiasm that it is easy to suppose that he had personal experience of the subject. This is consistent with his reputation as a womanizer, though of course he was a young man even when he died, and this theme is, in any case almost ubiquitous within comedy.

Wagner wrote at length about power struggles and the quest for ideals, themes which conspicuously parallel his tendency to be grandiose and ambitious in real life. Another theme that dominates several of his operas, that of gaining peace and salvation through death, also seemed to derive from a personal death wish. In a letter to Franz Liszt, Wagner (1851) wrote

> If I think of the storm of my heart, the terrible tenacity with which, against my desire, it used to cling to the hope of life, and if even now I feel this hurricane within me, I have at least found a quietus which, in wakeful nights, helps me to sleep. This is the genuine, ardent longing for death, for absolute unconsciousness, total non-existence. Freedom from all dreams is our only final salvation. (p.271)

Many observers have noted that Andrew Lloyd Webber's most successful work, *The Phantom of the Opera* contains autobiographical elements, particularly the central theme of a talented composer, highly introvert and insecure about his looks, who selects and elevates to stardom a beautiful soprano, with whom he falls tragically in love.

W.S. Gilbert is a particularly interesting writer from the point of view of psychological analysis. In a most compelling study of the relationship between Gilbert's life and writings, Eden (1986) traces his obsessions with torture and execution and large, dominant, aging women to emotional fixations derived from events occurring to him in infancy. To anyone familiar with the Savoy operas, this is a fascinating case study of how a writer's personality problems may be manifest in their works.

These examples illustrate that the themes selected for musical treatment by a writer, especially when unmistakably repetitive, give clues as to the personal nature and problems of that writer. Certainly, there is sufficient reason to believe that they *sometimes* do, though unflattering dynamic interpretations should be reserved until more straightforward, parsimonious explanations have been eliminated.

One such alternative theory (Chapter 2) is that these themes recur because they were selected by audience appeal and that the writer was simply supplying to his public what he knew they wanted. With respect to opera, we, the public, have taken to our hearts such a limited number of 'great' composers and their works that whatever they may or may not tell us about themselves, they certainly reveal something about ourselves.

ORIGINS OF PERFORMANCE

The role that theatre plays within human psychology is better understood through an examination of its origins. By this, I refer not to the history of theatre as conventionally taught, but to the instinctual and anthropological bases of the impulses that lead inevitably to the appearance of drama and performance in human society. Can we detect precursors of human performance in animal behaviour? Are there certain characteristics or capacities of the human brain that promote the development and enjoyment of performing arts? Can we gain insight into the psychic and social functions of performance by observing the rituals of so-called 'primitive' societies? And do the repetitive themes of classic and popular works of drama reveal anything about the central preoccupations and fantasies of human beings? These are the sort of questions addressed in this chapter.

PLAY AND FANTASY

One of the most obvious psychological roots of theatrical performance is that of *play*. All mammals, especially advanced primates, like to explore the environment around them, exercise innate skills and test the limits of their own physical and mental capacities. The survival advantage of such an instinctual tendency is self-evident. By means of play, the young animal becomes familiar with the environment and gains increasing control over it. Play provides a variety of sensory-motor experience and practice for life.

When two young monkeys engage in mock combat, they are establishing dominance (finding out who is boss) as well as rehearsing skills that may one day be called upon in real battle, either with a rival member of their own species or their natural enemies. The gaining of experience is the more universal function of play. In the game of 'cat and mouse' there is little doubt about who is dominant. The cat lets its prey escape and recaptures it again repeatedly so as to gain practice for future hunting episodes; but only when immediate hunger is not pressing. Solo play, as when a child climbs a tree, or a dog chases a ball, is likewise practising skills and learning the laws of physics for future occasions. It is no accident that dramatic works are called 'plays', for increased experience and rehearsal for life is one of the main rewards they offer.

But play is not just physical. Because of our advanced brains we have an innate capacity for, and inclination towards, mental play, which we call *fantasy*. Anyone who has observed children growing up will have been impressed by their facility for inventing little games, imaginary friends, enemies, fairies and monsters, talking to plants and insects in the garden and treating their inanimate toys as living creatures. This is not ignorance, and it is not a sign of autism or schizophrenia. On the contrary, it is a highly advanced, creative and healthy activity, the mental equivalent of play. Perhaps above all other human capacities, the ability to generate and manipulate complex images within our own head, is responsible for human pre-eminence within the animal kingdom. Unfortunately, the capacity of imagination appears to be progressively lost, or at least suppressed, as we grow towards 'maturity' and become self-conscious, 'responsible' beings. For the adult, theatre and films are among the last socially acceptable outlets for the instinct of mental play.

As noted in Chapter 1, one of the most important functions of theatre in human society is to give us experience of situations that we do not encounter often enough in real life (experience that is vicarious for the actors, and vicarious at one step further removed for the audience). This explains why horror, disaster, rape, death and other such gruesome themes are so popular in films and plays. These are things we do not, in the ordinary course of events, experience in real life. Our own death, for example, can be experienced only once in reality and the death of people close to us is a rare event. It is not surprising that we seek to prepare ourselves for exceptional contingencies such as these, rehearsing our reactions and hence gaining better control of them through fantasy and play, one formalization of which is theatre.

Psychodrama, which has gained considerable popularity in many parts of America and Europe, consists of the therapeutic use of the exploratory and rehearsal functions of theatre. By acting roles and trying out solutions to relationship problems in the safety of the clinic, patients (or clients, as they are more often called today) can practise interpersonal encounters without being drastically punished for mistakes. Music does much the same for the emotions. It provides an intense but temporary (and therefore safe) evocation of feelings. And rather in the same way that jogging compensates for our sedentary physical existence, music is a diversion from the typical emotional flatness of everyday, mundane life.

We have discussed the expressive, abreactive rewards of performance in Chapter 1. In non-human primates it has been observed that loud, rhythmic vocal hooting, rising to an intense climax, and followed by vigorous activity (such as chest-beating in the mountain gorilla) is a common response to intense excitement. This may be socially contagious, setting off similar noisy reactions in other members of the troupe, especially adult males. To the human observer this looks like an exhibitionistic display of the type we call 'showing off'. The similarity to the spectacle of an Italian tenor completing an aria, with the subsequent burst of applause from the audience is appealing. The longer the period of vocalization in which the tension is allowed to build, the more pronounced is the ultimate applauding activity.

Live performance is not just a simulation of everyday behaviour, it is a biological *stimulator* (Pradier 1990). Actors, singers and dancers, when performing effectively, actually energize their audience. One symptom of this physical activation is the clapping, whistling, screaming and stamping of feet that is evoked from an audience that is really 'moved' by the performance. Pradier notes that this is how watching a performance differs from dreaming. In dreams our motor system is disconnected so as to prevent any physical expression of the schemes manufactured in the brain. Sporting activities are almost the reverse: motor activity being stimulated while cognitive functions are largely at rest. Performing arts (especially the 'living' kind, as opposed to technological ones such as film and TV) restore the integrity of mind and body while still maintaining the playful mode. The active performance will induce incipient movements in the audience that could theoretically be measured. Hence, says Pradier, performance may be thought of as a 'tonic dream'.

IMITATION AND MIMICRY

Another human instinct that is basic to human performance is that of *imitation*. Watching other people behave is a perpetual source of curiosity and amusement, whether we are on the beach, in a commuter train or viewing a soap opera on TV. One of the reasons for observing others so avidly is so that we can incorporate certain aspects of their behaviour into our own repertoire (while at the same time rejecting others that are seen to be less effective). Imitation is the primary way in which we acquire many aspects of our cultural behaviour, most notably language, etiquette and courtship techniques. Although certain birds like parrots and mynahs are more celebrated for their powers of mimicry, such a capacity is highly developed in children, who are able to imitate facial expressions at birth (Reissland 1988). The evolutionary significance of imitation is apparent; it assists greatly in the assimilation of cultural behaviour patterns and in communication with other members of the species.

In dramatic performance we draw upon the skills of imitation and mimicry in many ways. Perhaps most obviously we adopt accents in a holistic kind of way (which is the skill of impersonators such as Danny Kaye and Peter Sellers). In addition, we learn lines, and especially songs, primarily by imitation, and the very word 'mime' suggests that body language is also largely acquired by mimicry. In fact, the Roman *mimus* consisted of an imitative dance describing animal life and erotic practices (Pradier 1990).

INFORMATION PROCESSING

The human predisposition to generate and appreciate art also has foundations in the cognitive functioning of our highly advanced brains. Our perceptual system is equipped with fine-grain discrimination of auditory and visual patterns, and a remarkable memory capacity – abilities which have great value, for example, in recognizing people's faces and assessing the significance of noises. The pleasure gained in the exercise of this capacity for detailed perception in the visual and auditory modes no doubt contributes to our interest in many art forms.

We also have a need to impose order upon random and complex stimuli and to seek recognizable form. In other words, we are compelled to 'make sense' of our environment. We do not see a hole in the area of the visual field corresponding to the 'blind spot' where the visual tract departs the retina for the brain; rather we fill it in by logical processes, if necessary perceptually completing the pattern of the wallpaper we are looking at. And it is virtually impossible to listen to a series of even drum beats without grouping them into twos, threes or fours (correspond- ing to the most common musical metres). Most importantly, we carry in our brain abstract concepts like the shape of a tree or the sound of a snake, blueprints which we try to fit to incoming sensations so as to identify them. Perceiving patterns in the environment assists memory storage and retrieval and enables us quickly to detect dangers in the environment.

These capacities have not evolved in order to produce art, but their appearance in the human brain makes art possible or perhaps inevitable. Much of our enjoyment of music as well as visual art is in the satisfaction of finding order and meaning in seemingly complex patterns of stimuli, that is, in the exercising of higher brain faculties. Great art frequently requires some degree of mental 'work' on the part of the viewer or listener before reward is reaped, but satisfaction is all the more for that. The information-processing theory of art (Berlyne 1971) suggests that there is an optimum level of familiarity or uncertainty for any artwork/audience interaction. If a work of art is too obvious and predictable we become bored. If it is so complex that we surrender in the attempt to detect meaningful patterns we may also become bored, or even anxious. Many people, lacking the background experience or processing capacity to make sense out of great music, regard it as an assault upon their ears. For them it is like the trauma of being immersed in an alien culture in which there is nothing familiar to cling to. The same applies to abstract visual art; if too disorganized it is boring or threatening.

CROSS-MODAL ASSOCIATIONS

Another cognitive capacity that is fundamental to artistic appreciation is that of *representation* or *metaphoric thinking*. We can think of a tone as being mellow or warm or a tune as grand or blue. This remarkably flexible ability, which is one of the keys to complex human thought (as well as being basic to art and music) may have evolved as a function of the striking lateralization of the human brain. That is, the left and right hemispheres of the brain are specialized for different purposes, yet can still co-ordinate activities across a linking bundle of tracts called the *corpus callosum*. Music processing is primarily a right-hemisphere phenomenon, but trained musicians learn to bring the left (verbal) side of the brain to bear upon musical skills as well, most obviously in identifying keys, pitch intervals and styles of music (e.g. baroque, jazz, heavy metal, etc) (Chapter 9).

The most common type of cross-modal association is that of describing sound in spatial terms. Calling the pitch of notes 'high' versus 'low' is an obvious example, which probably derives from the anatomical location of the resonating chambers used to produce sounds vocally (head versus chest voice). Talking about a sound as 'big' or 'small' is another example that draws upon the parallel of volume. Likewise, we have no difficulty understanding what is meant by music that is 'bright', 'dull', 'blue', 'sparkling', 'uplifting' or 'flat'.

A small proportion of people (perhaps about 1%) find these sound/sight connections so compelling that musical notes produce immediate powerful visual experiences. This phenomenon is called *synesthesia*, and it is one possible basis for the unusual ability to identify the pitch of a note or a musical key without any frame of reference (absolute pitch). Most reports of sound/colour synesthesia show that low-pitched notes produce dark, dim colours like brown and black, while high-pitched notes evoke light and bright colour sensations, such as yellow and white (Marks 1975).

When we speak of 'the mind's eye' we acknowledge the pre-eminence of the visual mode in human cognitive functioning and our ability to translate other sensations into visual parallels. It is no coincidence that theatre comes from the Greek word *theatron*, which means the place 'where you view'.

RHYTHM AND TONE

Music has other instinctual bases. The impact of rhythm has its beginnings in foetal experience of the mother's heartbeat. Music with a pulse similar to the mother's heartbeat (about 72 beats per minute) seems to have a soothing effect on babies. In fact, it does not have to be music. A simple recording of paired beats similar to a human heartbeat can pacify young babies, reducing their crying and helping them to sleep and gain weight (Salk 1962). Taking this experiment one step further, the *Science Museum* in London set up a dark room intended to simulate the inside of the womb and played a recording of sounds taken from inside a woman's uterus. Young children were observed to spend a remarkably long time sitting entranced in this secure, womb-like environment, of which the 'lup-dub-bing' sound of the mother's heart must have been a distinctive component.

Even if reminiscence of our mother's heartbeat is not the essential feature (and one attempt to replicate Salk's finding has failed; Tulloch *et al.* 1964) our own pulse may be a marker that determines the emotional intensity of a musical piece.

As we get excited our heart-rate naturally increases, and so music that quickens in tempo is judged as getting more exciting. Many musical passages seem to be arranged so that they first assimilate the normal heart-rate, then accelerate progressively, thus taking the heart-rate of the listener along with them to some extent. They may thus function as a kind of auditory pace-maker to increase bodily excitement. Some of Rossini's big ensembles such as the one in *La Cenerentola*, 'But I fear a storm is brewing', seem deliberately designed to build emotional intensity in this way.

Soibelman (1948) reports that various melodies produced increases in pulse rate of between 0 and 15 beats per minute. One of my own students (Le Clair 1986) replicated this finding by observing increases in pulse rate in six subjects (three male and three female) who were listening to a section of Prokofiev's *Romeo and Juliet* symphony. Over the course of the four minute passage, the pulse rate increased progressively from an average of 74 beats per minute up to 85 bpm. These increases were clearly related to the mood of the music, a sharp climb being observed during more exciting (*subito* and *crescendo*) phases, and a plateau (or even slight fall) during *pianissimo* and *diminuendo* sections. This topic is discussed further in connection with the therapeutic use of music (Chapter 12).

An extremely powerful, regular beat, as occurs in tribal dancing, military marches, religious chants and teenage rock music, can induce a trance-like state as the relentless sensory input and muscular movement is taken up by electrical rhythms in the brain. This results in a loss of volition, heightened suggestibility and sometimes ecstasy. It hardly needs to be said that the insistent pelvic thrusting that often accompanies such dancing can also heighten sexual arousal, even in the absence of the body contact offered by more sedate European dancing (Winkelman 1986). The masturbatory element to some forms of pop music is one reason why puritanical parents object to it and authoritarian governments denounce it as decadent. Yet more advanced forms of music are not without sexual significance. Wagnerian love duets, notably those between Tristan and Isolde and Siegmund and Sieglinde are blatantly orgasmic in structure, as though the composer had studied Masters and Johnson before writing them.

The vocal sound produced by a singer also has primitive significance. Basses and baritones directly suggest masculine power (cf. the hooting of the male gorilla) while sopranos on high notes simulate a plaintive scream (e.g. Tosca's distress as she leaps from the battlements). Tenors are also good for cries of anguish (e.g. Cavaradossi being tortured, Otello's pain of jealousy). Increasing loudness is perceived as threatening, since it suggests that the sound source (a monster?) is coming progressively closer. There is a section in Mozart's *Cosi fan tutte* in which Fiordiligi is being sexually harassed by Ferrando and her vocal line makes sudden excursions to a high note suggestive of a prim woman who has just been goosed. In one production I recall, the soprano's difficulty in singing this phrase was completely overcome when the director instructed the tenor actually to pinch her bottom at the appropriate moment just preceding her high notes. The expressive quality of the human voice is part of our instinctual system for communicating emotion, and singing makes use of this fundamental process. Together with the capacity of rhythmic sound patterns to drive our brain and visceral processes, this accounts for much of the excitement evoked by music. The origins of musical experience are more fully discussed in Chapter 8.

RITUAL

Social rituals are recognized by anthropologists as the birthplace of many aspects of performance. Ritual consists of the stereotyped repetition of activity for magical effect. The behavioural pattern is repeated not just out of habit but because it has acquired deep mystical significance. The origins of the activity may be arbitrary, accidental or forgotten, but they have become invested with important social or religious meaning (e.g. smoking a peace pipe, breaking bread).

The functions of ritual are various, but include the following:

1. To celebrate victories or remember great disasters (e.g. war remembrance).

2. To mark important social occasions, (e.g. weddings, funerals).

3. To promote group identification and proclaim values (e.g. circumcision).

4. To appease or influence deities (e.g. sacrifice, group prayer).

5. To exert magical influence upon the environment (e.g. rain dances).

6. To communicate with the supernatural world or departed relatives (e.g. séances, ancestor worship).

7. To extend consciousness by entering trance-like or ecstatic states (e.g. fire walking, sex orgies).

Among the components of ritual ceremony that have made their way into modern theatrical performance are:

- Chanting and mass singing

- Co-ordinated instrumental playing

- Formation marching and dancing

- Masks and elaborate costumes

- Special effects such as the use of fire, totems and scenery.

Ritual merges with performance in tribal societies in that there is frequently a division between performers (priests, shamans, etc.) and audience (congregation). The performers assume roles and imitate gods and animals in order to mystify, educate and entertain. The Australian aboriginals, for example, perform a 'snake dance' in which a senior male member of the tribe is decorated to look like a large snake which is venerated as a god, and wriggles about so as to imitate its movement. In other ritual performances, members of the tribe pretend to be hunters and kangaroos respectively, enacting a chase with the kill as a finale (a spear being shoved under the armpit of the victim as in an amateur play). At one level this can be seen as a demonstration to the young men of important skills that they must acquire. But the magical significance of the ceremony is highlighted by the fact that men become gods incarnate and women are excluded on pain of death. Hence entertainment is intertwined with the transmission of cultural values.

European nativity plays and oratorios and perhaps even football matches also link ceremony with entertainment, and operas have many elements reminiscent of magic rites. Opera frequently incorporates religious scenes (e.g. the Easter hymn in *Cavalleria Rusticana*), weddings (*The Marriage of Figaro*), patriotic choruses (*Aida*), traditional plays (*I Pagliacci*) and other social events such as competitions (*Die Meistersinger*). Wagner's works particularly play up the ritual connection, and *Parsifal* is so religious in flavour that audiences are traditionally asked to show respect by abstaining from applause.

The layout of a modern church has many elements in common with a theatre. The area of the altar (scenery) where the choir (chorus) and minister (leading man) conduct their performance is raised up and separated off from the main body of the church where the congregation (audience) is seated. This division functions in much the same way as a proscenium arch marks off the area where magical things happen (the stage) from the ordinary, everyday world (the auditorium).

Classical plays and operas are ritualistic in the sense that audiences enjoy seeing them repeated over and over with minimal change. Most people want their *Hamlets, Magic Flutes or Mikados* to be performed pretty much as they have always seen them before. Innovations are resented as interference with a sacred rite, rather as many Catholics resented the Vernacular Mass. Annoyance with the director or performer who tries to put a new slant on classical works may be justified on artistic grounds, but sometimes seems to reflect insecurity due to the loss of something familiar.

Some of the traditions of operatic performance become so inflexible and detached from their original purpose that they take on the character of rituals. Goldovski (1968) tells the story of a famous tenor who always walked upstage and looked out of the window at a particular point during his rendition of 'Your tiny hand is frozen'. His influence in the day was such that virtually all other tenors followed suit, assuming this to be the way it should be done, and the move became strongly traditional. Then, one day, a free-thinking young tenor who could not see any dramatic merit in the move had the temerity to question the maestro on his reason for doing it. 'Oh that', he replied, 'it's just that about that point in the aria I'm usually troubled by a build-up in phlegm, so I go up to the window to get rid of it'.

While some rituals continue to serve valid, albeit altered, social functions, others would appear to be totally obsolete vestiges of meaningless events. The human urge to create ritual is a source of artistic performance, but not always an admirable guide for current purposes.

SHAMANISM

A *shaman* is a kind of witch-doctor or religious leader who specializes in trance-travelling to other worlds in order to communicate with spirit beings such as gods or ancestors. The practice is widespread throughout the world, especially in Asia, Africa and South America, and is of very ancient origin. Currently, it appears to be on the increase in parts of the European world, being seen, for example, in Pentecostal Christianity and the revival of interest in witchcraft and spiritualism. It usually takes the form of a public performance with dancing, drumming, chanting, screaming and semi-epileptic bodily and vocal hysterics. The shaman's audience is convened for a particular ceremonial purpose, such as healing a sick person, supervising a rite of passage like birth, circumcision, marriage or death, or seeking advice from supernatural powers. They frequently participate in some way, for example, joining in a chorus of amens, hallelujahs or suchlike, or entering into a trance-like state, which may be assisted by drugs, music or dancing.

Shamanism is discussed by anthropologists in terms of the concept of *magic*. When an outcome is strongly desired by a person or society, and rational means by which it may be secured are not available, then they will often resort to magical rituals, such as rain dances, seances and prayers. Although not directly effective, these are helpful in raising morale and reassuring people that everything possible is being done. Occasionally, however, they may increase anxiety, as when the bone is pointed at someone who is said to be doomed or a priest is summoned to the bedside of a conscious patient, thus signifying that the medical experts have written him off. And, of course, magic may be dangerous if it means that constructive action (such as an appendicitis operation) is foregone in favour of the dubious benefits of witch-doctory.

Every so often the desired outcome does occur simply by chance. For example, a rain dance is performed and shortly afterwards it happens to rain. A causal connection is imputed, thus reinforcing the entire sequence. And because reinforcement is intermittent, superstitions are maintained for very long (historical) periods of time. More than that, faith-healing sometimes is beneficial in that it mobilizes the powers of suggestion, which can produce impressive gains in health.

One sleight-of-hand that is particularly characteristic of shamans throughout the world is the apparent extraction of some material from the patient (such as bone, stone, tuft of hair) that is supposed to be the cause of the problem. In fact, this has been concealed in his mouth or somewhere about his person, but, the procedure may, nevertheless, prove to be a very good placebo. It may also be performed symbolically, as when a faith-healer passes his hands across the sufferer without touching them. Another common practice among shamans is to drive out devils or evil spirits that have taken possession of a person by beatings, dunking in cold water or verbal exhortations. This is called *exorcism*.

The rituals of the shamans are basic to a wide variety of performing arts. Conjuring and illusions, ventriloquism, acrobatics, clowns, fire-eating, puppetry, stage hypnotism, masquerades and make-up all derive from the antics of the shaman and some historians believe that dancing, singing and acting originate partly from the same source (Drummond 1980).

Shamanism comes particularly close to theatre when good or evil spirits are represented by masked performers in combat (Cole 1975). Demons were originally representations of physical illness, but later came to portray psychological symptoms as well. This trend became more pronounced as physical medicine developed which was more effective with physical disorders than psychological conditions. Clowns were used to express lunatic tendencies, and deformed people of one sort or another. In the ritual play, these figures usually ended up being driven off, so that society might rid itself symbolically of freakish people. At other times in history, deformed people have themselves been used for entertainment. The hunchback jester, as represented in *Rigoletto* and *I Pagliacci*, was not untypical. Even today, circus freaks are treated as entertainment, and comedians who look pathetic or peculiar have a head-start in their profession. Laurel is skinny and appears dim-witted, Hardy is fat and smug, and Woody Allen makes capital out of presenting himself as impotent and unattractive to women (Chapter 7).

Many drama theorists (for example, Cole 1975) maintain that shamanism is the central ingredient of theatre. The essence of true drama, they say, is not just the reproduction of mundane social reality, but the presentation of a different order – one that is supernatural, surreal, or 'marvellous'. Originally, this was produced by trickery and the expansion of experience and physical abilities through trance states. Today, it is more often produced through 'special effects' such as lights, scenery, music, make-up and all the technological wizardry that is available to stage directors and film makers. The purpose is to transport the audience to another, usually more elevated, reality. Realistic theatre, such as kitchen sink drama, goes through short periods of fashionability, but there is a strong tendency to revert to the fantastic. The most widely popular forms of entertainment at any time (e.g. *The Wizard of Oz, Fantasia, Star Wars* and *Superman*) rely heavily on fantasy.

In an episode which highlights the relationship between modern performance and shamanism, Bates (1986) describes how film director John Boorman met a famous shaman called Takuma while researching *The Emerald Forest* deep in the South American jungle. Asked to explain his work to a man who had never seen a movie or TV he had great difficulty. 'I struggled and he listened intently. I told him how one scene would stop and another begin in a different time and place as it does in a dream. He lit up, grasping that. I told him of some of the tricks and wonders we get up to. Finally he was satisfied. "You make visions, magic. You are a *paje* (witchdoctor) like me!"' (Boorman 1985 p.88).

Spiritual leaders exist in all societies in parallel with political and military leaders and they are often equally, or even more influential. Macbeth was influenced by witches, King Arthur by Merlin and the Russian court by Rasputin. President Reagan was said to have taken advice from astrologers and the Italian government has always been respectful of the Vatican.

In modern society the phenomenon of shamanism has split several ways:

1. Doctors, psychotherapists and practitioners of 'alternative' medicine perform the healing role of the witch-doctors.

2. Evangelists and priests supervise contact with the supernatural order (God, heaven, the deceased, etc).

3. Pop idols, actors and singers crystallize powerful feelings such as sex and social rebellion.

All three groups are historically derived from shamanism and retain many of the major components of the shaman's skill. However, typical of the development of western society, they have diversified and become 'specialized'. It is the third group that is of major interest here.

POSSESSION

Some writers distinguish *shamans*, who make a journey to another world, from *hungans*, who are possessed by visitors from the other world. 'Hungan' is actually a Haitian term for a priest who specializes in being possessed by spirits, but the word is also used more generally. In that both shamanism and possession involve trance-like states and disruption of speech, the difference is difficult for an observer to determine. The latter is more likely to be seen as madness because it occurs to individuals who do not have priestly status in society. When such a person is taken over involuntarily by evil spirits, exorcism may be deemed necessary, or some modern equivalent such as electro-shock therapy. Acting may seem more like shamanism in the sense that all control is not lost, although some actors believe in being so absorbed in their role that a state of dissociation bordering on benign possession may be reached.

Bates (1986) is one psychologist who has argued that the concept of possession is central to the understanding of the acting process, even though, in our 'rational' age, we have repressed recognition of this. Bates interviews great actors and actresses to find components of shamanism in their approach. Among the examples he gives: Alec Guinness claimed to be prescient about the death of James Dean; Shirley MacLaine claims to reincarnate the spirits of past lives and to travel outside of her own body ('astral projection'); Glenda Jackson says that she sometimes steps on stage fearing that she is risking life and death – that her soul may be snatched away, leaving her to wither and die; Anthony Sher reports that his roles enter his life like someone he loves; another person is always present, always close (even though at the same time his own personality is probed, explored and expressed); Liv Ullmann feels that in performance she encounters and reveals her inner self, while also being filled by another character that possesses her – a spirit shared by actor and audience. Another example is that of actress Mel Martin who claimed to have been possessed by Vivien Leigh when called upon to act her in a TV biography called *Darling of the Gods*. In an interview with *The Sun* (7 July

1990), Martin said that she talked to Vivien and heard her voice telling her how to act in different scenes. 'I did not play Vivien Leigh, I became her. There were spells when her spirit took me over and I'm not sure I'll ever be totally free of her'.

Bates concludes that actors perform for our society the role of shamans, bringing a world of imagination and fantasy (an alternative reality) into believable existence. They are 'psychic illusionists, transforming mundane reality'. In order to achieve this, they need profound self-understanding, by 'tapping deep, spiritual, psychic and psychological levels within themselves'. Great acting, according to Bates, frequently involves unusual psychic ability, body awareness, spiritual power and intense dreaming – the harnessing of powers bordering on the paranormal.

It is possible that actors learn from drama school or elsewhere the jargon of shamanism and possession and hence use it to describe their experience. However, there is other evidence connecting performance with 'dissociated' mind states. Research on the personality of sleepwalkers (Crisp *et al.* 1990) has revealed only one, very specific group of traits on which somnambulists are distinguished – they tend to enjoy and have experience of dramatic situations, acting and being the centre of attention. Apparently, the 'performer personality' (Chapter 10) predisposes small groups of mental processes (corresponding to the role being enacted) to take over control of behaviour, hence breaking up the normal integrity of the mind. A simplistic interpretation of the link between sleepwalking and performance would be that sleepwalkers are just 'hysterics' who are acting and seeking attention when they sleepwalk. However, there is no doubt that sleepwalkers are in a dissociated (trance-like) state of consciousness at the time they are sleepwalking, and have genuine amnesia for their activities upon waking. Therefore, the alternative hypothesis, that acting partakes of dissociation-type processes (one of which is possession), is more plausible. If actors are hysterics, their hysteria seems to give them special, 'magical' powers, enabling them to set their mind in unusual modes.

ARCHETYPAL THEMES

We saw in Chapter 1 that recurrent themes appearing in the works of particular authors give insight into the psychology of that author. If that is the case, then themes which are widespread in mythology and drama across different authors give insight into the preoccupations of humanity in general. This is so regardless of whether the themes are being selected by authors or by audiences (hence factors like popularity and lasting power).

It is increasingly recognized by modern psychologists that certain images and ideas have had such profound evolutionary importance to us that we have stored prototypes in our brain that predispose us to react to them innately (Lumsden and Wilson 1983). Neural cells and circuits have been identified in the brain that react specifically to certain stimulus patterns – an infant's cry, the colour red, the shape of a face, or a mating signal. Ethologists call these *innate releasing mechanisms*, and the Jungian concept of *archetypes*, referring to inherited memories of profound and universal human significance, conveys a similar idea.

A good illustration of an archetype is the idea of a dragon which appears in the myths and fairy tales of nearly all cultures and which precedes the discovery of dinosaur fossils. Sagan (1977) has argued persuasively that the dragon myth represents a residual fear of reptiles dating from a time in evolutionary history when pre-human mammals struggled with giant reptiles for supremacy on the earth. Although the mammals won, and dinosaurs are now extinct, we have retained an instinctual loathing for reptiles that is out of proportion compared with our attitude toward tigers and wolves, which have been far more lethal to us in recent history. We even make pets out of tamed miniature versions of the latter (cats and dogs) which we feel affectionate towards, whereas few people feel any empathy with reptiles, however small and harmless. Yet our fascination with dinosaurs is evidenced by their popularity as toys and museum displays. As for the fire-breathing act of dragons, we could speculate that a second primordial peril of the evolving mammal might have been volcanoes and forest fires. Put fire into the mouth of the dragon (its most dangerous region) and we have the ultimate compound of prehistoric terror. Our use of the phrases 'mouth of the volcano' and 'crater of the stomach' demonstrate that we are easily able to formulate such metaphoric associations.

THE HERO

In his celebrated book *The Hero with a Thousand Faces*, Joseph Campbell (1949) drew attention to another common theme in literature, mythology and drama throughout history and the world. This concerns the epic journey or quest of a brave, if sometimes naive, young man who battles against tremendous odds to achieve triumph, which may be in the form of manhood, wealth, the love of a good woman, social deliverance, or all of these things. It is no coincidence that George Lucas, who created the *Star Wars* trilogy in the 1980s, was a friend of Campbell and consulted him directly concerning the script and characters. It is equally clear that as a mythological pastiche *Star Wars* has many similarities to Wagner's *Ring Cycle*, which was explicitly constructed from commonalities among ancient legends.

The heroic legends of many cultures follow a similar sequence of events:

1. They begin with the birth of the hero, which is usually in some way exceptional. His parents may be royalty, poor and humble, close relatives (hence incest) or killed immediately after his birth. He is likely to be banished but bear some distinguishing mark which enables later recognition. Often he is parented by gods or aliens but raised by ordinary mortals. He may be reborn from a previous existence.

2. The hero's childhood is threatened by enemies who recognize him as a potential threat or he is maltreated by foster parents. His exceptional talent is sporadically indicated but seldom fully appreciated by those about him.

3. The maturity of the hero is sudden and impressive with intimations of invulnerability.

4. Remarkable exploits follow, including the conquest of enemies, monsters (e.g. a dragon) and ultimately a beautiful maiden (princess). The maiden may be rescued from a villain or monster who holds her captive, or she is re-awakened from a long sleep that has been imposed on her.

5. Apart from concrete achievements there is a psychological transformation of the hero – a personal growth, fulfilment or transcendence. The personal triumphs are also likely to be synonymous with social deliverance, the whole of society being the beneficiary of the hero's journey.

6. The ultimate fall of the hero may then be described – death and destruction resulting from some inherent fatal flaw, which may be physical (e.g. the Achilles heel) or psychological (e.g. pride). Sometimes there is a journey to Hades after death.

No one story fits this formula exactly, but these elements occur in the myths of many countries and times (e.g. Beowulf, Oedipus, Siegfried, the Bible, St George and the Dragon, Sleeping Beauty and Superman). What, then, is the psychological significance of this universal story?

At the personal level there is an analogue in individual ambitiousness, or need for achievement. Most people, to a greater or lesser extent, are driven to succeed in life, to achieve mental and physical mastery, to build castles (real or 'in the air'), to conquer enemies and thus to win admiration and love. Heroic fantasies are particularly common in men, but women also dream of the shining knight on a charger who will bear them away from drudgery and strife and take responsibility for their welfare thereafter. The monster from whom the maiden is liberated may represent a restrictive father or over-protective mother, so it is not surprising that a sexual awakening is often thrown in.

Society at large also has need of exceptional men who will deliver them from troubles and enemies. If such a man does not already exist within their ranks, they tend to invent one. They may do this either by misidentifying some fairly ordinary person as being equipped to supervise their salvation (cf. *The Life of Brian*) and appointing him to the task accordingly, or by devising fictional characters who serve the same purpose in fantasy. Thus people seek saviours, idols and heroes in sport, music, politics and religion as well as in fiction.

The concern with the genetic background of the hero has fairly obvious evolutionary significance. Within limits, exceptional human beings can be bred like racehorses, so parents who are themselves outstanding are the most likely source of a hero. At the same time, we are often reminded in these stories, rightly, that a genius or leader may be spawned of perfectly ordinary, unprepossessing parents. The Nobel prize-winners' sperm bank that was recently established in California will raise the chances of producing a genius, but only slightly. The hero may emerge from the most unlikely of places: a lowly stable, a flying saucer, or a Swiss patents office.

The heroic legend, then, is founded in some combination of male ambitiousness and achievement fantasy, the female dream of a 'champion', and the importance that society ascribes to its exceptional leaders and prophets. According to McConnell (1979) heroes (and heroines) are versions of our 'own self in the making' which help us to invent a better story of our own. Thus they have an inspirational function as well as airing our fears and indulging our fantasies.

Wagner's particular treatment of the hero myth (Siegfried in the *Ring Cycle*) is extended to a history of the cosmos. The fall of Siegfried is shortly followed by the destruction of Valhalla, making way for a totally new order of freedom and understanding, rather as Christian mythology connects the anticipated second coming of Christ with the end of the world. This was expected to be fairly imminent around the time of the resurrection; now Christian theologians are unclear about the time scale. The prelude to Rhinegold at the beginning of the Ring Cycle commences with long-drawn monotonic sounds that seem watery and formless, representing the primordial void. Gradually they 'evolve' more meaningful structure, until the human voices of the Rhinemaidens emerge, initially pure and uncomplicated. After Alberich steals the Rhinegold (the primal crime) an irreconcilable conflict or 'lack' is created. The existing order becomes deficient and alienated and this is reflected in the vocal and orchestral music. The task of the hero is presumably to restore the original state of order (cf. *Genesis* in the Biblical account of the origin of the world).

The typical structure of the heroic myth could be extended to include the prehistory of the hero, in which some kind of problem or conflict is created (a fall from grace). The birth of the hero is anticipated and predictions made about his exploits. At the other end, we could note that the central problem is often solved as much by the death of the hero as by his actual exploits. Salvation may come about as a kind of by-product of his passing; he makes the supreme sacrifice so all may benefit. This pattern is clearly applicable to the Christian religion, but it is not unique to Christianity. Such a formula can be detected in the legends of a great many pre-Christian, even pre-literate societies.

Implicit in many cosmic myths is the belief that the existing order must be completely annihilated before a state of perfection (*nirvana*) can take its place and that the sacrifice of some highly valued individual is a prerequisite to eternal peace and joy. Thus the hero legend not only models an 'ideal' life, but it often attempts an overview of the entire history of the cosmos. In the pre-scientific age, such legends probably functioned to satisfy the same need for knowledge and understanding that is provided by scientific paradigms such as evolution theory and astronomy. The considerable success of the Bronowski TV series on *The Ascent of Man* and Carl Sagan's *Cosmos* may be noted in this context. Myth and science both cater to the natural curiosity that we have about ourselves, our origins, our future, and our place within the 'divine plan'.

ARCHETYPAL MEN AND WOMEN

The hero is only one of several character types that recur within dramatic writing. Stevens (1982) has brought together the work of Jungian psychologists who have analysed the religion, mythology and literature of a variety of cultures, both primitive and modern, to produce the following mapping of male and female types (Figure 2.1).

The four polar types of male are identified as (1) the *Father*, who is the leader and protector, concerned with the maintenance of law and order and the *status quo;* (2) the *Son*, who is preoccupied with personal interests and cares little for social responsibilities; thus necessarily pitting himself against the Father; (3) the *Hero*, who is active, ambitious and thrusting, and who strives for prestige within

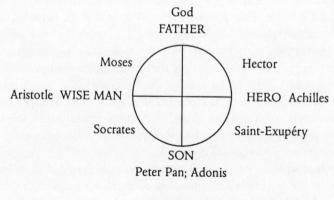

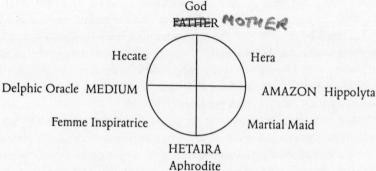

Figure 2.1. The main archetypes of men and women identified by Jungian psychologists. The four polar points for each gender may be thought of as social roles, typical people or conflicting aspects within ourselves. (From Stevens 1982)

a social context; (4) the *Wise Man*, who is a philosopher and teacher, concerned with ideas rather than action or the personalities of people.

The primary female types are: (1) the *Mother*, who is impersonal and collective, and concerned with nurturance, child-rearing and home-making; (2) the *Hetaira*, who is opposite to the Mother in that she is the eternal mistress, concerned with getting her man and relating to him at an intensely personal level, rather than assuming the social responsibilities attached to the wife/mother role; (3) the *Amazon*, who is independent, active and goal-oriented, functioning as a comrade or competitor to men rather than a wife, mother or mistress; (4) the *Medium*, who is uncanny and clairvoyant, immersed in subjective experience and speaking with the conviction of an oracle.

These archetypes can be thought of as social roles deriving from age, sex and aptitude, as recognizable personality styles that can be observed in the modern world, as frequently occurring characters in drama and literature, or as aspects of the personality of all of us.

Although this classificatory scheme has no empirical validation, it is nevertheless intuitively appealing as a descriptive system. It is easy to think of characters, particularly in classical drama and opera, who correspond to these ideal poles, and possible to place most other characters within the two-dimensional map appropriate to their gender. Hamlet is primarily the Son, King Arthur is a Father figure, Antony is a Hero and Merlin a Wise Man. Mama Lucia in *Cavalleria Rusticana* is the Mother type; Manon the Hetaira. Ulrica in *Un Ballo in Maschera* illustrates the Medium, while Brunhilde is an Amazon. Even when characters cannot be slotted easily into one of the four pigeonholes, these elements can be seen in their character. Carmen, for example, displays clear components of Amazon (willingness to fight for what she wants), Hetaira (seductiveness and refusal to be tied down to one mate) and Medium (reading her own fate in the cards). The appeal of this categorisation is that it points up readily recognisable key aspects of the psyche of males and females respectively, which connect logically with what is known about the instinctual basis of sex differences (Wilson 1989).

LOVE AND DEATH

One of the most recurrent themes in literature is seen particularly clearly in romantic opera. This concerns the death of somebody beautiful, virtuous and well-loved or some other juxtaposition of love and death.

Death may arrive too soon, frustrating what otherwise could have been a perfect relationship (*La Traviata, La Bohème, Tosca, Il Trovatore, Luisa Miller, Manon*). Sometimes it comes almost as a welcome relief, seeming to be the only solution to a hopeless situation or relationship against which the fates have conspired (*Romeo and Juliet, Tristan and Isolde, Rigoletto, Carmen, Aida, Faust, Madam Butterfly, Antony and Cleopatra*). The lovers may die together in each others arms, death affording them a kind of ultimate refuge, a permanent intimacy with which nobody can interfere.

The sense of tragedy is often heightened by the fact that the person who dies need not have died, or should not have died. They may die because of unfeeling authorities or stringent moral codes (*Suor Angelica, Billy Budd, The Rape of Lucretia*), because they have been misjudged in some way (*Un Ballo in Maschera, Otello*) or because they sacrifice themselves in some noble cause (*Rigoletto, Don Carlos*). Those who survive are left with a devastating sense of loss, distress or regret.

Why should death so often be the theme and climax of great drama and opera? Given that one major purpose of drama is to create an intense emotional impact on the audience, then death is an ideal event to portray. Nothing could be more disturbing than the death of someone we admire and love (except perhaps our own death, which we are generally unable to react to). In so far as drama is rehearsal for life, then death is bound to be salient. It is an experience which we all have coming to us at some time (death of loved ones, or worse still, our own) but we have limited opportunity to practice our emotional reactions to it. Drama provides us with second-hand experience of death, helping us to explore our feelings and reactions to it in advance, a kind of 'safe-run' by which we prepare for the actual eventuality.

Fictional death reminds us of our mortality and the mortality of others. In drama we see people who are regretful about having caused the death of another or about not treating them well enough while they had the opportunity. Such an experience may teach us to live our lives and treat others as though we might not get the chance to put the record straight or deliver apologies. This may be one of the most important personal and social virtues of tragic drama. There is also the feeling that 'it's good when it stops'. Whatever problems one has in life, they are seldom half as bad as those faced by Mimi or Macbeth. The lightness one sometimes feels after watching a tragic drama may be attributable to relief that it is not for real. It is like waking from a nightmare and discovering that some horror you have dreamed has not after all come to pass. This could be part of what the Greeks called catharsis.

Within the general category of love and death it is possible to identify some common subtypes:

1. *The perfect love match frustrated by death.* This theme is seen in many operas such as *La Bohème, Luisa Miller, Tosca* and *La Traviata*. Even though there may be other difficulties with the relationship that have to be dealt with along the way (for example, parents and jealousies) the death of one partner appears as the major obstacle to an otherwise idyllic union. *Love Story* is a modern example of this genre.

2. *Death resulting from the frustration of perfect love.* Any opera goer will have noticed that the characters in grand opera run a high risk of dying at their own hand. In the nineteenth century, particularly, suicide 'vied with tuberculosis as a major cause of operatic death' (Feggetter 1980). In an analysis of the plots of 306 favourite operas in the current

repertory, Feggetter found 77 completed suicides, 7 cases of murder followed by suicide and 12 attempted suicides. Most of these were 'romantic' suicides, in which the characters took their own life because they had lost their lover, killed them through some misunderstanding or believed them to be unfaithful (for example, *Madam Butterfly, Luisa Miller, Tosca*).

3. *Death due to a lover's jealousy.* This is a theme central to much Italian opera (for example, *I Pagliacci, Cavalleria Rusticana, Otello, Il Tabarro*), and no doubt reflects the cultural recognition of crimes of passion, sometimes called 'divorce Italian style'.

4. *Death as the ultimate consummation of love.* This is more typical of the German romantic movement, especially the operas of Wagner (*Tristan and Isolde, The Flying Dutchman, Twilight of the Gods*), and taken up to some extent by Verdi in *Aida*. The idea is that perfect love transcends mortal barriers and finds its proper dimension only in eternity.

5. *Death caused by the lure of love itself.* French opera is particularly obsessed with fallen women who are either corrupted by the society around them, or corrupting of the men who fall under their spell. The latter theme appears to reflect the interface between Parisian lust and the Catholic conscience which tends to project the blame for male weakness onto female seductiveness. Carmen is the archetypal 'femme fatale', but Giulietta in *The Tales of Hoffmann*, Manon and Maddelena also fit this category more or less, as does Cleopatra in the Shakespeare play. Historically, overtones of the 'black widow' legend can be seen from Homer's sirens to the 'brides of Dracula' in Hammer films.

The frequency with which men are victims of women tells against the feminist idea that the destruction of women in so many operas (by murder, suicide or disease) is a male chauvinist plot to 'put women down'. Clément (1989) argues that the death or 'taming' of a heroine (the prima donna) that is the central theme of so many 'bourgeois' operas is a reflection of the male insecurity of the writers – an attempt to bolster the patriarchal social order. A simpler interpretation, however, is that women, being more beautiful and 'helpless', are better value than men for evoking sympathy. As already noted, some writers, such as Charles Dickens and Benjamin Britten, prefer boys for this purpose and the killing of children (or even the possibility of children) is another popular tragic theme (Simon 1988).

Some operas and tragedies manage to combine more than one of the above love/death themes in the same story. There is, however, no great advantage in trying to do so because each is likely to be diluted in the process. There is also a risk that the work will not be taken seriously, and instead be perceived as slightly ridiculous. There is danger of this happening with two of Verdi's operas, *Il Trovatore* and *The Force of Destiny*, though they remain popular because of their musical vigour.

It would be possible to elaborate further on the various ways in which love and death intermingle in many of the most evergreen (hence audience-selected) of plays and operas but suffice to note that this combination is particularly potent as an emotional catalyst. Love, which is probably the premier component of the two, is at its most passionate and painful when obstructed or terminated prematurely. 'They lived happily ever after' would be a dull outcome of a relationship from the dramatic point of view, even if it were credible.

THE NEED TO SACRIFICE

One particular death theme that seems to have very fundamental 'archetypal' significance is that of *sacrifice*. Primitive tribes feel compelled to offer sacrifices to the gods, frequently human and highly valued (such as a young, beautiful, innocent, virgin). In more recent times historically, animal substitutes may have been used (for example, a lamb or goat). The sacrifice may even be totally symbolic. In Christianity, the one-off sacrifice of God's favourite (only) blameless, perfect 'son' is deemed sufficient to atone for the sins of all mankind forever, provided people make themselves party to the event in some way (for example, eating bread, drinking communion wine, 'accepting' Christ as Saviour).

Several psychological mechanisms seem to be involved in the urge to sacrifice. First, there is guilt-expiation – the feeling that someone has to suffer for our sins and those of society, but preferably someone else (our representative). Second is our feeling that the gods will be better disposed towards us if we deprive ourselves in some way. The more perfect and desirable the object that we give up, the more pleased, and hence forgiving and generous will be the deities. A third mechanism involved in sacrifice rituals is the idea of incorporating some valued attribute of the victim into oneself – partaking of the spirit in some way.

The origins of the word 'tragedy' are illuminating in this connection. In the ancient Greek cult of *Dionysis* (also known as *Bakkhos*) the vegetation god was worshipped with ecstatic dancing aided by the chewing of ivy leaves and mushrooms. These rites, which were the preserve of women called *bakkai*, took place on mountains in winter and ended with the symbolic killing of Dionysis in the form of a goat (*tragos*) which was torn to pieces and eaten raw. The celebrants thus became *enthusiastikos* ('having the god inside them'). Later on, many city states held festivals of Dionysis, which were transferred to the spring and enlivened with *tragoidiai* ('goat songs'). By the end of the sixth century B.C. the festival of Dionysis in Athens was specializing in plays that we now call 'tragedies' (Glover 1990).

It is tempting to suppose that the death of the operatic heroine (e.g. Mimi or Violetta) or the destruction of the perfect hero (Achilles or Siegfried) is some sort of remnant of our sacrificial tendency. Myths, tragedies and opera may then be seen as descendants of ancient sacrificial rites.

POWER STRUGGLES

Another common theme in drama and opera concerns alignments and struggles for ascendancy between men. Sometimes the extent of loyalty or betrayal is of central interest and sometimes there is an open battle for supremacy between two or more men. Among the classic and popular stories in which male competition is a dominant theme are *Macbeth, Hamlet, Julius Caesar, Il Trovatore, Robin Hood, The Godfather* and *Dallas*. The competition may be for power, territory, or women, but these three are interconnected in that the male who wields power and controls wider tracts of territory is, in nature, able to attract more females (Ardrey 1966). Occasionally there is a female equivalent of this theme, with competition between women appearing as central (e.g. *Aida, Der Rosenkavalier*), but this is much less common.

The motive force for this obsession derives from the Darwinian importance of *intermale competition*. In most mammalian species, males engage in hierarchy struggles for control of territory and females because of their biological capability of breeding with several females in parallel. When successful, this strategy results in a wider diffusion of the male's genes, and consequently it has greater survival value. Females have more limited opportunity to breed, so it is not in their interest to be promiscuous, but rather to attend to the quality of the particular male that impregnates them, and to be concerned about his ability and willingness to help them look after any offspring that are produced. These differing strategies have become enshrined in the genes of males and females respectively, and manifest themselves as instinctual mating tendencies and personality characteristics (Wilson 1981). Man the hunter and explorer (of both land and women) has evolved greater fighting skills and aggression to support such tendencies. Woman, the nurse and educator, has evolved greater empathy, social insight and communicative skill. The natural concern of both sexes with the mechanism and outcome of status struggles is basic to the repeated appearance of this theme in drama, opera and films.

The theme of intense *loyalty between men* that also occurs frequently in Shakespearean and operatic plots might initially seem to be the opposite of inter-male rivalry, but on closer examination it turns out to be the other side of the same coin. As throughout mammalian history males hunted and fought for territory, they evolved a co-operative capacity that gave them an edge over rivals and enemies that operated as individuals. Thus men, rather more than women, are instinctively inclined toward forming close bonded teams for tackling common problems (Tiger 1969). This tendency is apparent in teenage gangs, football teams, political groupings, masonic lodges, clubs and the 'old school tie' tradition, and it is manifested in literature and drama as alliances between men that are 'true unto death'. When women sacrifice themselves in real life or in drama, it is usually for their children or the man they love; such tight-knit bonds within pairs or small groups of women are much less conspicuous than they are with men.

TRIUMPH OF THE YOUNG INTERLOPER

The most recurrent of all themes in comic opera corresponds to a specific aspect of inter-male competition which may be dubbed 'the guardian outwitted' or 'there's no fool like an old fool'. *Don Pasquale, The Abduction from the Seraglio, The Barber of Seville, The Marriage of Figaro, The Secret Marriage, Iolanthe, Falstaff* and many other comic operas (as well as Act II of *La Bohème*) tell the story of a high-ranking, selfish old man who is tricked out of his claim to an eligible girl by a younger man and his ingenious collaborators. The old man (normally a buffo bass) is the butt of the humour, while the young couple (tenor and soprano) provide romantic interest with lyrical love duets. The young ones are assisted by likeable friends (usually baritones, like Figaro or Malatesta) while the older man has villainous and ludicrous allies (often comprimario tenors like Don Basilio or Bardolph).

The plot is appealing because the situation is familiar, yet nobody identifies with the old fool. Women in the audience imagine themselves either as the girl who gets the youthful lover of her choice, or as the wife whose errant husband is suitably humiliated. Men of all ages identify with the young suitor, if necessary recalling the triumphs of their own younger days. Few people, men or women, are able accurately to conceive of themselves as old. Thus is the universal theme of inter-male rivalry for the scarce commodity of attractive females rendered pleasurable to all consumers.

There are various other figures of fun that occur with some frequency in comic plays and operas: for example, the fat and ageing woman with whom some male character is lumbered as punishment for his misconduct (Katisha, Marcellina), the hypocritical puritan whose selfishness and weakness for pleasure are publically exposed (Tartuffe, Don Basilio) and the adulterous husband who gets his come-uppance (Count Almavira, Eisenstein). These themes, and most others that could be identified, in comedy as well as tragedy, concern familiar patterns and conflicts that occur within the perennial mating game.

Why are we so obsessed with love and sex? The reason can again be understood in sociobiological terms. The 'reproductive imperative' is a powerful instinctive urge, and one that almost certainly underlies the greater part of our motivation and behaviour. Furthermore, it is complicated, in that, unlike others such as hunger and thirst, it necessarily involves co-operation with at least one other person, and usually competition with many others. After stunning the world with his principle of natural selection, Darwin (1883) went on to demonstrate the special importance of sexual selection. What we are today is largely a product of the sexual preferences and successes of our ancestors, so the whole sexual arena instinctively fascinates us. As Schopenhauer put it, even earlier, in 1819: 'The final aim of all love intrigues, be they comic or tragic, is really of more importance than all other ends in human life. What it all turns upon is nothing less than the composition of the next generation'.

There are many other common themes and characters in theatre (ancient and modern) that could be analysed in terms of their fundamental psychological significance. The above examples have been taken to illustrate the fact that the evolution of the human mind parallels the origins of performance.

CHAPTER 3

SOCIAL PROCESSES IN THEATRE

Theatre is a social arena. What makes the experience of a live play, musical or other performance different from viewing films and television is the feeling of being part of a social occasion or 'happening'. Many of the phenomena that occur in the theatre can be understood in terms that social psychologists have used to describe group events and activities in general. This chapter is concerned with the application of established principles of social psychology to the theatrical experience.

Social communication in the theatre involves three groups of people: (1) writers or creators, (2) performers and (3) the audience. It might seem that the major line of social influence runs in that direction, with writers providing material for performers and performers having an impact upon the audience. But this is an over-simplification; both performers and writers are sensitive to audience reactions (whether in terms of immediate feedback or long-term reassessment) and indeed, each group influences the other two. Ultimately, theatrical enjoyment depends upon a 'conspiracy' among the three (Arnold 1990).

AUDIENCE FEEDBACK

Consider first the sensitivity of performers to audience reactions. Producers of long-running TV serials make adjustments on the basis of popularity ratings and reviewers' comments, but audience feedback in the theatre is much more immediate and direct. Signs of sympathy, amusement or appreciation in the audience are transmitted back across the footlights to the performers, reinforcing and encouraging them in various ways. Ideally, a spiral of enhancement develops, with the audience expressing appreciation, the performers gaining in confidence and improving their performance, the audience enjoying it even more, and so on.

But feedback effects are not always positive. The equivalent negative spiral can also occur. And even if the initial reception is good, inexperienced performers have been known to 'go over the top' in response to audience appreciation that they are unused to, exaggerating their lines and moves to the point where sympathetic contact with the audience is lost. It is because of this danger that drama instructors inveigh against the 'adrenalin high' which lures many novice actors to destruction.

According to the type of theatre, audience reaction has to be taken into account to some extent. At the least, it is necessary for performers to pause for applause or laughter. All good comedians learn to wait until the laughter has just peaked out and is beginning to fall into rapid decline before delivering their next line. This causes the audience to suppress the tail-end of their laugh in order to hear what comes next, though the residual mirth is carried through silently to cumulate with the subsequent 'official' laugh (Figure 3.1).

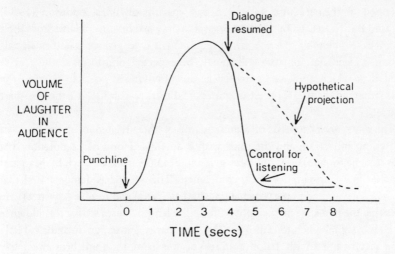

Figure 3.1: Diagram to illustrate the timing of laugh lines in the theatre. Dialogue is resumed just as the natural decay of laughter commences so that the comic impetus is maintained

Sometimes, as in melodrama, pantomime, or Edwardian music hall, actors and audience enter into a kind of impertinent exchange. This may vary from friendly to antagonistic, depending on the sort of rapport that has been established and the amount of alcohol imbibed on the two sides of the proscenium. At times it approximates to the 'heckling' that politicians have to contend with in speechmaking. Such banter can be quite inappropriate to the intended mood of the drama. The story is told of a famous actor in the last century playing Richard III, who was offering his kingdom for a horse, when a naive and over-helpful member of the audience called out to offer his own steed. Somewhat annoyed at the interruption, the actor called back to him 'Come up yourself, an ass will do'.

For the most part, audience feedback is beneficial to a performance, and it is because television lacks this element that comedy shows are often recorded with a live audience. There are practical difficulties involved in doing this, but such a technique is recognised as superior to any form of dubbed laughter. Films also lack feedback, but are different again in that they are normally intended to be shown to large cinema audiences who can at least interact among themselves and thus generate a warm social atmosphere.

TIMING AND 'CLAPTRAPS'

Timing is one of the most important skills that an actor, and especially a comedian, must acquire. Audiences need firm guidance as to when they should pay particular attention because something very important is about to happen, when they should laugh and when they should applaud. This information is contained in the structure, inflection and spacing of lines. Atkinson (1984) analyzed the tricks used by political orators to draw maximum applause from their audiences, concluding that the prime requirement is to give preparatory signals making it clear that applause will shortly be expected, and to make the precise moment at which applause is invited as unambiguous as possible. Among the devices commonly used for these purposes are the 'three-part list' and the 'two-part contrast'.

The *three-part list* consists of a presentation of three related ideas, the first two with rising inflection, and the third with a downward ring of completion that gives the cue for applause. Atkinson gives an example from a speech by Margaret Thatcher at a Conservative Party conference: 'This week has demonstrated that we are a party united in purpose (*pause*), strategy (*pause*) and resolve (*applause*)'. He notes that the items are marked out with similar length pauses so that the audience has a clear signal when to clap. This 'On your marks, get set, go' formula is likely to be accompanied with 'baton gestures' of the hand, the third beat effectively 'bringing in the chorus'. A similar strategy is followed when a stage compère introduces an artist: 'We now present for your enjoyment a man who is no stranger in this part of the country (*pause*); a man whose entertainment career has spanned more than three decades (*pause*); Mr Secondrate Comic (*applause*).' Again, the purpose of this build-up is not just to impress the audience with the artist's credentials but also to prepare them to commence applauding at a precise, simultaneous moment.

The *two-part contrast* consists of a juxtaposition between similarly-phrased, but opposite-meaning assertions about 'them' and 'us'. An example is given from a speech by James Callaghan: 'In this election I don't intend to make the most promises (*pause*); I intend that the next Labour government shall KEEP the most promises (*applause*).' Again, the audience can sense in the phrasing of this statement exactly when it is their turn to join in. In fact, in this instance the applause began immediately after the word 'keep', which is pivotal to his rejigging of the first phrase, the final few words being taken for granted. This use of contrasts is very similar to the way in which a comedian uses punchlines to extract focused laughter from an audience. Provided the structure and timing in the delivery of the lines is correct, a basically sympathetic audience will laugh even if there is no joke at all. (They may even laugh louder in case those about them detect that they weren't clever enough to get the joke.) What is critical is that the audience knows exactly when the performer intends them to laugh.

Various other claptrap devices are used in the theatre, such as the drum roll which signals that a magician or acrobat is about to perform a spectacular feat, followed by a percussive burst at its climax, and the musical signature tune that accompanies a popular singer's arrival on stage so that the audience claps the first phrase of the song with which he or she is most strongly identified. Also in this category is the loud staccato passage that frequently occurs at the end of 'tour de force' Italian arias; this functions as simulated orchestral applause to evoke and reinforce clapping from the audience.

The timing of curtain calls at the end of a theatrical performance is most important. Although the orchestra and performers maintain a high energy level in order to appear proud of themselves, the curtain is 'milked' for as long as possible by various contrivances such as keeping it down until the applause is about to decline before raising it again on a new applause-worthy line-up of performers. The goal is to stretch the reception for as long as possible without the audience running out of enthusiasm or feeling conned. And when the curtain closes for the last time quick-step music is played to get everybody out of the theatre in high spirits and minimum time.

IDENTIFICATION

Audience involvement in drama depends upon an important psychological process called identification (Wrightsman 1977). This is the ability of people to project themselves mentally into the position of the characters in the play so that, however vicariously, the things that happen to the performers on stage happen to them also. Identification is a powerful type of human fantasy, without which social living as we know it would not be possible, and it is an equally essential ingredient of dramatic appreciation (Schoenmakers 1990). When a character has a long soliloquy (e.g. one of Hamlet's speeches) the whole audience enters his head with him, and when Isolde sings her 'love-death' aria at the end of Wagner's *Tristan and Isolde* everybody shares her passion. If this does not happen, somebody has failed in the chain of dramatic communication from writer, through interpreter to audience. Ignorance or ill-preparation on the part of the audience may be responsible for the failure of the performance as much as those who set out to communicate.

Individual members of the audience may identify with one character more than others, usually the character that appeals as being most like their actual selves, or their ideal selves (the principle most often used in selecting models for television advertising) or quite simply the one that they like the most. But it is normal to 'get inside' other characters as well to some extent, seeing and feeling the situation from each person's point of view respectively. In the words of Arthur Miller, 'No one could write a good play unless he were able to shift his point of view every time he writes a line. It's a constant shifting of empathy; I'm with one man at one moment and then I have to go right over to the other side and be with the other man for a moment... We think Shakespeare is universal for one reason, and that is that he obviously could share the inner life of a variety of personalities to such a degree that he himself has rather vanished into his plays' (Evans 1981, p.18). As it is with the playwright, so it presumably is with the audience.

Identification depends on the ability to sympathise, and sometimes the author intends that this will apply to certain characters only, and not to others. In Kafka's *The Trial* we identify with the victim of unfeeling bureaucracy, not the bureaucrats. In *Billy Budd* we identify almost entirely with Billy, the likeable deckhand who is sacrificed to the rule of law, although it is possible to see the captain's position to some extent.

The characters upon whom we project ourselves need not necessarily be good. Skilful dramatists can easily put us inside the heads of the most unscrupulous villains and psychopaths, such as Macbeth, the child murderer, Don Giovanni, the seducer of women, or Alex in *A Clockwork Orange*. The ability to identify with villains is not restricted to dramatic audiences. Studies of the behaviour of concentration camp inmates during the Second World War (Bettelheim 1943), turned up a phenomenon called 'identification with the aggressor'. In order to survive, mentally as well as literally, some prisoners would adopt the defensive strategy of internalising the attitudes, values and goals of their guards and tormentors. While behavioural collaboration (doing what you are told) would seem a sensible, prudent course of action, these prisoners went a step further – they sought mental comfort by, in effect, 'becoming one of the enemy'. A similar defensive strategy has since been observed in hostages held under conditions of isolation, fear and hardship by fanatical terrorists. If in real life it is possible for us to identify with psychopaths, we can do so all the more easily through imagination in the theatre.

Although the character with whom we identify does not have to be virtuous, he does need to be believable, and bad casting or acting can impair the identification process. An excessively fat soprano may destroy the credibility of Violetta's imminent death from the 'wasting disease' and a short tenor may have difficulty conveying Radames, the hero of Egypt. Similarly, gross overacting only succeeds in drawing attention to itself; it usually fails to evoke real feelings.

CHARISMA AND IDOLIZATION

People are particularly excited by the immediate presence of performers who have exceptional appeal due to looks, self-confidence, voice, fame, wealth or suchlike. Charisma (meaning magic or charm) is the modern buzz-word for this commodity (Spencer 1973) and it can be powerful enough to cause members of the audience to scream in ecstasy or faint in awe. The presence of 'stars' in films or on television may be similarly effective to some extent, but being relatively remote, is much less compelling.

The 'power of presence' that we call charisma is partly based on *personal attributes*, such as sexual attractiveness (Marilyn Monroe), physical stature (Arnold Schwarzenegger), assertiveness (Humphrey Bogart) or voice (Pavarotti). However, charisma is also derived from *social position*, as in the case of royalty or political leaders. Prince Charles, Henry Kissinger, Ringo Starr or Woody Allen are not, perhaps, intrinsically very prepossessing men but their aura of social power and accomplishment has made them attractive to women. Hence, while charisma may lead to fame, fame itself can be sufficient to impart charisma. Even simple *familiarity* contributes to charisma, such that plain people who read weather forecasts on television every day or 'bimbos' that score game shows rapidly acquire celebrity status. While we may find charismatic people likeable (e.g. Benny Hill, Gorbachev, Muhammed Ali), this is by no means a necessary virtue. People who appear cold, surly and abrasive may also be acknowledged as charismatic (e.g. Margaret Thatcher, Clint Eastwood, James Dean). As Bates (1986) says, *self-assurance* (which is a more central aspect of charisma) may usefully be viewed as 'the strength to resist the need to be liked'. In other words, people may transmit social power by appearing unconcerned about the impression they are making on others.

It is an interesting fact that notorious psychopaths frequently exert great charm over people. For example, Ted Bundy, the good-looking serial murderer who was believed to have killed up to 100 women around his home town of Tacoma, Washington had many female admirers by the time of his execution in 1990. Five books were written about his life and when his story was made into a television film women from all over America wrote to him proposing marriage. Similarly, when in 1991 a young Italian man cold-bloodedly battered his parents to death upon their return from church one evening in order to hasten his inheritance of the family vineyard, the publicity accorded him at his trial led to his name being chanted in admiration at football grounds. We should not, therefore, find it strange that brutally repressive leaders such as Adolf Hitler and Saddam Hussein, and badly-behaved sports stars like John McEnroe and actors like Ryan O'Neal have little difficulty in attracting a following. Ruthlessness and villainy have a certain masculine 'charge' that women in particular often seem to find exciting.

While some actors submerge their own personality in the role they are playing and seldom appear as the same person twice (e.g. Peter Sellers, Robert De Niro), others depend upon their own charisma (e.g. John Wayne, Charles Bronson, Marilyn Monroe). These personality 'stars' as they are known, have phenomenal fame and acquire 'fans' (from *fanaticus*, meaning someone inspired to frenzy by devotion to a deity). Bates (1986) relates this sort of idolatry to shamanism. We become attached to the 'persona' of the star and even though they play different parts, their screen image (spirit) remains much the same. Our expectations even carry over to their private life, where we demand the role is maintained. Hence, like the shamans of primitive society, they 'incarnate' for us, or 'crystallize' certain feelings about sexuality, freedom, power or whatever is of special concern to us as individuals or society at a particular period.

Conrad (1987) goes further by suggesting that charismatic idols are sometimes effectively sacrificed by their fans. He gives the examples of Marilyn Monroe, Elvis Presley and Maria Callas, all of whom had devoted followings, suffered premature deaths after artistic failure or exhaustion, and became cult figures, with relics being traded, death anniversaries celebrated and attempts to reincarnate them with imitation or imagination (such as the 'Elvis is alive' stories in the tabloids). Conrad maintains that these people function as 'sacrificial victims', being elected to take on the stress, anguish and terror of us all; eventually we cast out these bogeys by calling upon the gods to ravage them alone. They volunteer, as does the shaman, to embody our desires – hence our idolatry – but they do so at great detriment to themselves. 'Chosen to enact our dreams, they must make themselves over to us utterly, resigning tenure of their own existence.' They end by losing the distinction between their private and public self and are hounded to death by the media in a state of excess and gross self-caricature. Presumably this is not the fate of all celebrities, but the pattern is nevertheless recognizable.

A more direct kind of sacrifice is the increasingly common phenomenon of stars being murdered by their fans. The most famous case is that of John Lennon who was shot by an obsessive fan waiting outside his New York apartment. The reason is obscure, but the fan may have wished to be remembered in history beside the name of his idol. Actress Rebecca Shaeffer, who starred in Woody Allen's *Radio Days*, was murdered after refusing to accept an admirer's gift of a five-foot teddy bear, and John Hinckley apparently shot President Reagan so that Jodie Foster would notice him. The motives in such cases are complex and mysterious and may have nothing to do with shamanism, but celebrities often need protection, especially from people who claim to be their greatest fans.

POLITICAL PERSUASION

Charisma is an attribute that is important not just to actors, singers and dancers but also to the members of many other occupational groups who have a strong performance element to their work, such as salesmen, evangelists and politicians. Because modern political campaigns are fought so much on television, candidates depend heavily upon advice from professional image consultants, or 'spin doctors' who guide them in how to dress, speak and behave so as to create the best impression with the voting public.

There has been much research over recent years on what determines voter preferences, some of it being based on reactions to videos of presidential debates and campaign broadcasts (e.g. McHugo *et al.* 1985, Lanone and Schrott 1989). The main conclusion is that the visual aspects of the candidate's performance (height, clothes, gestures, facial expressions) are most influential (accounting for

55% of variance). Second most important are the non-verbal aspects of speech (how deep, quick, unfaltering or monotonic the presentation is) carrying 38 per cent of weight. What the politician actually says (the content, message or policy) accounts for only 7 per cent of variance. Hence, many Americans who, on paper, would have preferred the policies of Dukakis, apparently voted for Bush in 1988 because he was taller and had a voice like John Wayne. Certainly, the body language of Bush was somehow more reassuring to the American public than that of Dukakis. However, in 1992 Bush had to contend with the equally impressive Bill Clinton, and lost.

Many analysts have noted that in Western democracies there has been a progressive shift towards personal image and 'performance' as critical factors in political success. This leads towards a merging of the occupations of performer and politician (cf. Ronald Reagan and Glenda Jackson). Politicians who do not have backgrounds as performers are often given training in television techniques. They are taught, for example, to prepare what they want to say and to say it regardless of the question, to suppress unfortunate mannerisms and to minimize smiling (because that can appear flippant or submissive). Margaret Thatcher was taught to speak in a lower register and wear dark blue suits in order to increase her apparent authority. British Labour leader Neil Kinnock was advised to control his head thrusting and airpunching which came across as pugnacious; he also took to wearing glasses during the 1992 election campaign, which is known to increase apparent intelligence (though not sufficiently, as it turned out). When John Major first became British Prime Minister he proclaimed that 'the image-makers will not find me under their tutelage... I shall be the same plug ugly I always was'. Although this statement was consistent with his 'honest John' image, he was soon wearing better tailored, double breasted suits and new (non-reflective) spectacles and his hair had been tidied up. It is virtually impossible for modern politicians to ignore their public image.

Another modern trend which affects political performance is the speed with which impressions are formed. Increased exposure to television (and tabloid newspapers) has taught people to interpret complex signals in ten second news and advertisement 'bites'. Politicians and other celebrities therefore learn to deliver their message (and more especially their image) within these very tight constraints. According to Harvey Thomas, advisor to many eminent people including Billy Graham and Margaret Thatcher, 'You have to earn the viewer's attention; it's not a right'. And the attention span of modern audiences is becoming increasingly short.

A research technique that has been developed to evaluate the effectiveness of political communications such as speeches and election broadcasts is called *vote-metering*. A representative sample of around 50 to 100 people are assembled in a studio to watch an experimental broadcast and are given a dial which they turn up when they are favourably impressed and down when their reaction is negative. As the video proceeds, a computer monitors average reactions of the audience, grouping them in various ways so that detailed connections can be made between what happens on screen and how different types of people react. For example, the audience might be grouped into Republicans, Democrats and uncommitted voters, so that when an issue like abortion is raised its impact on the three groups can be compared. However, the information stored by the computer will also allow the data to be split many other ways retrospectively, for example, into male and female, young and old, Northerners and Southerners. In this way, political campaigns can be aimed more effectively at their targets.

AUDIENCE RESEARCH

Vote monitoring is just one form of audience research that began at Iowa University some decades ago (Mabie 1952). Among the methods used to study spectator variables in the theatre have been rating scales (e.g. bipolar adjectives), psychophysiological monitoring (EEG, heart rate, skin conductance, pupil dilation and eye movements), video registration of facial expression, recordings of applause level, and attention as determined by subsequent memory for events in the performance (Schoenmakers 1990). Squirming has been used as a boredom indicator, with seats being wired to record buttock movements, the presumption being that attentive people sit still and fidget less.

Research using such methods has shown that audience reaction to plays depends upon factors such as age, sex, education, personality and social attitudes. Not surprisingly, older and more conservative people react less favourably to controversial (e.g. sexually explicit) material on stage. We noted in Chapter 1 that extrovert, sensation-seeking people prefer more 'shocking' kinds of material, such as X-rated movies and depictions of extreme violence. Generally speaking, men tend to like westerns, war films, slapstick comedy and sport more than women, whereas women prefer themes concerned with romance, marriage and family life (e.g. TV soaps, sit-coms and royal events) (Austin 1985). More educated people like documentaries, whereas people of lower socio-economic class prefer quiz/game shows. Interest in news, classic films and programmes about royalty increases with age.

GROUP AROUSAL

The larger the audience, the easier it is (paradoxically) for each individual to attend to, and become involved in, a performance. When many people are assembled for a common purpose, for example to enjoy a particular musical or drama, a quasi-religious atmosphere is generated. As the lights go down in a theatre such as at Covent Garden or La Scala, a hush ensues that is intense and full of anticipation, and this 'charge' is proportional to the size and density of the audience. The close presence of many other like-minded people, jointly intent on appreciating the performance, 'concentrates the mind wonderfully'. If all the people around you wish to be quiet and focus their attention on the stage it is difficult not to do likewise. Indeed, anyone talking or rustling sweet packets after a performance has begun will be glared at or told to hush.

Social facilitation has been demonstrated in many other contexts (Zajonc 1965; Crandall 1974). For example, despite the widespread belief among teachers and parents that small classes are educationally 'better', there are some circumstances in which children may learn more in large classes. This is due not just to increased competition, but also to general social enhancement. When there are a lot of people around us doing the same thing we somehow feel 'we must be in the right place' and are therefore less distractible. Perhaps the child who sees only a few other pupils about him wonders at some level of consciousness if he should be off fishing instead. Whatever the precise reason, large classes sometimes engender a social energy that promotes performance.

The presence of other people (i.e., an audience) is particularly likely to facilitate performance on tasks that are simple or well-learned. This is in accordance with the *Yerkes-Dodson Law* that will be discussed more fully in relation to performance anxiety (Chapter 11). In a review of studies on the effects of an audience upon various kinds of performance, Bond and Titus (1983) conclude that the presence of other people is basically arousing or motivating, and that arousal will facilitate output on tasks that we have a good command of, but may interfere with performance on tasks that are very exacting and upon which our grip is tenuous. This is apparently because high levels of emotion lead to mental distraction and are not helpful in circumstances where a clear head is required.

There is widespread agreement that a night at the theatre is generally more pleasurable and exciting when there is a full house. Awareness of this leads many theatre managements to give away complimentary tickets in order to 'pad the house' at press previews or at off-season times when audiences are scarce. This practice may help in providing word-of-mouth publicity for the show, but it also makes for a more happy and receptive atmosphere in the theatre and draws better performances from the cast.

Against this must be set the disadvantage that a conscript or free-loading audience is by nature different from one with more commitment to enjoying itself. The price of admission is an investment that guarantees sincere interest, and the more the tickets cost, the more determined people will be to get their money's worth. Laboratory experiments dealing with what are called *cognitive dissonance* effects (Brehm and Cohen 1962) suggest that people will generally be less appreciative of a performance for which they have not paid. A parallel case is psychotherapy, where it has been found that one of the few variables that predicts a patient's report of having benefited from treatment is the amount of money that has been charged for it. It follows from such research that managements are ill-advised to be indiscriminate in issuing complimentary tickets.

When other people laugh, applaud, feel sad or shocked there is a fairly direct knock-on effect to ourselves. Human emotions (or animal for that matter) are readily transmitted from one individual to another without a spoken word. Animals reverberate to the emotions of their own species in particular, for vital evolutionary reasons. The presence of predators may need to be communicated to other members of the group without giving away their location.

Ekman *et al.* (1983) conducted experiments on the effects of emotional expression on people themselves, and those around them. They found that the mere act of flexing the facial muscles into the patterns characteristic of joy, sadness, anger and so on, could produce immediate effects in the nervous system that normally accompany those emotions. Expressions of happiness, for example, produced a lowered heart rate, while sadness led to lowered skin temperature and electrical resistance. These responses occurred even when subjects viewed pictures that might be expected to induce a contrary emotion, such as adopting a smile while looking at a picture of the Ku Klux Klan in action or frowning at a scene of children playing innocently. Ekman also found that people tend to mimic the emotional expressions of those around them, with the result that similar effects are induced in their nervous system also ('Smile and the world smiles with you'). This could explain the effectiveness of advertising in which smiling models are used, and the tendency for smiling faces at parties to be infectious.

Emotional contagion might also account for much of the impact of theatre. Human emotions tend to be magnified in proportion to the number of people present. This amplification of feelings is apparent to anyone who has witnessed the fighting of young men at football matches, the screaming of teenagers at pop concerts, or any other type of group hysteria, such as the Jonestown mass suicide or the Harrods winter sale. The group passions that can be aroused at mass demonstrations and political meetings by charismatic leaders and demagogues are well-known. Hitler, who was a skilled manipulator of mass emotion, made it a rule only to address live crowds. A more benevolent example is the aura created by the Pope's periodic delivery of messages to massed assemblies in St Peter's Square.

There may be factors other than social contagion involved in the crowd excitement that is seen in pop concerts, political rallies and riots (such as those that occurred in Los Angeles in 1992). Tomkins (1991) argues that shouting loudly produces a lifting of the taboo on infantile emotion and behaviour. In much the same way as instructing people to write slowly can lead to the recovery of early handwriting, so shouting can produce a liberation of childish tendencies. 'The individual under such permissive conditions can be captured by deep excitement and rage he has not given expression since the nursery' (p.2). According to Tomkins, intuitive political leaders and pop stars are skilled in arousing and orchestrating these infantile passions for their own purpose.

Pradier (1990) discusses group facilitation effects in terms of biological factors such as brain chemistry and pheromones. He suggests, for example, that the collective euphoria experienced by crowds at demonstrations, rock concerts or special theatrical events may be related to the release of endorphins – opium-like substances produced internally by the brain which induce feelings of cohesion and social comfort. Pradier proposes that performance is a *contact event* that fulfils much the same purposes as social grooming in other primates, even if direct physical touching is not involved. The 'encounter group' movement that flourished in California in the 1970s took this further by promoting the actual laying on of hands, as of course do many religious and healing rituals. Finally, Pradier suggests that the bodily odours of performers and audience may contribute consciously or unconsciously to the sum total of human communication. These biological arousers remain speculative but it is probable that some effects of this kind are operative.

ANXIETY, AFFILIATION AND ATTRIBUTION

Events that are frightening, either in real life or in theatre, have power to bind people together emotionally. This occurs as a result of a well-established psychological process called *affiliation under anxiety*. In a celebrated series of experiments, Schachter (1959) showed that when people are placed in a threatening situation, where they expect to have to go through an ordeal together (for example, waiting to be used as subjects in an experiment involving painful electric shocks), they develop strong and affectionate ties which persist well after the danger has passed. This tendency for anxiety to increase social affiliation may be responsible for a wide variety of social phenomena. The 'old school tie' effect is more striking in schools that are very strict, illicit sex is frequently more exciting than married sex, people in bomb shelters develop a great spirit of comradeship, and, as noted above, hostages often sympathise and collaborate with terrorists. All of these well-known tendencies may be partly explained by the Schachter effect.

The ethological basis of this effect is the principle of safety in numbers (Wilson 1981). An infant monkey, when frightened by anything in the environment, runs and clings to its mother's fur so as to be transported away from the scene of the danger. Human babies also seek physical comfort when distressed, whether it be with someone they trust or a familiar cuddly toy. Young lovers engage in a great deal of intimate contact, but this manifestly diminishes as the relationship (and especially marriage) wears on. When they reach old age, however, physical and verbal reassurances are likely to reappear, which could be a reaction to increasing anxiety with the approach of infirmity and death.

The urge to affiliate in the face of mutual threat is the motive force behind some of the most intense and passionate love scenes in opera, for example, that between Tristan and Isolde who fall in love during a stormy sea crossing (with the additional help of a love potion), and Radames and Aida who are sealed together in a tomb. People about to die together feel very close to each other, and this is understood by the audience, who therefore share these intense feelings with them to some extent. Not only do they count themselves fortunate that they do not have to die like the characters in the opera, but they are likely to go home feeling closer to their companion.

Another psychological principle that helps to explain why love is so often paired with death in theatre and film is that of *emotional attribution*. Because most forms of emotional excitement, whether anger, love or fear, share a similar physiological basis (all the changes following activation of the sympathetic nervous system – increased heart rate, blood pressure and respiration, dry mouth, sweaty palms, etc.) it is easy for us to confuse our emotions. Under certain circumstances it appears that negative emotions such as anger or fear can be misinterpreted as romantic passion, or at least can potentiate the experience of love. As far back as Roman Empire days, insightful poets/philosophers recommended that men take their girl friends to the Coliseum to render them more amorous. It seems that they intuitively grasped the idea that the spectacle of a Christian being devoured by lions would not only cause a woman to cling physically and emotionally to her escort, but the emotional upset evoked by witnessing such horror would be liable to misidentification as sexual passion. In an experimental study of this hypothesis, Dutton and Aron (1974) found that men were more liable to make passes at a sexually attractive interviewer if they were approached on a dangerous suspension bridge overlooking a 200 foot drop onto jagged rocks than if they were crossing a secure road bridge. Although in this particular study the outcome may have been partly due to the anxiety/affiliation effect, there is other evidence that one emotion has the power to magnify another through a process of misattribution (Schachter and Singer 1962), and dramatists have implicitly realized this in using the horror of death (or impending death) to heighten the passion of fictional love.

CONTAGION OF LAUGHTER

Laughter is very much a social phenomenon. While we may inwardly think something is very funny when we are on our own, we seldom laugh except in company (Chapman and Foot 1976), although the other people present do not necessarily need to be laughing themselves. Experiments show that we are most likely to laugh at jokes if other people present are also laughing, but that we are more likely to laugh in the presence of other people who are not themselves laughing than if we are alone. Thus, laughter functions as a social communication device. The individual who laughs is probably trying in some way to share the joke with others about him. He might, for example, hope to be asked 'what's so funny?', so there is an excuse for bringing others in on the joke.

Although people laugh more at a joke in the company of others, this does not necessarily mean they will afterwards report it as any funnier. People seem quite capable of judging humour as funny even though they have first encountered it in solitude and not laughed. What is disastrous from the point of view of a comedian or comic playwright is the discovery that his material evokes no laughter from a large group of people. This is called 'dying on stage' and is equivalent to a consensual 'thumbs down'. Such a performance is certain to be reported afterwards as unfunny.

The fear of group silence prompts some television producers to use dubbed laughter in their comedies, a technique that would seem to be most necessary when the material is not intrinsically very funny. As one researcher put it, 'the effect of taped laughter is to make people look for a joke somewhere'. Various kinds of laughter and applause machines have been invented for salvaging mediocre television comedies, some of them looking rather like typewriters, with keys corresponding to various expressions of mirth – 'giggle', 'guffaw', 'chuckle', 'roar', etc. However, they are seldom completely effective because the pattern of laughter is critical. If hysteria hits an instant peak after the punch-line it sounds artificial and if the same growth and decay curve is used repeatedly the audience soon becomes aware of its mechanical origins. Laughter recorded from a live audience is much better, but this is often impractical, as when a show is made on location rather than in the studio. In this case what is often done is to play a video recording to a studio audience and add any laughter that occurs spontaneously onto the soundtrack. Depending on the basic quality of the comedy, this procedure may have to be repeated several times until sufficient laughter has accumulated. Another technique, (which comes across as rather desperate) is to have professional actor-laughers contribute chuckles and chortles to the soundtrack at appropriate points.

American television producers use dubbed laughter more than British, some-times to an extent that seems intrusive to British audiences. The BBC occasionally requires the removal of synthetic laughter from an American comedy series as a condition of purchase. This was the case with the comedy series *Mash*, set in a Korean war field hospital, which contained a sophisticated brand of humour that the BBC reckoned was diminished by the dubbed laughter.

SOCIAL COUGHING

Coughing in an auditorium is also socially contagious. Pennebaker (1980) devised a 'coughogram' in the form of a seating plan which showed the frequency and location of coughs occurring during a short period within an audience. With this method he was able to show that people cough more in large groups than small groups and when others are coughing. The coughing tends to spread away from the starting point in a radial pattern reminiscent of the ripple created by dropping a pebble in a still pond – each person triggering coughs in others beyond them. Pennebaker suggests that the contagion effect may be due to people paying extra attention to throat sensations that normally precede coughing. Alternatively, it might come about because of social disinhibition ('if they can do it, so can I'). Both factors are likely to contribute.

Not surprisingly, seasonal effects were also found; people coughed more in winter when throat ailments and irritations are rife. Pennebaker also showed that if concentration is high (as when an audience is watching a segment of film independently judged to be highly interesting) coughing is less frequent. People probably save their coughs for the less absorbing parts of a performance, or for applause at the end of an item. It is possible therefore that coughing could be used as an index of boredom if director or performers are trying to tighten their show after opening night.

The Baltimore Symphony Orchestra experimented with the distribution of cough drops to concert-goers before performances and during intermissions in the winter season, and found that it was an effective way to reduce the amount of coughing in the auditorium. Any direct medical benefits were almost certainly outweighed by the psychological effects of having something to suck on, plus the hint that coughing is disapproved. And for every cough thus suppressed, several more 'reflected' coughs would have been averted.

CONFORMITY AND CLAQUES

Social contagion of various types operates so as to create pressure towards group conformity. This can lead to idiosyncratic responses on the part of entire audiences. The same show presented on two occasions may produce almost opposite audience reactions. Performers talk of good and bad audiences (irrespective of size) and there is definite truth in their observation. The effect can be studied by reactions to movies, which provide identical performances each time. they are shown but receive inconsistent audience response. What apparently happens is that a few dominant individuals are accepted as leaders by the crowd and the overall atmosphere (accepting or rejecting; excited or bored) is pushed powerfully one way or another according to the way these leaders react.

Social conformity effects were demonstrated in a famous series of laboratory experiments by Asch (1956). People asked to judge the relative length of two lines can be swayed remarkably by patently incorrect judgements given confidently and unanimously by accomplices of the experimenter. Since the criteria for judging artistic performances are less objective, the conformity effect is likely to be that much more powerful in the theatre.

One application of the conformity effect to theatre is to seed the audience with a *claque* of professional applauders who try to lift the rest of the audience with raucous laughter, clapping, shouts of 'bravo', or whatever is appropriate. Mechanical claques, like laughter machines, have been tried, but are less successful than skilled people who are sensitive to the needs of the moment. The trouble is that if the claque does not succeed in *assimilating* the audience (i.e., taking them along with them), they might actually have the reverse effect and create what social psychologists call *reactance* (Brehm and Brehm 1981). If credibility is strained beyond a certain point, the claque may be recognized as agents of the performers and resented, or they may be perceived as dissidents rather than leaders. The result is that they are socially excommunicated, while the mass of the audience becomes even more cold and hostile as a means of dissociating itself from the outcasts.

The way in which the claque is dressed and spatially deployed will affect the way in which it is perceived by the rest of the audience. Ideally, it should be distributed in small groups throughout the auditorium, not massed in one spot, and members of the claque should be dressed in a respectable, bordering on trendy, manner (depending on the nature of the performance and the kind of audience present). Claques often occupy the royal box and upper balcony slips because these areas are vacant and accessible. This usually works all right provided they do not look too out of place and too obviously members of the company or theatre staff. These positions are also strategic for throwing flowers on to the stage at the end of the performance, which is a task sometimes assigned to the claque, particularly when adulation is sought for a female star.

Claques are not limited to theatres. Pop groups may arrange them for airport receptions so that swooning and screaming fans will be photographed by any media present. Even *The Beatles* were provided by their manager with this kind of boost in their early days, however unnecessary it was to become in later years. In opera, especially Italian opera houses, individual singers have their personal claque comprised either of paid supporters or genuine enthusiasts. Top sopranos and tenors are particularly competitive and hope to give the impression that they are the outstanding stars of the performance. This competitiveness may extend to *anti-claques*, in which the supporters of one singer go along to boo and disrupt the performance of a rival. Again, a delicate balance needs to be struck; if this ploy is too crude and unconvincing the public will react against it and give an even more positive reception to the intended victim.

Social communication among members of the audience is relatively weak in the movie theatre. Without the presence of live actors to offset against the audience (cf. the contrast of priest versus congregation or military leader versus army) the movie audience tends to fragment into its own subgroups – smokers versus non-smokers, pairs of lovers, and so on. This may be one of the reasons why many people find live theatre to be a more exhilarating experience than watching a film; the social role ascribed to the audience is more clearly defined and there is greater cohesion among them.

There may be some family rapport generated while watching a television show, but not much, what with all the interruptions and freedom to move about the house. However, there is sometimes discussion of television programmes by an entire nation the next day and this may be an important basis of community identity and social change. Some years ago, *Cathy Come Home*, a British television film, aroused a great deal of public concern about the plight of the homeless. Similarly, *The Day After*, which dramatized the impact of a nuclear attack on an average American city caused great emotional and political stirrings throughout the world. Today, documentaries about the environmental impact of deforestation or global warming have the potential to promote feelings of world community.

PRESTIGE SUGGESTION

Asch found that conformity effects operated more powerfully when the model has an aura of prestige. This is not surprising when it is considered that a large part of what we call charisma is derived not from the unique characteristics of the charismatic individual but from the social power or 'status' associated with their role (Spencer 1973). The person who is introduced as 'President of the United States', 'star of the show' or 'top of the pops' is automatically invested with a certain amount of charisma regardless of his or her personal attributes – or lack of them. The 'halo effect' is such that people believed to be of high social status are even perceived as being substantially taller than if they are believed to be lower ranking people (Wilson 1968).

Theatres make use of prestige suggestion in various ways. It is common practice to feature favourable quotations from newspaper critics in advertisements and billboards outside the theatre. Sometimes these quotes are deliberately taken out of context to the extent that a hostile critic appears to praise the show. One of London's West End theatres used the quote 'this magnificent quartet' to promote a four-star musical play, when it fact, the critic had described the play as so bad that 'this magnificent quartet would do better to stay home in bed'. Sending complimentary tickets to famous people in the hope that they will attend the performance and that some of their prestige will rub off onto it is also common practice. One man in England who changed his first name to 'Lord' by deed poll was amazed by the welter of free sample products, business propositions, social invitations and theatre tickets that arrived through his mail box.

Prestige suggestion concerning a composer's background has been shown to affect the quality of an orchestra's playing. A jazz band asked to play new works by composers variously represented as untried hopefuls versus highly talented, established writers was found to like and remember better the works attributed to reputed composers, and to perform them better in the opinion of independent judges (Weick, Gilfillian and Keith 1973).

There is little doubt that the reputation of a playwright, composer or performer will significantly influence our appreciation of their work. Other things being equal, we perceive greater artistic merit in the person whom we believe has been previously acclaimed. However, there are occasions when 'reactance' can occur instead. If somebody has been puffed up in advance beyond the limits of credibility, audiences and critics may react even more negatively than they would otherwise have done, denouncing the artist vituperatively as failing to justify his or her reputation. This happened to the Greek soprano Elena Souliotis at Covent Garden after she had been widely billed as 'the new Callas'. Although her performance was well up to international standard, she was given a hostile reception by critics and loudly booed by some members of the audience who felt that the claim that she could replace Callas was presumptuous. (Performers and agents should perhaps bear in mind the possibility of this kind of reaction when preparing biographies for programme notes.)

CHAPTER 4

ACTOR TRAINING AND ROLE PREPARATION

The veteran American comedian George Burns once said: 'The most important thing about an actor is sincerity. If he can fake that, he's made'. Within this terse directive are incorporated the two major approaches to acting, which may be called the *imaginative* and the *technical* systems. The latter is sometimes called the *French system* because it was systematized by François Delsarte at the end of the last century (Schreck 1970). The main distinction between the two schools is whether the actor works from the inside out, or the outside in – whether he concentrates on 'feeling the part', or projects himself into the position of the audience, seeing it largely from their point of view. For this reason, the two attitudes may be called 'internal' and 'external' respectively (Table 4.1).

Table 4.1: Summary of the differences between the imaginative and technical approaches to acting

Imaginative	Technical
Focus of attention on internal thoughts and feelings of the character.	Mental 'viewpoint' is external i.e. that of the audience (standing back and looking at oneself).
Associated with Stanislavski and Strasberg's 'method'.	Associated with the French school (Delsarte) and British directors such as Guthrie and Olivier.
Main concern is with sincerity.	Main concern is communication with audience.
Favours preparation based on 'emotional memory', character analysis, improvisation and self-talk.	Preparation based on modelling, feedback, discipline, body language and manipulation of audience attention.
Suited particularly to avant-garde theatre and intimate film work.	Suited to classic stage, opera and epic films.

IMAGINATIVE VERSUS TECHNICAL APPROACHES

The imaginative approach is most commonly identified with the name of Constantin Stanislavski and the *Moscow Arts Theatre*. Stanislavski felt that European theatre around the turn of the last century had too much concern for the outward manifestations of character such as posture, gesture, and vocal projection, and so tried to redirect the attention of actors to inner processes. In his best-known book, *An Actor Prepares*, originally published in 1936, Stanislavski outlines the means by which actors should contrive to experience for themselves the situations and emotions that the dramatist imposes upon the characters. More specifically, he recommended that actors should 'feel' themselves into the part, imagining what it would be like to be in the situation dramatized. They should think to themselves: 'What would I do, if I were in this situation?' This 'if', which Stanislavski called 'the magic if', was said to be the key to effective imaginative projection. A second faculty that Stanislavski felt should be exercised and developed was that of *emotional memory*. Actors should try to recall occasions when a similar circumstance had occurred within their own life and reconstruct the emotion felt at that time. This emotion and the gestures inspired by it are then incorporated into the dramatic portrayal. The job of the actor, is therefore to discover material within himself that can be adapted to the part.

A more recent exponent of the imaginative approach is the Austrian-born director Lee Strasberg, who in 1948 established a training school for the stage in New York called *The Actor's Studio*. In following decades the reputation of the Studio grew enormously, and Strasberg's approach was dubbed (rather grandiosely) 'the Method' (Strasberg 1988). Strasberg's stress was upon psychological analysis of the character and a somewhat introvert attitude that led to naturalistic, though sometimes brooding, interpretations of a role. This approach was suited to American *avant garde* theatre and the increasingly important medium of cinema rather more than classical stage plays. Among Strasberg's more famous students, who (significantly) made their mark in films rather than on the stage, were James Dean, Marlon Brando, Rod Steiger, Marilyn Monroe, Paul Newman, Al Pacino and Jack Nicholson.

Critics of Strasberg say he misunderstood the message of Stanislavski, who sought only to superimpose his psychological approach upon a secure background of traditional technique, not dispense with it entirely. An absence of fundamental stage discipline is held to account for the fact that Strasberg's disciples were most successful in portraying inarticulate, common people, in intimate media where inadequacies of vocal and other technique are less obtrusive. Certainly, Strasberg's training was less geared to equipping actors for the portrayal of the elegant, lofty characters more typical of epic films or the traditional stage. Some proponents of 'the method' appear to believe that if appropriate emotion is truly felt by the performer, the correct actions and gestures will follow naturally and the performance will appear totally realistic. It is by no means clear that this was Stanislavski's position and it is not necessarily true.

Directors and actors who prefer a more technical approach, such as Tyrone Guthrie (1971) and Laurence Olivier (1982), point out that many aspects of technique have no connection with feelings or realism. For example, the actor has to be aware that there are times when he should face the audience so that they can hear his lines. This can be facilitated by gaining an 'upstage' position, or it may be necessary to 'cheat out'. Similarly, classical actors learn as a matter of basic stagecraft that, except in very unusual circumstances, a moving character should cross downstage (on the audience side) of stationary characters. These may be obvious examples, but sufficient to remind us that if an actor 'loses himself' in the part too much his egocentrism would be disastrous to the team effort.

There is also a danger that excessive feeling on the part of the actor, particularly when it is displayed demonstratively, may cut across the ability of the audience to sympathize with the emotions projected onto the character. Real crying on a stage, for example, often seems embarrassing or ludicrous to the audience, and may paradoxically be less affecting than showing great control in a situation that is clearly very emotion-provoking. Suppose a scene in a play involves a soldier delivering to a young mother the tragic news that her son has been killed in battle. If she breaks down screaming and sobbing in response to this news, the audience is in a sense relieved – she is showing a normal, healthy, grief reaction. If, however, she looks somewhat vacant and invites the messenger inside for a cup of tea, much greater tension and interest is developed in the audience. The woman is admired for her ability to maintain composure and gains more sympathy because of this, yet at the same time there is the uneasy feeling that at any moment the realization may strike, with an impact all the more turbulent for its delay.

It is necessary to distinguish between the actor feeling the character's emotions and maximizing second-order feelings of the audience for the character. In the final analysis it matters only that the audience feels powerful emotion, not the actors on stage. 'Method' training may help an actor feel the emotions that are appropriate to a character and situation but it does not guarantee that these emotions will be transferred to the audience. (See Chapter 5 for a further discussion of this issue.) The emphasis of the technical actor is, therefore, on sophisticated skills in voice, movement, costume and make-up to create illusions. Among the better known exponents of this approach are Jeremy Irons, Ben Kingsley, Vanessa Redgrave, Peter O'Toole and Alan Bates (significantly all British).

The distinction between 'being' and 'acting' is described by Olivier (1982) in relation to a flirtation with method-style acting he had in the 1920s (well before Strasberg):

> The 1920s brought forth a generation of actors, to which I belonged, who fell under the influence of the 'natural' actors, led by Charles Hawtrey and followed by Gerald du Maurier. They deceived us into believing that realistic acting was, in fact, realistic behaviour; those marvellous artists hoodwinked us. Their influence upon us was pretty disastrous. We all assumed

that acting wasn't acting at all, it was just 'being'. We had
insufficient experience to appreciate that they were such brilliant
artists that they were able to conceal their special techniques.
After a period of inaudible performances and mystified
audiences we were forced to reject this highly specialized school
and leave it to the experts. (p.47)

Olivier visited The Actor's Studio several times and was scathing of Strasberg's
'off the cuff sermonizing'. However, he did admit that the 'method' sometimes
produced results. When directing Marilyn Monroe in *The Prince and the Showgirl* he
found himself quite unable to discover any way of infusing a spark in her at a
certain critical point in her first meeting with the Prince. Paula Strasberg (Lee's
wife), who according to Olivier knew nothing about acting but attended rehearsals
as moral support for Marilyn, finally achieved the breakthrough by telling her,
'Marilyn, just think of Coca Cola and Frankie Sinatra'. Suddenly, there was a new
vivacity in her performance, said Olivier, and he had to concede that this approach
would never have occurred to him.

Another anecdote in support of 'method' acting comes from the autobiography
of Alec Guinness (1985). Playing the part of Yakov the butler in *The Seagull* one
evening, Guinness had won a laugh and round of applause on his exit. Passing
Edith Evans in the wings, he looked proudly at her. Next night there was no laugh
or applause and he asked Edith why. 'You're trying too hard', she said. 'You didn't
know how you got it in the first place, but it's natural to you; one day you'll find
it again. Take it lightly. But when it does come make a note of what you were
feeling *inside*.' We are not told if this advice was useful, but Guinness was certainly
impressed by the grand lady's wisdom.

Technique and imagination are no doubt both necessary for effective performance. Each school of acting seems to maintain that the other's emphasis comes
fairly naturally, and so they argue that training should concentrate on the other
aspect which does not. In this respect there might seem to be more truth in the
technical position, since it could be argued that most people have learned to
empathize with other people's problems and feelings well before they arrive at
drama school. This seems largely a matter of instinct and difficult to develop
through training. By contrast, the great technical actors go on perfecting their
technique throughout their career. According to Olivier's wife, Joan Plowright, he
was still doing voice lessons and working on his technique in his fifties. 'Even in
the bathroom, shaving, he's suddenly doing Shylock in the mirror. It just never
stops'. (*Sunday Times*, October 1982).

Of course, Olivier is not universally admired. He does have his critics and their
complaint is mostly that his technique is too obtrusive. When Olivier performs
Othello or *Henry V* they say, one is too conscious of a great actor going through
the motions and displaying his skills like a kind of gymnast. In this view,
awareness, even awe, of the performance detracts from involvement with the

character. It is possible, however, that this perception is a product of the training of the critic. Olivier's technique may be less apparent to lay audiences.

The theory that an actor should actually experience the emotions his character would feel in the dramatized circumstances is probably more relevant to early rehearsal than eventual performance. Olivier could not possibly have felt Othello's full passion every night over a three year run; it would probably have killed him. Certainly he would be running short of adrenalin by the end of the third year. But feeling genuine suspicion, jealousy, anger, grief and suchlike once or twice in the early stages of reading the part and rehearsing it with other cast members might well have helped him to plot his moves, gestures, voice tones, and so on. By the time he reached performance of the role, he would probably have been in a position to produce the prearranged series of signals (gestures, voice tones, etc.) almost from 'cold'.

Stanislavski would perhaps agree. It is significant that the title of his first and most famous book was 'An Actor *Prepares*', not 'An Actor *Performs*'. Modern proponents of 'the Method' seem to misunderstand this. They tend to concentrate their interest on Stanislavski's first book and rather overlook his later works, such as *Building a Character*, which run much closer to the technical viewpoint.

As noted, 'the Method', with its emphasis on realism and the commonplace, is more suited to intimate TV, films and experimental theatre in the round. Technique is relatively indispensable to classical theatre and opera, and to epic film acting. Often a work is stylized in such a way that a degree of almost military-like discipline is necessary for effect (e.g. geometric spacing of performers, synchrony of movement – or absence of movement, as in a frozen tableau). In such a context, individual actors 'feeling their parts' all over the stage would be nothing but a nuisance to the director and other performers.

Imaginative and technical approaches to acting each have something to contribute and so should be thought of as complementary rather than incompatible. The best actors draw upon each system in accordance with the requirements of the particular role. There are times when movements on stage must be executed with preplanned precision, and other times when the actor is best to 'get into the part' like a form of self-hypnosis.

CHARACTERIZATION AS POSSESSION

The discovery that many great actors and actresses feel 'possessed' by the character they are playing (Chapter 2) suggests that something may be gained in 'apparent sincerity' by total involvement during the actual performance. Indeed, possession may be regarded as an extreme form of imaginative acting, so it is appropriate now to consider this phenomenon in greater detail.

According to Bates (1991), a type of possession occurs when an actor puts himself into a character, or indeed allows the character to 'enter into himself', to the extent that he feels the emotions *of that character*. Actors offer a *channel* through which the feelings of the character can be expressed, though of course these are derived from the actor's own reservoir of emotions. Inevitably, there is some fusion of the two, but sometimes actors report being surprised by the way their character has responded to a situation, for example, crying when they did not expect them to. Some actors fear that the possessing character may become too strong and take control of them, to the detriment of the performance and possibly even threatening their sanity.

Bates maintains that possession is an everyday phenomenon, not just the preserve of actors. A large part of each day is spent in daydreams and reveries in which we talk to ourselves in much the same way as we might talk to someone else (although not out loud). We say to ourselves, 'I'd better hurry up' or 'You're going to be late again'. Sometimes we hold a conversation with ourselves, asking and answering questions. This inner talking is equivalent to the trance state of possession in that the mind is engaged in activity that excludes awareness of external reality. In both cases, says Bates, we have 'lost our mind' in the sense that it has been relieved of the moment-to-moment checks against the social environment that are the hallmark of normal waking consciousness. Whenever we are alone (e.g. driving a car) we enter a mild trance and carry on a dialogue with a presence which resides within us. But whereas the character possessing us does so privately and silently, the character played by the actor possesses publicly and is expressed externally. Actors deal with the imaginary characters within themselves in much the same way everybody else does, though we often forget that our inner self is 'an imaginary construction, a trick of the mind which allows us to negotiate with our life experience in the form of an inner character' (Bates 1991).

Bates points out that the allowing of creatures within oneself is a process of self-revelation. Actors are not just mediums, but they penetrate and possess themselves. A character that takes over an actor in performance, or maintains a presence in the mind afterwards, is an aspect of his inner self, which (unusually) is being experienced, confronted and digested. Hence creating characters may involve actors in calling up hidden, repressed experience and it may be this that leads many of them to report the experience of 'possession'. In Bates' view, acting is not just self-presentation, but the focusing on special aspects of the self which may not often get favoured airing.

It is unclear how useful these concepts are in understanding the acting process, or how widespread the phenomena. No doubt they can be detected in certain cases and may lend special electricity to a performance. However, the majority of work-a-day actors probably have no need of the concept of possession and yet communicate effectively with their audience.

IMPROVISATION AND CHARACTER ANALYSIS

Improvisation and character analysis are two derivatives of the imaginative approach to acting that are widely used in modern drama schools. Although useful in script-writing, they are of dubious value with respect to improving eventual performance. It is tempting to suppose they are popular because they are good fun, occupy time and are easy for drama instructors and directors to implement, requiring no preparation on the part of anyone. The story is told of a pretentious young director who was inflicting various trendy exercises upon a troupe of actors preparing for a short season of a Chekhov play in a West End theatre. After a week of apparently pointless activity he started another morning with what he described as a valuable 'warm-up'. Members of the company were told to run, one at a time, from the back of the stage to the footlights and scream into the auditorium the most obscene profanity that occurred to them. All was going well, with plenty of four-letter expletives being delivered, when the most experienced professional in the cast pounded into position and yelled, 'We open in three weeks!'. His point was well understood, to the embarrassment of the director, and work on the play itself commenced soon after.

Character analysis may be useful in the context of deciding how to read a particular ambiguous line, or how to motivate a particular piece of action in the play, but again, much time can be wasted with actors sitting around discussing their personalities and relationships in the abstract. Generally, it is better that these emerge in the course of a floor rehearsal where all technical requirements, such as the geometric placing of people on the stage, are simultaneously satisfied. It is no good developing a broad preconception of one's character if some of the lines and actions are later found to be inconsistent with it. The most significant discoveries about character and motivation are made in the course of bringing the play to life on the stage. Introverted psychoanalyzing is of little use in itself.

Goldovski (1968) describes an incident in his opera school in which a visiting director was asked to teach a group of students a complete act of Verdi's *Simon Boccanegra*. According to Goldovski, four solid weeks of work culminated in a public performance so dreadful that it might have been a first rehearsal.

> Remembering the countless hours of practice and the favourable comments of the students, I was extremely curious to find out just what had been going on in these daily sessions. Questioning (as diplomatically as I could) a few of the singers, I discovered to my surprise that they had obtained an amazing knowledge of the most obscure details of this opera and an extraordinary understanding of the ramifications of the plot. A veritable psychoanalytic study had been performed on each of the personages in the drama, and their most hidden impulses had been laid bare... The only trouble was that all this precious information remained solidly locked up in the minds of the

singers, and the audience that witnessed the performance remained just as solidly unaware of all these compelling dramatic insights. (p.34)

It is not enough for the director and actors to appreciate the motives of the characters in a drama. These motives have to be communicated to the audience by external means, and this usually requires a degree of technique. Many actors can perform a role very effectively without any deep understanding of the character's motives, just as most people go about their daily life without awareness of the instinctual springs of their own behaviour. It is the job of the director to ensure that the signals emitted by the actor convey the desired motives and evoke the desired effects regardless of how much role analysis that actor has or has not undertaken.

FEEDBACK

The external approach to acting stresses the importance of the audience perspective. One of the most obvious ways an actor can check how he looks from the audience point of view is by some sort of feedback. This is an important element of what the director contributes to a performance. Professional critics also provide a kind of feedback, however destructive, as do friends and relatives in the audience who offer little comments such as 'couldn't hear you; why don't you speak up?', or 'your make-up was too dark and your hair was shadowing your eyes'.

The Scottish poet Robert Burns pleaded:

O wad some power the giftie gie us
To see ourselves as others see us.

A mirror does this, of course. It reverses left and right, but otherwise gives a perfect and immediate representation of our expressions and actions. Stanislavski was known to examine himself in a mirror and practice gestures before going on stage – so was Laurence Olivier and a great many modern actors. Tyrone Guthrie used to set a complex move briefly at rehearsal and then, rather than embarrass the actor by having him attempt it repeatedly in public, would say: 'go away and practise it in your bathroom and astonish us in the morning'. Presumably the bathroom was recommended because it is private and equipped with mirrors.

Some singers find it useful in preparing for an operatic role, to set up the living room with major props such as chairs, swords, coats and hats, and to move around miming to a recording (or singing lightly on top of it) while watching the effect in the mirror. Especially on the day of the performance itself, this saves the voice while consolidating words, music and movements.

Sound recordings of one's own voice and videotapes of performances are also powerful feedback devices. They are not as immediately reinforcing as a mirror and do not allow quick readjustments and experimentation, but they do have the advantage that they show the performer exactly what he or she is like in performance and at a time removed from the feelings involved in generating the performance in the first place. Many amateurs (and some professionals) are afraid to risk such revealing self-scrutiny for fear that their confidence will be shattered, and so avoid it. Others refuse to believe that the technology has accurately represented them, claiming that for some peculiar reason they, alone among their colleagues, 'do not record or photograph well'. (It couldn't possibly be that they do not sing or act well, yet strangely, everybody else seems validly represented.) Such reactions are childishly ego-defensive and must be worked through, unless self-deception is preferred to professional development.

The actor in performance needs to be involved with the part to some extent, but equally important is the continuous monitoring of performance in 'the mind's eye' from the audience point of view. This may well be the difference between performance and egocentric self-indulgence. The effects of self-hypnotic identification with the character one is portraying may in a sense be parallel to the effects of alcohol; the actor's vista is restricted such that he feels convinced he is doing magnificently, but the audience does not necessarily share this conviction. From their perspective he often loses contact to the extent that he becomes immersed in his world of fantasy.

OBSERVATION AND MODELLING

While most actors would agree with the 'Method' suggestion that internal resources are used to create a character, there comes a point where the boundaries of the actor's own self are reached and more is needed. At this point it may be necessary to incorporate material that is based on the observation of others into the role.

> Often you are called upon to understand something in a part you yourself have never experienced. So throughout life you need to have a kind of snapshot shutter than comes down very much without you knowing it. (Judi Dench 1990, p.313)

Actors, especially those who are skilled as impersonators (as opposed to the charismatic 'stars') develop their powers of observation so they can use aspects of the people they meet to round out a character. In creating Basil Fawlty in *Fawlty Towers*, John Cleese presented a conglomerate of certain aspects of himself with several other eccentric men that he had encountered. One of them was almost certainly a ferociously right-wing publican called De la Teste Tickell, who was something of a celebrity in Cambridge. This man wore jackboots, bellowed commands at his helpers and had a reputation for assaulting his clientele if they offended him by such things as wearing T-shirts, sporting beards or putting ketchup on his ham. Fawlty was, in fact, only a slight exaggeration of this real-life character.

The classical actor Anthony Sher (1985) has provided a fascinating account of his preparation for the role of Richard III for the London stage. This included observations of a serial murderer called Dennis Nilsen, who was under public scrutiny at the time, and the behaviour of various predatory insects. These components were put together to produce an impressively grotesque and chilling portrayal of the King who was reputed to be deformed in body and mind.

Clearly, observation and mimicry are major sources of an actor's inspiration and important for role preparation. It is not unusual for them to immerse themselves in the sub-culture they have to represent before undertaking a role or to go out seeking individuals they can impersonate to a greater or lesser degree.

PERSONALITY THEORY

A knowledge of the psychology of personality can be useful to an actor in preparing a role. For example, there has been much research on how various *traits* tend to cluster together into broad groupings like extroversion, emotionality and adventurousness (Eysenck and Eysenck 1985). Extroverts are not only sociable but inclined to be stimulus hungry in all respects (liking bright colours, loud music and variety in their experiences). Highly emotional people are over-reactive in all their emotional responses, being fearful, anxious, volatile and 'hysterical', but also highly empathic (sensitive to the feelings of others). Studying the way in which personality attributes typically relate one to another may help an actor produce a character that is consistent and credible.

Other theoretical approaches to personality also have much to contribute. One is to classify personality in terms of an individual's *dominant needs*. Some people are driven primarily by ambition, some by a need for affiliation (company and social support). For some people sexual lust and novelty is the main objective, for others it is the avoidance of social humiliation and embarrassment. It is useful for actors to keep in mind what it is that they really want when they are developing their character. In addition, drama teachers advise that the actor should keep in mind the major obstacles to their goals. These may be material (e.g. lack of money), internal (e.g. Hamlet's conscience) or they may be other characters with conflicting motives.

Another major approach to personality is the *psychodynamic* view of Freud and his followers. The central idea is that people are usually unaware of the instincts that drive them because, being mainly sexual and aggressive, they are unacceptable to consciousness and hence have been repressed. With the help of Freud's biographer Ernest Jones, Olivier produced a *Hamlet* which emphasized his sup- posed Oedipus complex. Hamlet's mother was played by a young, attractive, woman whom he caressed in a blatantly sexual way. Similarly, an *Othello* was produced in which Iago was portrayed as overtly homosexual (the idea being that he was homosexually attracted to Othello and thus intent on eliminating his rival Desdemona). The problem with these interpretations is that if the supposed sexual motives were unconscious and repressed, they should not be so explicit. Indeed, it would be equally arguable in psychoanalytic terms that reaction-formation (bending over backwards in the opposite direction) would be observed by the audience.

Despite these dangers in psychoanalytic stage portrayals, there are subtle ways in which underlying motives can be communicated to audiences. For example, a woman who is sexually attracted to another character may betray this by preening, or checking her blouse buttons, or dislike may be 'leaked' by a false smile (Chapter 5).

ADVANCE 'CHOREOGRAPHY'

A major principle of technical acting is that, with the help of the director, but more especially through homework, every move, gesture and timing of lines should occur in a preplanned, well-rehearsed sequence. Geographical aspects of the performance, for example, should never be left to happen accidentally or be decided on the night. There are several reasons for this. First, it is inconsiderate to other members of the cast not to be predictable in movement. An actor who is in the wrong place at the wrong time is likely to upset someone else – other performers, or the lighting technicians perhaps. Stage performance is supposed to be teamwork coordinated by the director. It must not degenerate into a competitive struggle among actors, trying to upstage one another, 'hog the spots' or 'steal the show'.

Another reason for preplanning movement and timing is that such discipline is paradoxically liberating to the performer. Freed of spatial uncertainty (not having to make ongoing decisions about what to do and where to go next), the actor is better able to concentrate on other aspects of his or her performance, such as inflexions in lines, facial expressions, or even 'living' the role with sincerity. The singer, similarly, is better able to concentrate on music and voice production. Full preparation gives confidence and facilitates memory. Consistent connections between location, movement, lines and music (if any) make sequences easier to remember.

The fact that unexpected events on stage can give rise to memory lapses is illustrated by an incident that occurred in a Covent Garden production of *Rigoletto*. The baritone singing the title role had performed the part many times in English, but was now making a debut in Italian. Just at the beginning of Rigoletto's main aria, where he demands the return of his daughter from the courtiers who abducted her, a piece of scenery collapsed backstage and the distraction caused him to regress momentarily into the more familiar English. 'Filthy rabble, vil razza, dannata', he sang, to the astonishment of the audience.

CONTROL OF ACTION

The technical approach to acting puts as much emphasis on what the actor does *not* do as what he does do. The mark of the bad amateur is the discomfort that he displays unless doing something. Inexperienced actors tend to fidget with their hands and shuffle their feet, and these unnecessary movements come across to the audience (usually accurately) as anxiety. This is related to one of the reasons why many people have difficulty in giving up smoking. They are addicted not just to nicotine or the smell of smouldering tobacco, but to the ritual of pulling the packet out of their pocket, striking matches, lighting up, putting it in and out of their mouth and tapping off the ashes. Without all this activity they feel at a loss for something to do with their hands and, if prone to social anxiety, they feel especially deprived of their ritual when in company. Hollywood directors of a few decades ago, in recognition of this difficulty many of their actors faced, had their characters light up a cigarette in virtually every scene (in fact, whenever they were not running, fighting, shooting or kissing). Actors in classical plays and modern films are seldom permitted such luxuries. They have to hold attention largely by words and facial expression, and so have to learn control of hands and limbs that might otherwise cause distraction.

The danger that 'Method' actors may talk themselves into inappropriate emotional displays and a flurry of inconsequential action arising from their internal 'hype' has been noted. The example given was that of a woman receiving news of the death of her husband, where a stunned silence is more likely to be the real life response than an immediate burst of tears. This is also more effective dramatically because it maintains and builds tension rather than release it. Another example would be Butterfly's discovery that Pinkerton has returned with an American wife; people resolved to suicide are not usually demonstratively unhappy. Rather they appear composed and placid, a fact which derives more readily from psychological knowledge than sympathetic imagination.

Minimization of bodily movement is more effective because it has clarity and projects confidence. The fewer gestures and movements an actor makes the more significant each becomes and the more powerful his presence is felt to be. A good example is Olivier's performance in the classic film version of *Wuthering Heights*. Olivier's Heathcliff arguably derives its power more from what he does not do, than what he does. In one memorable scene he remains totally passive facially until a critical juncture upon which he simply raises one eyebrow. Yet few people who recall the emotional impact of his performance in this film would be aware of the extent to which restraint was the key to it.

Control is especially important in opera, where emotion is often carried so much by the situation in which the characters find themselves, and the associative meaning of the music, that anything added further from the singer would threaten to push it 'over the top'. At times all the singer needs to do is assume the role of a screen upon which the audience project the appropriate emotion. He does not have to do anything; they know from the context what he must be feeling inside.

For example, the famous baritone aria 'Eri tu' in *Un Ballo in Maschera*, which explores Renato's hurt following the discovery of his wife's involvement with the man he has loyally served, is preceded by some intensely exciting bars of orchestration. Most directors recognize that the temptation to have Renato storm about in a manner parallel with the mood of the music should be strenuously resisted. The music is better used to represent his internal passion than a random strut around the stage. The latter would only succeed in letting off steam, rather than building it up to the point of Renato's expression of righteous anger as he fixates the portrait of the Count and begins to sing.

Actors also need to learn how to control movement so that audience attention is not diverted toward them at times when it should be focused elsewhere. The director should have determined that at every moment during a performance the audience is following significant action. The job of other performers is to assist in this focus, often by attending to it themselves so that they point the direction of gaze of the audience appropriately (even if this means turning their back on the audience). At the very least, they should not distract by sudden jerky movements, facial contortions, audible intakes of breath or other attention-getting devices (Chapter 6). The chorus member who wants to be noticed by his aunt in the back stalls is a perennial problem for the director; as is the inconsiderate actor who wants to be the focus of attention all the time at the expense of his fellow performers.

OPERATIC ACTING

Opera singers are notoriously bad actors. This is a reputation that is partly deserved because some singers are selected on the quality of their voice alone. Nellie Melba was reputed to have two gestures: passion (depicted by one arm extended) and extreme passion (two arms extended). Italian tenors, in particular, have a reputation for being hopelessly egocentric. At Covent Garden one was seen to stroll off into the wings and light up a cigarette, leaving the unfortunate soprano to address a long aria to his imagined presence downstage. Another had a habit of dumping the heroine, with whom he was singing a duet, whenever he came to a big note, in order that he might come down to the footlights and belt it straight into the auditorium. There is an element of competitiveness in this; tenors and sopranos sometimes hang onto *ad lib* top notes *ad infinitum*, striving to outlast the other (much to the detriment of dramatic credibility).

In defence of singers, it should be said that operatic acting presents special difficulties. Singers need to watch the conductor's beat, and even though they can do this quite well out of the 'corner of their eye' (the retinal equivalent of which is replete with movement receptors), they tend to look glassy-eyed and peculiar when doing so. They also need to generate an internal beat, whether or not they can see the conductor, in order to anticipate entries. Reliance on the conductor's beat alone would result in their slipping behind tempo. What they need to do is match an internal tempo with that supplied by the conductor, and this necessitates a subliminal beating action in some part of their anatomy. Some singers beat time visibly with their hand, head or entire trunk, which is irritating to the audience and other performers (especially if their beat is slightly out of synchrony with that of the conductor). More experienced singers learn to beat time with some invisible part of their anatomy, such as the big toe inside the shoe.

Some singers, during the course of their training, develop gestural analogues of vocal dynamics, the most common of which are supporting an upward moving phrase with a vigorous scooping movement of their hand or standing on their toes to reach high notes. This is all very well during voice coaching sessions, but some later have difficulty in suppressing such movements in performance, with the result that obtrusive mannerisms detract from their characterization.

Operatic acting often requires moves to be elongated while feelings are explored musically. Singers need convincing that the voice and eyes alone can be sufficient to carry several phrases of music with no extra action interpolated. Gestures need to be stretched into accordance with musical structure. Arm movements that are snatched back straight after being initiated (like a boxer's left jab) look out of place against a background of legato music. Sometimes the effect that needs to be created is like the slow motion violence seen in movies. Although quite possibly motivated by sadistic voyeurism, the latter can be justified as representing perceptual experience. Horrific events that evoke exceptionally high mental arousal do sometimes seem to occupy more time than the split-second in which they actually occur. So it is with the passions and dilemmas of operatic characters. Many ensembles can only be treated as frozen moments of time, in which tortured thoughts and feelings are expressed against a static tableau.

For reasons such as this, operatic acting can never be naturalistic in the sense that acting in modern intimate plays and films usually is. Singers must always depend upon a certain amount of technique, and especially when ensemble work is involved, there must be advance planning so that a mutual understanding is arrived at concerning where everybody is and what they are to be doing in relation to the music.

LEARNING LINES

One of the practical problems faced by actors and singers is that of committing large tracts of material to memory verbatim. Developing the capacity to memorize parts quickly is particularly important to professional actors; if they are playing in repertory they may be required to learn several roles simultaneously.

One way to investigate strategies for learning lines is to ask the experts how they do it. However, actors seldom agree as to which strategies are most effective and which are most preferred by other members of the profession. They even disagree as to whether or not it is important to understand the lines fully and develop a meaningful framework as they are being learned, or whether simple repetition is all that is necessary. Some argue for a 'photographic' approach.

A famous Victorian actor, Harry Edwards, described his personal experience of rapid learning in a letter to Professor Harry Osborn (Osborn 1902):

> The faculty of 'cramming' a part, or as we call it, 'winging' it, i.e., learning it at the wing, is undoubtedly only to be acquired by practice and long experience, and is in these days of long runs unknown amongst our younger actors. When the bill of the night was changed much more often than is now the case it was a matter of necessity that the words of a part should be quickly acquired, and it was then no uncommon occurrence for a man to take a part in the morning and play it at night, reading it as he came off the stage at every scene and fixing mechanically upon his memory the shape of the written part, the very hand-writing, the position of each speech upon the paper, the sequence of the same, and all details which would present themselves to his physical eye. Thus he would acquire the words, not always perhaps the sense, as he would have no time to think about the context; and in some cases if a wrong cue were given it would probably tend to throw the student off the track and upset him altogether. I have known many ludicrous incidents occur as a result of such misadventures. In my early days I had to do a great deal of rapid study and cramming, and soon after I began to play leading business I studied and played six long parts in one week with only two of which I was at all familiar. I once took Sir John Falstaff at twelve o'clock and played the part perfectly at night. I need not say to you that I could not get at the meaning of the character under such circumstances. One result of these hurried studies is that the words do not remain. They seem to fade from the memory as rapidly as they were acquired.

Intons-Peterson and Smyth (1987) studied 'repertory memory' by comparing experts (experienced actors) with novices (psychology students matched for age and sex) as regards strategies used for learning long verbal passages. Subjects were videotaped as they worked out loud to commit prose passages to verbatim memory. They found that certain key words, usually the beginnings of sentences, paragraphs and long phrases were rehearsed more frequently, as though being used as landmarks to define manageable chunks. Although apparent in both groups, this tendency to focus on particular words that would serve as retrieval cues was more marked among experts than novices. The experts were also more likely to focus their efforts by self-testing in order to discover whether a chunk was properly memorized. In addition, they were observed to gesture with their head, hands or feet in such a way as to mark rhythm during the learning of the texts. Presumably as a result of these strategy differences, experts showed faster learning of the passages than novices.

Research of this kind enables psychologists to give performers a number of hints on how to commit material to memory most efficiently:

1. *Chunking.* After reading or listening through the complete work to gain some overall impression of it as the audience will ultimately receive it, the material should be split into manageable units, each of which will comprise a sub-goal in the learning process. Initially these chunks will be about one sentence, one couplet or one musical phrase long, and they should have some meaning, coherence or 'completion' in themselves.

2. *Grouping the chunks.* Once the individual chunks have been mastered they should be put together into larger sections, for example the entire first entrance to exit, the first verse of a song or the first section of a musical work. After this has been successfully achieved, grouping should proceed to the next unit size, for example, the first act, first aria or first movement. And so on, until the complete work is mastered.

3. *Self-testing.* At each stage from the first set of chunks, memory should be tested by forcing oneself to repeat it without looking at the text or music. This diagnoses areas of special difficulty so that further repetitions can be focused more efficiently and saves wasting time on the parts that are already known. It also serves to consolidate the memory trace more thoroughly and gives reassurance that progress is being made (a form of feedback and reinforcement). To aid in this process, some actors prepare a tape of their cues, leaving sufficient space for them to insert their own lines; this can be used to test memory even when out driving in a car that has a cassette player.

4. *Spacing of practice.* It is advisable not to work so long at a time that fatigue and confusion set in. This is not just uneconomic, it may even be stressful. Most people cannot effectively concentrate on learning for more than 30 or 40 minutes at a stretch. Rather than force oneself to carry on and cram remorselessly it is better to take a walk in the garden, do something else, or just rest. The breaks are not wasted because memory consolidation carries on, even when we are asleep. In fact, getting the full amount of sleep that is needed (a regular seven to eight hours for most people) is probably the most important thing of all, both for learning and eventual performance. It is now believed that an important function of dreams is to store daytime experiences in places with sufficient associations that they can be retrieved when required.

5. *Learn within context.* As far as practicable, material should be learned within the total context of the eventual performance, on the actual stage (or some space that simulates it as closely as possible), with the same props, costumes, fellow performers, musical instruments, acoustics, and so on. Lines are better remembered in relation to moves, positions on stage, scenery: indeed any such cues will help. This is why a considerate director will block moves as early as possible in rehearsal and will not expect lines to be learned by heart before that. It is so much easier to learn lines once you know where you are on the stage and what you and the other performers are doing at the time they are delivered. By the same token, self-testing is all the more exacting when stripped of all context, so the actor or singer who wants to be sure he has a thorough grip on his material may go through it in his head on the evening of the performance just to be sure.

6. *State-dependence.* An interesting fact about learning is that we remember things better when we are in the same biochemical and emotional state as we were at the time of acquisition (Goodwin *et al.* 1969). This is a special case of a context effect. If, for example, you heard a joke while drinking with friends in the pub, you have a better chance of recalling that joke when you are similarly intoxicated. By corollary, material that is learned while sober is better reproduced when sober. So unless a performer is proposing to act in a drunken state, rehearsals should be conducted in a state of sobriety. The state-dependence effect applies to a wide variety of drugs, both recreational and medicinal, and it also works for mood (Bower 1981). Things learned while happy are better remembered when we are similarly happy and things learned during a state of depression are better retrieved when feeling miserable. The effect may be small, but is of considerable theoretical interest and performers may also find it useful to know about.

7. *Overlearning.* Beyond the point where we can recall material with deliberate, conscious effort is a level of memory which is like replaying an automatic tape. Most people know *The Lord's Prayer* or the *Pledge of Allegiance* to the point where they can reel it off without having to think about it. Pianists experience the same thing when they have played a piece so many times that their fingers seem to find their own way around the keyboard. This does not necessarily make for a more artistic, 'feeling' performance of a work, but overlearning may be useful if any sort of stress is anticipated during performance (e.g. when doing an audition or broadcast). The automatic tape is less likely to be affected by fear or distraction than a consciously controlled performance.

8. *The method of the loci.* A useful adjunct to memory that performers may utilize is the 'method of the loci'. This is attributed to the Roman orator Cicero, who would remember the main points of a speech by wandering around a geographical location, such as a room, in his mind's eye, following a fixed route along which he had placed objects which would serve as cues in a fixed order. Today, speakers use phrases like 'in the first place' that reflect implicit use of this method. Since actors and singers are able to move physically about a stage this method is particularly effective. For example, a particularly left-wing sentiment may be delivered on the left side of the stage, followed by a cross to the right when mention is made of writing a letter. An imaginary bee may be located downstage to prompt the speech 'To be or not to be'. And so on; the only limitation is the ingenuity of the performer.

9. *Mnemonics.* Where it is necessary to learn a list of items that has little logical structure it may be useful to devise a personal prompter of some kind. There are many famous mnemonics that schoolchildren use for memorizing things like the periodic table in chemistry, but performers have to develop their own according to need. For example, the song 'There's a place for us' from *West Side Story* ends with the words 'somehow, someday, somewhere'. Since there is no particular logic to this sequence it helps to think of the Texan greeting 'howdy'. This gives the first two items (how and day) in order, leaving the where in last position. However awkward such gimmicks may sound at first, they do provide memories that are long-lasting.

CHAPTER 5

EMOTIONAL EXPRESSION

Humans use two quite separate languages, which sometimes concur in their messages and sometimes conflict. One is the verbal or spoken language with which we are all familiar, be it English, French, Arabic or some other. This is good for passing on information about facts and things, for logic and problem-solving, and it can be written down. But there is a more mysterious language, called 'body language', which is used unconsciously and which expresses the more truly human aspects of ourselves – feelings, emotions, needs, attitudes. This language is more difficult to write down but is probably more important in interpersonal relationships and is of particular interest to actors, dancers, mimists and other performing artists.

Watch a couple talking on the other side of the room at a noisy party. Paradoxically, their true feelings and intentions are all the more transparent because the content of their dialogue is masked by the background hubbub. This is called the 'cocktail party phenomenon' and it illustrates the power of non-verbal communication, through channels such as posture, gesture and facial expression. You can get this effect by turning down the sound on a TV soap opera such as *Dallas* or *Dynasty*. Just watching the characters interact tells us a lot about their relationships and feelings towards one another. People may be talking about the weather while blatantly flirting, detesting or competing with each other.

Scientific research on the subject has been boosted greatly with the advent of video-tape analysis techniques in which the impact of sight and sound can be compared (e.g. Mc Hugo *et al.* 1985, Bull 1987). As noted in Chapter 3, research on the Presidential debates in the US has shown that people form impressions and judge the winner much more on the basis of body language than what is actually said.

ORIGINS OF EMOTIONAL EXPRESSION

In his classic book *The Expression of Emotions in Man and Animals*, Darwin (1872) noted that much of our emotional expression derives logically from behavioural tendencies. For example, clenching the teeth and fists are obvious preparations for fighting and hence display *anger*. Because his teeth are clenched, the 'tough guy' is inclined to talk out of the side of his mouth and breathe hard through his nose in approximation to a snorting bull. Equally brutish in origin is the open-mouthed, teeth-baring laugh, which derives partly from a primate threat signal (indicating readiness to bite). The face of an angry person is characterised by a deep frown (the eyebrows being pulled low over the eyes), a tightly compressed mouth (projecting the jaw and teeth), a pallid complexion (blood supplies being directed to areas more vital for fighting such as the biceps), and the head is thrust forward as if to 'butt' the opponent.

Fear or shock is displayed in the following ways:

- The freezing of movement and silence (so as to avoid detection and locate the source of the danger).

- Eyes wide open and alert, with head moving from side to side (also for the localisation of the danger, especially by means of sound).

- Body muscles tense and 'sprung' (ready for hasty escape once the optimal direction is determined).

- Breathing pronounced (so as to increase the oxygen supply to the muscles – part of the general adrenalin reaction).

- The seeking of physical contact or proximity with people or other objects. If walls or trees are available, the frightened individual will gravitate towards them, hold onto them or flatten him or herself against them in order to feel more secure.

Worry or anxiety are usually indicted by 'nervous' movements such as pacing up and down, scratching the head, snapping the fingers and punching the palm. This may be understood as a problem-solving orientation, with the physical movement serving to maintain arousal, thus 'tuning up' the brain, as well as providing a continually changing perspective on the environment which might prompt a fresh idea. However, restless movement may represent behavioural conflict, or it may be due simply to a need to burn up excess adrenalin. After all, the human stress reaction dates from a time in our evolutionary history when crises called for a physical reaction more often than a mental solution.

Relaxation is the opposite of fear and anxiety and hence is displayed by a lack of muscle tension (which amounts to an absence of preparation for doing anything). It is also indicated by the open teeth smile which, by contrast with percussant laughter, is a friendly, happy, appeasing sort of gesture.

Darwin also noted that children express *disgust* by poking out their tongue and making a bleating sound. This, he says, derives from the primitive reflex of vomiting or rejecting something distasteful. The very derivation of the word 'disgust' would seem to support such an interpretation. Even the 'civilised adult' shows contempt with a tone of voice produced with an open throat, for example, the sneering, superior way in which a typical snob would say 'Oh really'.

The *scream* appears to have three major evolutionary components, which are mixed in various proportions according to the situation: a warning to conspecifics so they may escape the danger; the summoning of aid from any strong enough to help; and an attempt to frighten off the enemy.

This latter aspect is traditionally used in bayonet practice in the military and in martial arts like ju-jitsu. Apart from its potential for striking fear into the hearts of the enemy it may also function as a means of helping the warrior to cope with his own fear (a morale booster like whistling or bagpipes).

Crying and whimpering are fairly universal expressions of milder or more chronic forms of distress. These derive from infant signals which are calculated to evoke parental/protective instincts in stronger adults. Along with certain facial characteristics such as large eyes and soft complexion, these 'helpless' signals are more often deployed by adult females than males.

Some facial expressions of emotion appear so early in babyhood that they are almost certainly innate. Babies only a day or two old can discriminate and imitate happy, sad and surprised faces posed by the mother. Likewise, gestures which are universal across different cultures are also presumed to be innate. For example, people in all parts of the world 'flash' their eyebrows (lift them in an expression of pleasant surprise) when greeting an old friend that they have not seen for some time. The smile and nod also have the same friendly significance in all cultures, and hence are used copiously in meetings between peoples who do not understand each other's language (e.g. a meeting of American and Japanese businessmen).

It is not just facial expressions that have universal significance. Postures of the entire body (as opposed to gestures restricted to one limb or part of the body) also have power to express feelings, and often when the person is not deliberately trying to signal information about their emotions. We usually have little difficulty telling whether a person is happy, sad or frightened by the overall orientation or 'attitude' of their body (e.g. upright and expansive versus drooping and crumpled). As we shall see in Chapter 6, ballet may be considered as the artistic expansion of postural language. Dance sequences convey feelings such as masculine or feminine, proud or humble, exhilarated or sorrowful.

SOCIAL RULES

Although many gestures are primitive in origin we may modify their display in accord with social norms and politeness. Sometimes we qualify an expression by adding another one as a comment on the first. For example, we may smile after anger or sadness, as if to say 'I won't go too far' or 'I can take it'. Some emotions are suppressed because they do not show us in a favourable light, while others, not actually felt, may be manufactured if social circumstances demand. Generally, negative emotions such as misery and hate are suppressed, while positive, friendly ones are faked or exaggerated when we are in public.

In reading body language it is important to be able to distinguish gestures which are of biological origin from those which are culturally learned. It may also be vital to understand local codes. Captain Cook was apparently killed by Hawaiian Islanders when they mistook his offer to shake hands with their chief as a threat to attack. More recently, two British swimmers were shot by Albanian coastguards because they misread a downward-palm beckoning gesture as a signal to go away: North Europeans signal 'come here' with a palm up gesture, while much of South Europe uses the palm down (Morris *et al.* 1979).

An actor wishing to portray a person from another culture may need to study the characteristic gestures of that group to be convincing. Not only do Italians gesture more than North Europeans, but some of their gestures appear obscene to Americans and British. For example, an Italian man is often seen to stand on the curb and check that his genitalia are in order by groping his crotch before venturing to cross the road. No doubt the Italians see some of our behaviour as equally extraordinary.

Against the argument that gestures should be appropriate to the culture of the character is the view that the culture of the audience should also be considered. In his memoirs, the famous Russian actor/bass Feodor Chaliapin (1933) describes how offended he was when a particular Italian Iago employed vulgar, parochial gestures which he thought were unacceptably crude even if it were credible that the real Iago might have used them. Some directors would therefore prefer that gestures, as well as words, are in the vernacular of the audience. It also needs to be considered whether stage gestures are out of character with the dignity of the work being played. Difficult decisions often have to be made in satisfying these conflicting demands.

READING EMOTIONS

People vary in the extent to which their emotions can be read by others (Ekman 1972). On average, women are more expressive ('transparent') than men and better at receiving messages from others ('intuitive'). Research suggests that men are better at concealing emotions ('poker faced') but not so good at reading them ('insensitive') (Hall 1978, Noller 1986, Walk and Samuel 1988). These sex differences may explain the frequent complaint of women that their male partners do not 'communicate' sufficiently, and the reciprocal male complaint that women expect them to be mind-readers.

There are also cultural differences in emotional transmission: Oriental people really are inscrutable in that they can read the faces of Europeans more accurately than they can people of their own ethnic group (Shimoda *et al.* 1978) and, as already suggested, South Europeans are more 'transparent' than North Europeans.

The term 'leakage' refers to the transmission of feelings that the sender is trying to suppress or camouflage. For example, a false smile is detectable if it is switched on or off too quickly, or if it appears only at the mouth, not the eyes. Gripping the hands together very tightly, or touching or hiding the face, sometimes signals stress or anxiety that the individual is attempting to conceal. When we see a person laughing, while at the same time hiding part of their face with their hand, it usually means that they are amused, but at the same time realize that it is no laughing matter. Their hand has therefore come up to 'censor' the face. When there is conflict of this kind, the more anti-social (less respectable) gesture probably indicates the 'true' feeling. Despite the odd 'Freudian slip', the veneer of civilization tends to be thinner for body language than for the spoken word.

It is sometimes difficult to read other people's emotions from facial expressions and gestures because they are themselves in a state of conflict about how they should react, and their mixed feelings are reflected in ambiguous signals. It is common, for example, for a threat posture to combine components of both hostility and fear, because the individual is unsure as to whether fight or flight is the best option in the circumstances. When the urge to attack predominates, the frown is deeper, the mouth tightly compressed, the head thrust forward and the skin more pallid. When a greater amount of fear is present, the eyes are open and staring, the mouth shows a snarl that exposes more teeth, the neck is withdrawn and the skin is slightly reddened (Morris 1977).

DETECTING LIES

Recalling George Burns' comment that acting amounts to 'faking sincerity', it is clear that the study of leakage is of central interest to performers. We shall therefore look more closely at how insincerity is betrayed.

When people try to conceal their emotions they often succeed quite well in controlling their face but give themselves away with body movements. Lying is not easily detected in the face but Ekman and Friesen (1974) found that it may be betrayed by unnecessary movements of the hand towards the face (partial attempts to cover the mouth and stop it from lying). Touching the face does not necessarily mean the person is lying, but it often indicates tension of some kind. People who are lying also increase their use of hand shrugs, as though responsibility for verbal untruth is being disclaimed by some other part of the personality. They also squirm a great deal, as though generally uneasy or wanting to escape from the situation.

Even when facial expressions are apparently normal, slow-motion photography of people who are lying sometimes reveals fleeting, anxious micro-expressions, such as grimaces lasting only a fraction of a second. Apparently, a higher brain centre is cancelling a mood expression that is automatically initiated at a lower level, effectively telling the face to 'shut up'. Frame-by-frame analysis of videotapes is now used as a way of checking the intentions of potentially hostile foreign politicians.

More recent research (e.g. De Paulo *et al.* 1988) has looked at the non-verbal cues associated with *highly motivated* lying. These include pupil dilation, raised voice pitch, shorter utterances and speech hesitations. Compared with less motivated liars, people who are trying hard to lie successfully are inclined to over-control some of their gestures. For example, they blink, avert gaze and move their head and body *less*. This shows how complicated the detection of deceit can be. In our culture we tend to think that shifty-eyed people are liars, and we would hesitate to buy a used car from salesmen who displayed this characteristic. Yet if people are lying and trying hard to avoid discovery, they often deliberately try to over-ride any signals that they think might give them away and end up by exaggerating the amount of eye contact that they use. Rather than glancing away intermittently they will stare you straight in the face while delivering the lie. At the same time they will be taking pains to avoid blinking and squirming, because these are also widely known to be telltale signs. Hence any publicity given to early research on the detection of deceit may render the discovery useless – the *reverse* effects may then become the cues to look for (i.e., magnified 'honesty' signals.)

A related line of research (e.g. De Turck and Miller 1990) concerns the things observers actually look for when they are trying to detect lying. This shows that the main cues used by people for judging deception are, in order of importance: slowness to begin talking; averting the gaze; more postural shifts; unfilled pauses in speech; reduced smiling; slower speech; raised pitch and speech errors. The interesting thing about this list is that it corresponds poorly to the actual non-verbal cues that accompany deception. Raised pitch and slower, more hesitant speech are correctly used cues, but the others are fast becoming non-valid indicators (as we have seen, when the motivation to deceive is high, the number of posture shifts may be a reverse indicator because it is deliberately minimised by the deceiver). The cues that are currently valid but overlooked by the majority of observers are pupil dilation, reduced blinking, fewer head movements and shorter utterances.

Thus research on the body language of deception reveals a complex game of second-guessing in which the liar tries to suppress giveaway signs of deceit and the judge looks either for direct signs of lying or blatant attempts to suppress the appearance of lying. As people learn more about body language the more sophisticated they become at covering up their lying. Whereas children simply hide their mouth behind their hand (a sign of guilt that is transparent to most adults) with adults we increasingly have to look for more subtle signs of leakage.

Personality differences in deception ability have been studied. Riggio, Salinas and Tucker (1988) had students make videotaped presentations on sociopolitical issues, some of which were counter to their own attitudes (deceptive) and some in accord (truth-telling). The presentations were then judged by others as more or less believable. Outgoing and energetic people were the most successful deceivers (good actors?) whereas apprehensive, insecure and guilty people came across as less convincing. Subjects who seemed motivated to 'fake good' on the personality test (producing a high 'Lie' score) were also more successful deceivers on the videotape task. It would seem to follow that self-confident, extroverted people who are keen to present themselves in the best possible light would make the best actors and politicians.

FAMOUS LIARS

There have been several instances in which famous people have made very public statements which have subsequently turned out to be patently false, giving us an opportunity to look back and see if there were any telltale signs in their expressions and gestures. One of the best-known examples is that of Kim Philby, a highly placed official in the British Secret Service whose sudden defection to the Soviet Union confirmed suspicions that he was a Russian agent. After two of his colleagues (Burgess and Maclean) had defected, Philby appeared on a British newsreel denying that he too was a traitor. Although he appeared superficially self-confident, slowing down the film revealed facial twitches indicative of stress. Also now recognised as significant, he produced a rather silly grin immediately after his major denial of being a spy. Presumably this reflected an inner voice saying 'how embarrassing' or 'what a joke me sitting here and saying something so ridiculously false'. The same inappropriate smile was seen on a Midlands student who appeared on TV appealing for the safe return of his missing girlfriend whom, it turned out, he had murdered a few days earlier, hiding the body under the floorboards of her Oxford flat.

Although stress signs may be detected, it is not always possible to be sure what they mean. At the height of the hunt for a serial killer of young women dubbed 'The Yorkshire Ripper', police received taped messages from a man claiming to be the Ripper and taunting them for their inability to catch him. Voice print analysis was used to conclude that the Ripper was under great stress which at that stage was presumed to derive from guilty conflict over the horrific nature of his crimes. In fact, the messages were sent by a hoaxer whose real problem must have been something else entirely, perhaps hatred of the police or fear that they might trace him.

There are no doubt some idiosyncratic gestures accompanying insincerity that are consistent within a particular individual but unique to that individual. During the Watergate era it was reported that body language experts had determined that Leonid Brezhnev was lying when he raised his eyebrows, Edward Heath was lying when he scratched his ear and Richard Nixon was lying when he opened his mouth. This, of course, is a joke, but it illustrates a valid principle that is taken account of by political analysts – that the meaning of some gestures is personal rather than cultural or instinctual. Once a particular politician's personal code has been cracked, his subsequent pronouncements can be examined for veracity.

Deceit is probably a necessary skill for politicians and diplomats because they have to represent the interests of their party or country even if these conflict with their personal opinion. Politicians also tend to be expedient in that they say what the electorate wants to hear in order to be elected. But the capacity for deceit is even more obviously the stock-in-trade of the actor, who depends upon creating an illusion of sincerity, regardless of how closely his own character or feelings correspond with those of the role he is playing. This is why the area of non-verbal 'leakage' of emotion is of special relevance to the performer.

WARMTH AND COLDNESS

One of the most important things we need to know about another person in everyday social interaction is whether or not they like us. Hence warmth versus coldness is a primary dimension of body language. Apart from the obvious social rituals such as handshakes, embraces, greetings and gifts, warmth is expressed by making eye contact, pupil dilation, smiling, attentiveness and openness of posture (making oneself accessible to the other party). Coldness is communicated by the opposite gestures such as turning away, frowning and setting up barriers between oneself and the other, for example, holding a lit cigarette out front in such a way as to defend personal space. Other gestures which betray disapproval or disagreement include backing away from the other person (as though they are talking too loud or have body odour), wiping a finger across the nose, screwing up the eyes and picking imaginary lint off one's clothing.

A detailed list of warm and cold gestures has been provided by Gerald Clore and colleagues at the University of Illinois (1975, see Table 5.1). In these lists the gestures are ordered in terms of importance, those at the top of the list being rated by judges as the clearest indicators of acceptance and rejection respectively. Thus eye contact and touching are unequivocally warm gestures, while a cold stare, a sneer or a fake yawn are especially strong signals of rejection.

When people are in groups of three or more it is often possible to tell who is attracted to whom simply by the way they arrange various parts of the body. For example, whenever we sit down and cross our legs we have a choice as to whether we bring the left leg over the right or the right over the left. While some people have natural preferences they will also adjust their behaviour according to their attitude to those about them, using the leg cross either to turn their body inwards and open themselves up to another person or to create a barrier between themselves and the person next to them. When people are standing, the direction that their feet are pointing may be particularly diagnostic. We tend to point our feet in the direction we would like to go, which of course has the effect of turning our body towards the person we like. At the same time we may use our shoulder, a hand carrying a glass or a cigarette as a kind of barrier to exclude someone from our conversation or social circle.

One of the more subtle indicators of warmth towards another person is called *mirroring*. When two people are 'in tune' with each other (i.e. getting along well and feeling agreeable and cooperative) they tend to reflect each other's postures, gestures and movements (La France 1982). Other names for this are 'synchrony' and 'postural echo' (Morris 1977). This is a largely unconscious process which

Table 5.1 Non-verbal signals of acceptance and rejection: How a woman expresses warmth and hostility to a man without uttering a word

Warm gestures	Cold gestures
Looks into his eyes	Gives a cold stare
Touches his hand	Sneers
Moves towards him	Gives a fake yawn
Smiles frequently	Frowns
Works her eyes from his head to his toes	Moves away from him
Has a happy face	Looks at the ceiling
Smiles with mouth open	Picks her teeth
Grins	Shakes her head negatively
Sits directly facing him	Cleans her fingernails
Puckers her lips	Looks away
Nods head affirmatively	Chain smokes
Raises her eyebrows	Pouts
Licks her lips	Picks her hands
Uses expressive hand gestures while speaking	Looks around the room
Has eyes wide open	Plays with her split ends
Gives fast glances	Cracks her fingers

Source: Clore *et al.* 1975

conveys the silent message 'See, I am just like you'. The term 'good vibes' that was fashionable in the 1960s probably referred to this feeling of synchrony. Research in California singles' bars (e.g. Moore 1985) shows that mirroring is a particularly good predictor of who will go off together, with breaches in synchrony heralding the end of a budding relationship. Although mirroring implies that the individuals concerned share the same attitude, it is not necessarily a positive attitude. Cold mirroring may also occur, as for example, when a couple turn their back on each other so as to create mutual barriers. Analysis in terms of who is mirroring whom gives clues as to which individual is dominant. Generally speaking, the person who *initiates* changes in posture which are copied by the other is dominant, although in some circumstances a high status individual may deliberately mirror a subordinate in order to put him at ease (as in the case of a job interview).

COURTSHIP AND INTIMACY

When a couple are courting all the warm signals tend to be magnified. They gaze into each other's eyes with dilated pupils, listen attentively, divulge intimate personal details, smile and laugh a lot and mirror each other's movements (Morris 1977, Marsh 1988). They also tend to tighten their body muscles so as to pull themselves upright and look more youthful and vigorous. Their heads are frequently tilted back to give extra height and an impression of balletic lightness. They orient themselves front on to the partner, making the vulnerable parts of their body accessible (while at the same time closing other people out of the circle). Either because one is pursuing the other, or they are trying to burn up surplus adrenalin, their excitement may cause them to rotate in a slow, circling 'dance', while maintaining their face-to-face position.

Preening is another classic courtship signal. When people are keen to be seen as attractive by somebody else, they make little adjustments to their clothing such as straightening their tie or playing with the buttons on their blouse. They also tend to groom their hair, effectively combing it with their hand, and draw attention to their genitals with hand placements. When a man places his thumbs in his belt in the classic macho posture his fingers point to and converge upon his 'marriage tackle'. Just as a woman might wear a low-cut dress and tight, split skirt when she is feeling flirtatious, so her body movements will be geared to the provocative display of sexual signals such as breast cleavage, thighs and pouted lips.

Lovers tend to talk in low tones so their messages are not overhead. They whisper 'sweet nothings' and use baby talk that revives memories of parental care and devotion. They advertise their bond by holding hands, putting their arms around each other and gazing longingly into each other's eyes. As a result they may be oblivious to what is going on around them.

EYE CONTACT

The eyes are perhaps the most powerful social signallers that we have; hence they are sometimes called the 'windows of the soul'. Therapists who are concerned to improve a patient's social skills usually find it necessary to correct deficiencies in deployment of eye fixation, and the same applies to stage directors working with inexperienced actors. Some people appear shy and awkward because they avoid eye contact too much; others appear rude because they stare excessively.

In conversation, people normally look at each other's eyes for about one-third of the time – much less suggests guilt, boredom or inattention, and much more usually comes across as threatening in some way. But this is a rough average, and research has revealed a number of meaningful variations (Argyle and Cook 1976):

1. People tend to make more eye contact when they are listening than when they are talking.

2. A glance at the other person is frequently used to 'pass the ball' of conversation on to him or her.

3. Friendly people tend to look into the eyes of another person more than do unfriendly people, and women tend to do so more than men.

4. As noted above, lovers tend to gaze into each other's eyes to express intimacy; they also dilate their pupils as a sign of interest and arousal.

5. There are cultural differences with respect to the use of eye contact. Italians, for example, tend to look longer than English, with the result that they think the English cold, while the English find them over-familiar.

6. Staring can be used as a means of establishing dominance. The 'battle of the eyes' is a well-known game among children, and adult equivalents can be observed. Submissive people and people who are socially outranked tend to withdraw in the face of challenging eye fixation. As a result, they are likely to spend a great deal of time looking at their feet.

Eye contact can therefore be used either as a means of seeking intimacy or an attempt to intimidate. It follows that avoidance of eye contact may represent either a means of evading intimacy or an act of social submission. In the case of young women, the escape from eye contact may be part of a modesty pattern that is perceived as appropriate and attractive. According to some anthropologists (e.g. Eibl-Eibesfeldt 1989) this has a flirtatious connotation because it originated as a ritual invitation to chase. In support of its instinctual basis they cite the fact that it occurs in young girls who have been blind from birth and who therefore could not have acquired the pattern through imitation. Whether or not this theory is correct, use of the eyes is gender-specific in that certain patterns appear normal or enhancing to one sex but not to the other.

Actors need to 'lead with the eyes' since these are usually the focal point for the audience and should be the first part of the body to register new ideas. A gesture or comment should therefore be preceded by a mental process that is first displayed in the eyes. In the worst of amateur productions an actor may be seen to point at something shortly before seeing it, or announce an idea just before thinking of it.

FACIAL EXPRESSIONS

Since the face is such an important organ of emotional expression, it is not surprising that operations intended to remove wrinkles such as taking tucks under the eyes are of limited use to performers and may even be counter-productive. Although performers may look younger in static photographs after cosmetic operations they often lose expressiveness and the ability to smile warmly. At worst they end up looking like wax dummies of their former selves.

The importance of looking youthful might explain the fact that some observers claim there is a preponderance of blue eyes in modern Hollywood films. One critic complained that apart from the lead, who was black, everyone in *Beverly Hills Cop* was blue-eyed. This may be an exaggeration but many top stars do seem to be blue-eyed (e.g. Paul Newman, Robert Redford, Steve McQueen) and according to the manufacturers of contact lenses blue is the colour most often requested. Blue eyes look young because they are associated with babies (in the same way that natural blond hair is more common in children than adults). On the other hand, blue may be preferred by film-makers simply because it is more colourful. Before 1940, dark-eyed heroes and heroines (such as Olivier) may have been preferred because they look more striking in black and white movies.

The left side of the human face is generally more expressive than the right. This conclusion derives from studies in which people are asked to identify an emotion that an actor is attempting to convey from photos of his face that have been separated into left and right halves (Sackheim *et al.* 1978). A possible explanation for this finding is that the right hemisphere of the brain 'feels' more emotional than the relatively cold, logical left side, and this feeling is transferred to the contralateral facial muscles controlled by that side of the brain. If this effect was large enough for practical consideration (which is doubtful) the actor on stage left should be at an advantage with respect to facial expressiveness. However, the tendency for emotional expression to be left-faced may be true only if the emotion is simulated (deliberately manufactured) rather than truly felt (Skinner 1989). Some researchers find that heartfelt emotion pervades both sides of the face and that only a consciously initiated expression is stronger on the left. Separate neural pathways seem to be involved, with conscious expressions being cortically mediated, and hence lateralized, while spontaneous emotion is mediated by subcortical parts of the brain (Rinn 1984). There are two contrasting neurological disorders. In one, you tell the patient a joke and he smiles, but if you ask him to smile he cannot. The other is the reverse of this; the patient does not respond to a joke but can produce a smile upon demand.

It has been suggested that there are individual differences with respect to 'facedness'. Smith (1984) maintains that people can be classified with respect to facial dominance, with the majority being 'right faced' and a minority 'left faced'. Dominance is determined by looking for the side of the face that is more open with a greater distance between jaw and brow, fewer dimples and wrinkles and which is tilted towards the listener when speaking. The mouth is said to open wider on the dominant side during speech. Smith claims that although about 80 per cent of people are right-faced, musicians tend to be predominantly left-faced. Nearly all great composers, singers and orchestral musicians were judged as left-faced (presumably because this reflects a more developed right brain hemisphere). He further claims that scientists, athletes, orators, actors and dancers are particularly likely to be right-faced because these specialities depend more on 'cognitive articulation' which is controlled by the left-brain. This interesting research has so far not been independently replicated.

Schwartz *et al.* (1980) studied the way in which activity of facial muscles connects with emotional feeling. When men and women were asked to imagine situations that might be expected to produce happiness, sadness, anger and fear (e.g. 'You inherit a million dollars', 'Your mother dies') women showed more muscle activity in the face. This is consistent with the idea that women transmit emotional signals more powerfully than men. However, they also report a more vivid experience of the emotion, so it is possible that women express more emotion because they *feel* more emotion.

NON-VERBAL ASPECTS OF SPEECH

The words that people use are often less significant than the manner of their delivery (Davitz and Davitz 1989). Many things can be vocally communicated to foreigners, young children and even animals without the words themselves being understood. A popular exercise in drama school is to say one thing while meaning something else, and it is surprising how effectively the true meaning can be communicated. Apart from body and facial gestures, the measurable characteristics of speech, such as volume, pitch, tone and speed, carry information about the emotional state and true intentions of the speaker.

People who talk in loud voices are not necessarily dominant; they may have learned that they have to speak up or nobody else will listen to them. A quiet voice may be more threatening because it implies barely controlled rage (cf. the Godfather making somebody 'an offer they can't refuse'). If the initial hurdle of persuading people to hush so they can hear what is said is successfully passed, then a certain amount of social power has been exercised already, so the connection between whispered instructions and dominance is partly circular. Still, the optimum, as Theodore Roosevelt maintained, is to 'speak softly and carry a big stick'. Once you are in position of real power you don't have to shout to be heard.

A sudden increase in volume comes across as assertive and is used for special emphasis. Some military officers adopt a style of throwing out an occasional very loud word or phrase almost on a random basis when addressing the troops in order to maintain attention and submission: 'You will all ASSEMBLE, at nine o'clock PRECISELY, with your rifles CLEANED and at the READY...'

Low pitches sound strong and masculine because they are linked with male hormones, which are a major source of social dominance. It is probably for this reason that men tend to be more successful as hypnotists, evangelists, salesmen and advertising voice-overs while, reciprocally, women are more susceptible to such persuasion. Higher-pitched voices have the advantage that they have fewer masking noises to compete with and therefore carry better through the air. They also tend to sound plaintive and are thus geared to evoking the helpful, heroic instincts in other people – especially men. Victims in opera are usually soprano or tenor while kings and villains are bass or baritone. The carrying power of high voices may help to explain why sopranos and tenors are particularly prized in the opera house.

Female and higher voices show greater variation in pitch than male and lower voices – a difference in flexibility that is paralleled by the fact that 'coloratura' arias (those full of thrills and spills) are much more commonly written for sopranos than basses. Connected with this is a tendency for monotonous voices (as cultivated by many American politicians and businessmen) to be seen as dominant. However, monotony sometimes indicates depression rather than dominance.

The emotion of fear is usually expressed by variable pitch and volume and by an upward inflexion at the end of sentences. Breathy, resonant tone tends to sound emotional and sexy (a speciality of mezzo-sopranos and 'red-hot mamas'), while thin sound is more formal and communicative, being relatively free of 'noise'. Speed of delivery is also significant. People who speak quickly come across as intelligent, well-informed, confident and energetic. However, if taken to extremes fast talking appears nervous and overcompensating, especially if it is high-pitched and includes stammering. A nervous man trying to impress a woman sometimes talks like a machine-gun and a woman on a date with a man she finds unattractive may talk excessively to forestall physical advances.

The assessment of emotion from non-verbal aspects of speech depends on a variety of complex cues, many of which are processed unconsciously. For talented actors, most of these principles are intuitively understood and operated and it may seem patronizing to outline them in simplistic form. Yet a formal appreciation of such general rules may not only be of intrinsic interest to performing artists but also helpful in creating special effects, or in understanding the mechanism by which they are achieved.

EMOTIONAL SYNTHESIS

A group of European psychologists (Bloch *et al.* 1987) have proposed a system for training actors based upon coldly simulating the body language of various emotions. They claim that actors can learn to project emotions to an audience on the basis of deliberately controlling three groups of non-verbal signals:

1. Body posture (muscles tensed v. relaxed, directions of approach vs avoidance).

2. Facial expression (position of the eyes and mouth – open v. closed, etc.).

3. Breathing patterns (amplitude and frequency).

Table 5.2 The differentiation of six primary emotions by effector patterns. Posture is classified as (T, tense or R, relaxed) with the direction being either Approach or Avoidance. The last column shows the main breathing pattern and mouth position

Emotion	Posture	Direction	Main Breathing trait
Happiness	R	Ap	Saccadic expiration (mouth open)
Sadness	R	Av	Saccadic inspiration (mouth open)
Fear	T	Av	Inspiratory apnea (mouth open)
Anger	T	Ap	Hyperventilation (mouth closed tight)
Eroticism	R	Ap	Small amplitude, low frequency (mouth open)
Tenderness	R	Ap	Small amplitude, low frequency (mouth closed in a relaxed smile)

Source: Bloch *et al.* 1987

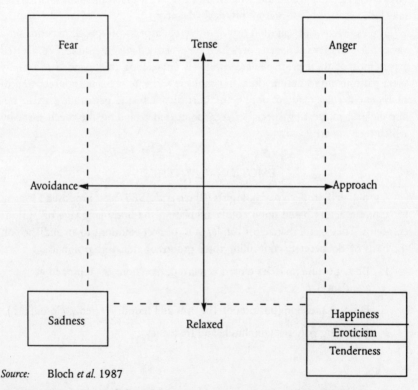

Source: Bloch *et al.* 1987

Figure 5.1 Representation of the six basic emotions in terms of postural tension/relaxation and approach avoidance parameters

These three areas were chosen as the major visible effectors of emotion that are under voluntary control and hence suitable for training. Most other features of emotion, such as heart rate and blood pressure, are less apparent to the outside observer and are probably naturally carried with the above in any case. Bloch *et al.* identify six primary emotions:

1. Happiness (including laughter, pleasure and joy).

2. Sadness (crying, sorrow and grief).

3. Fear (anxiety, panic).

4. Anger (aggression, attack, hate).

5. Eroticism (sex, sensuality, lust).

6. Tenderness (filial love, maternal/paternal feelings, friendship).

Each of these is said to have a unique combination of effector patterns (Table 5.2). With respect to two postural axes (tension/relaxation and approach/avoidance) the six basic emotions are classified as in Figure 5.1. Differentiation of happiness, eroticism and tenderness depends upon other cues (facial expressions and breathing patterns).

Detailed descriptions of the typical body/face/breathing patterns are given for each emotion and these are then trained in a totally detached way. In complete contrast to the 'method' approach (Chapter 4) it is presumed that actually experiencing the emotion concerned is unnecessary or even counterproductive.

Later on, after the primary emotions have been taught, various composites are considered

for example, pride = joy + anger (combined in suitable proportion)
jealousy = anger + fear + eroticism.

The results of this approach to actor training have been assessed empirically. Consistent with the findings of Ekman *et al.* (1983), simulating the effector patterns of an emotion initially induced the subjective feeling appropriate to that emotion. But later, after a period of training, Bloch *et al.* found that subjective activation was by-passed and became unnecessary. The effectiveness of the training procedure was evaluated in two ways:

• Physiological measures showed that actors trained in this procedure produced similar polygraph records (skin conductance, blood pressure, etc.) as non-actors hypnotized and given a suggestion to feel a particular emotion. This is equivalent to comparing the technical and imaginal approaches to acting, and they appeared indistinguishable (at least by the measures used).

• Dramatic scenes performed by actors trained in the detached method were independently judged as more 'expressive' than the same scenes rehearsed by other actors using a Stanislavski approach featuring 'emotional memory'.

As unlikely as these results might seem intuitively, Bloch *et al.* have described their procedure in sufficient detail that others might replicate it and find out for themselves. They claim the following advantages to their system over traditional actor training methods:

1. It clarifies emotional expression, separating intended emotions from irrelevant activation (e.g. stage-fright, awkwardness, adrenaline 'high').

2. It provides a language of communication between actor and director that is externally rooted and independent of feelings that are often elusive and difficult to communicate verbally.

3. It protects the psychological health of actors by doing away with the need to delve into their own past distress to recover feelings that can be genuinely painful or to manufacture feelings which might spill over into real life, producing identity confusion, relationship disturbances and so on.

4. There may be therapeutic side-effects to this training. An example given is that of an actress who had a problem of mixing eroticism with fear. Once trained to separate them, she reported an improvement in her private sex life.

No doubt many teachers and aspiring performers will find this approach cold and unappealing and it will require more evidence of superiority before most people will be convinced. Nevertheless, it is an interesting illustration of the way in which scientific principles of non-verbal communication may be applied very directly to the performing arts.

CHAPTER 6

Motivation, Movement and Use of Space

The last chapter described how emotions are communicated by non-verbal means such as facial expressions, tone of voice and gesture. It emerged that actors need to work on covering personal emotions that are inappropriate to the character being portrayed, while projecting with clarity the feelings that are 'in character'. The application of the study of body language is now extended to motivation, movement and the use of space. Among the topics covered are: (1) the distinction between whole-body postures and specific gestures; (2) the creation of credible characterization by posture and gesture; (3) the use of personal space and territory to convey dominance and submission; and (4) the manner in which actors and directors use movement and visual effects to manipulate audience attention. Because these topics are of central interest to dancers, we end with a discussion of the body language of dance.

POSTURE VERSUS GESTURE

Lamb and Watson (1979) argue that the key to reading body language is to look past gestures to the more emotionally determined and all-pervading postures. They define *gestures* as movements confined to specific body parts, such as the hand or the eyebrows, which are usually consciously selected and used deliberately in order to communicate some message to others. As a result, they are culturally variable to a considerable extent.

Postures are distinguished as showing consistency of meaning throughout the body. Since they tend to be unconscious they may conflict with messages stated by words and gestures, thus 'leaking' the more genuine underlying attitude. Because postures are more basic in evolutionary terms (i.e., instinctual rather than learned) they tend to be uniform across cultures. An example of this difference would be pointing out a parked car with a single arm and index finger extended ('That's my car over there'), versus pointing to a car that is out of control and careering dangerously in the direction of a friend ('Watch out for that car!'). In the latter instance there is a great deal more urgency, and tension pervades the entire body from head to toe; a total attitude of warning is conveyed.

This distinction seems to be primarily one of emotional involvement. Postures stem from deep feelings, whereas gestures are a form of social communication that may be used instead of, or in addition to, words. Insincerity is often seen in the failure of gesture to be backed up with a consistent posture, like the smile that involves the mouth only and not the rest of the face (like the enigmatic *Mona Lisa*), or a cheery wave that starts only at the shoulder and is contradicted by a slumped, indifferent body. Incompatibilities of this kind are sometimes used deliberately by actors for comic effect, as when a clown shivers violently in an icy jet of water but maintains a grit-teeth smile. But assuming the actor is not usually trying to convey insincerity, it is easy to see why he may find it useful to feel the correct emotion before moving – this way he produces a posture rather than a gesture. As proponents of 'the Method' would argue, unfelt gestures are likely to come across as empty and isolated. That is not to say the actor must 'lose himself' completely, for as we have noted (Chapter 4), there are certain dangers in that, but it may help to evoke appropriate feelings to some degree in order to make movements convincing.

When there is conflict between various elements of posture, gesture and speech, how is it possible to tell which is genuine? In fact, it may be very difficult to do so, but here are some generalisations that may help.

- Negative signals (e.g. of hostility and anxiety) are more likely to be true than positive (desirable and flattering) ones, since it is negative emotions that we more often seek to conceal.

- Posture is usually more sincere than gesture (for reasons discussed above).

- Non-verbal cues leak true feelings more than the meaning of words, which is the basis of the 'cocktail party phenomenon' (Chapter 5).

The interpretation of gestures is vexed because they are sometimes voluntary and conscious and sometimes not, and they have variable meaning, according to context. Fidgets and facial mannerisms, for example, are usually taken to mean nervousness. But while it is true that such gestures do increase with nervousness, it is not possible to argue backwards with any degree of certainty. 'Irrelevant' movements may signify anger or agitation (if situation and posture suggest that) or they may simply represent an effort to increase arousal by self-stimulation – a kind of self-treatment for boredom that is particularly characteristic of impulsive, extrovert, sensation-seeking people. Examples of such fidgeting are the student who taps her fingers on the desk during a tedious lecture, the businessman who bangs his knees together rhythmically under the table during a board meeting, or the man at a party who constantly jingles coins in his pocket.

The cultural context is also important. We should not imagine that the Japanese businessman is actually humble just because he nods his head in a ritual bow and smiles a great deal. There may have been a time in Japanese history when it was important to be humble, but the need for humility has long since passed and what we observe is a ritual remnant of submissive gestures which can be very misleading to European competitors. Even within Europe there is enormous variation in the employment and meaning of gestures. This applies to the extent of use of gestures as well as their actual meaning. Mediterranean peoples use their hands in conversation more than North Europeans. It has been said (lightheartedly) that a Neapolitan is rendered inarticulate by handcuffs.

USE OF GESTURES

Gestures may be employed for many different purposes. Benedetti (1976) distinguishes *illustrative* gestures (e.g. 'the box was this high and wide'), *indicative* ('he went thataway'), *emphatic* (a Russian leader pounding his shoe on the podium as he makes a political point) and *autistic* (not intended for communication at all, but nevertheless expressive of the self). The example Benedetti gives of the latter category is that of a person concealing hostile feelings by crossing his arms and squeezing himself under the shoulders. This, he says, may indicate a secret desire to strangle or crush the other person. This type of gesture approximates to what Lamb and Watson (1979) would call a posture. In fact, Benedetti's four types of gesture could be ordered on a scale that runs from gesture to posture within the Lamb-Watson typology.

Generally speaking, the gestures used in a dramatic performance should not mimic words as if the audience is composed of people who are either deaf, blind or totally moronic. The argument that some people may not hear the words properly is not a good enough excuse for banal duplication that irritates everyone else. A case in point is Rose Maybud's song in Gilbert and Sullivan's *Ruddigore* in which she addresses the following to the innocent Robin Oakapple who lacks courage to express his love for her:

> If somebody there chanced to be
> Who loved me in a manner true
> My heart would point him out to me
> And I would point him out to you.

In performing this song, there is a temptation for Rose to start pointing in various directions (to her heart, to herself, and to Robin in quick succession). Taken to extreme, this could actually be effective as a comic device (the piece is a parody anyway), but if done seriously it becomes tedious and distracting. The same applies to Robin's subsequent song: 'Now take for example my case [points to self], I've a bright intellectual brain [points to head]', etc.

There is a particular danger of gestural redundancy in foreign language opera, where the director or singers may be so determined to prove that they understand the words or desperate to communicate at least something to a largely non-comprehending audience that they clutter their delivery with visual parallels. Leporello's aria in *Don Giovanni*, in which he catalogues his master's sexual conquests around the world, is verbally very funny, but singers performing it in non-vernacular language frequently fall back on a Marceau-type pantomime in the hope of extracting laughs.

Most directors would agree that this is not the ideal way to use gestures. Ideally, gestures should *add something* to the text, not just duplicate it. At the very least, they should emanate from the character's thought and feeling rather than illustrate them mechanically like boy scout semaphore.

Not all forms of drama are intended to be totally realistic. Stylization is likely to occur when the characters are historically and culturally far removed from ourselves. If the characters in a play are ancient Egyptians, contemporary speech and demeanour seem out of place. Therefore, both language and gesture tend to be poetic and grand. The same applies when the characters are meant to be superhuman (e.g. God or heroes); vernacular language and behaviour are likely to seem inappropriate in this context as well. Similarly, when the characters are played as contemptible, as in farce or satire, they are likely to be exaggeratedly silly in language and behaviour. Realistic language and characterization is fairly new in the theatre. Some date its origins from Shaw's demythologising of characters like Joan of Arc and Caesar, though such a demarcation is bound to be arbitrary. Realism in the theatre is used only when characters occupy roughly the same social planes as ourselves and so became a particular preoccupation in the era of 'kitchen sink' drama.

Attempts to be too realistic may seem incongruous in classical drama and opera. Zeffirelli's film version of *Romeo and Juliet* struck this problem; when setting and acting are very realistic, high falutin Shakespearean lines begin to sound wordy and over-intellectualised. Much the same happens when opera is adapted for television; if there is too much realism in the production the audience becomes excruciatingly aware of the singer's tonsils and facial distortions. They are likely to wonder, 'Why is he declaiming like that when the other character is right beside him and we, the audience, only a few feet away from the screen?'. Opera evolved as a distant medium and really only makes sense when viewed from a distance.

TYPES OF POSTURE

James (1932) produced an early classification of postures, identifying four major kinds, arranged as pairs of polar opposites.

1. Approach: attentive and forward-leaning.

2. Withdrawal: the opposite of approach, including various negative orientations such as drawing back or turning away.

3. Expansion: proud or conceited, involving an erect head and chest and open limbs.

4. Contraction: downcast, dejected, drooping.

This typology is still recognised as useful today, though the four types are often called warm, cold, dominant and submissive respectively. Generally speaking, attraction is marked by approach and repulsion by withdrawal, social power is conveyed by broad, upright postures and submission by curling into a ball with flaccid muscle tone. However, dominance may also be expressed by a relaxed, sprawling seating position (a boss dictating to a secretary) and submission by a tidy, formal, self-presentation (e.g. the timid man at a job interview who sits with his feet and knees tucked neatly together, holding his hat over his genitals or crossing his hands on his lap geometrically).

Source: Rosenberg and Langer 1965

Figure 6.1: The Meaning of Some Postures
   (a) curious; (b) puzzled; (c) indifferent; (d) rejecting; (e) watching; (f) self-satisfied;
   (g) welcoming; (h) determined; (i) stealthy; (j) searching; (k) watching; (l) attentive; (m) violent
   anger; (n) excited; (o) stretching; (p) surprised, dominating, suspicious; (q) sneaking; (r) shy;
   (s) thinking; (t) affected

An interesting application of posture to characterization occurs in David Cronenberg's film *Dead Ringers*. Jeremy Irons had to play twins, one of whom (Elliot) was dominant and successful, both occupationally and sexually, while the other (Beverly) was submissive, sensitive and less successful in life. Irons was faced with the problem of differentiating the two personalities. This was done partly by hair style, and having Beverly wear glasses, but Irons confided that he used one main body language cue: Elliot walked on his heels, giving him an upright, expansive stance, while Beverly walked more on his toes, causing him to lean forward with an apologetic demeanor. Although Irons maintained that this just provided the 'switch' by which he himself could shift character mentally, it was probably instrumental to a major degree in providing the astonishing differentiation between the two personalities that he achieved.

The two dimensions of warmth and dominance implied by James' typology do not exhaust the possibilities of postural expression. The stick figures shown in Figure 6.1 reveal a great diversity of feelings, attitudes and intentions. Note that these are identified consistently by people from most cultures around the world even though they involve no cues from facial expression.

Table 6.1 Some Psychoanalytic Interpretations of Postures

	Posture	Interpretation
Arms	1. Folded arms, self-wrapping	Self-protection, especially of breasts, withdrawal
	2. Bodice of dress clutched	Fears of bodily damage
	3. Shoulders shrugged, palms out	Passive helplessness
Legs	1. High crossing (females)	Self-protection, withdrawal
	2. Uncrossing	Flirtation
	3. Exhibitionistic leg crossing (females)	Flirtation
	4. No movement in pelvis	Sexual inhibition
Trunk	1. Stiff, military bearing (males), prim and upright (females)	Imprisoning anxiety
	2. Vain, affected bearing	Conflict between flirtation and shyness
	3. Drooping, listless, immobile	Helplessness, request for help
	4. Nestling into chair, languid, erotic manner	Expresses sexual impulses

Source: Argyle (1975)

In recent years, psychoanalytic theories have influenced the interpretation of body language. Based more on intuition than empirical evidence, the analytic viewpoint seeks to attribute outward posture to supposed internal conflicts (usually of a sexual nature). The person who walks with minimal movement of the pelvis is presumed to be sexually inhibited ('uptight'), the man with a stiff military bearing is thought to be defending against anxiety, while the woman who is excessively aloof and affected is said to be caught in conflict between flirtation and shyness (Table 6.1).

There is no doubt that people do formulate dynamic hypotheses such as these on observing others, whether justifiably or not, and actors may find it useful to adopt such ideas in the process of characterisation. Few would question the validity of using compulsive restraint of movement and emotion as a device for portraying a state of impending nervous breakdown. Psychologists know that as the brain approaches overload there is usually an attempt to reduce input, and determined immobility is one strategy for achieving this. When Olivier plays Othello, he is seen to make concerted attempts to control himself and retain dignity between explosive outbursts of jealousy.

TERRITORIALITY

James (1932) used the terms expansion and contraction with respect to posture quite wisely. Expansive gestures signify dominance because they effectively stake out a claim to a larger amount of territory (Mehrabian 1969). When an actor, singer or dancer tilts his head backwards and spreads his feet and hands wide apart he marks out a broader area of body space for himself. If all peripheral parts of the anatomy (hands, limbs etc.) are tucked inwards towards the chest and genitals like a startled hedgehog, there is a minimal claim to territory – only a determination to protect the little that is left. The former posture expresses exultation, triumph and power; the latter suggests shame, depression, weakness and insecurity. When the Toreador in *Carmen* or Figaro in *The Barber of Seville* prepare to sing their somewhat pushy, egotistical arias they do not normally stand in one place during their introductory music. Rather they set the scene with a demonstration of social dominance which usually entails wide, sweeping arcs around the stage with hands outstretched. This serves figuratively (and literally) to mark out personal territory and clear space around the performer, before he delivers his statement of physical and social power. The audience may gain this impression without necessarily being aware of how it is achieved, but it is nevertheless useful for performers and directors to understand the concept of territoriality.

In their everyday dealings, people mark out territory for themselves in much the same way that animals do with scent and droppings (Ardrey 1966). They build fences around their property, put their name on their office door and reserve tables and chairs in restaurants and theatres by leaving coats, bags and personal effects lying about on them. In social groups, men lay claim to female partners by putting an arm around them and they guard them from usurpers by creating barriers with their elbows and shoulders. People at parties form themselves into circles that exclude outsiders from conversation and social contact. Social power and property rights often have institutional reinforcement, ranging from the impressive bench and regalia of a judge to the wedding ring of a married woman, which possibly originated as a symbol of bondage (Morris 1977).

There is a memorable scene in Chaplin's film *The Great Dictator* in which Hitler prepares for his vital first meeting with Mussolini. Hitler's advisers have sought to compensate for his lack of height by having him seated on a high platform behind a very large desk, with a much lower chair opposite for Mussolini to sit on. The plan is that *Il Duce* should enter through doors at the back of an empty hall and have to walk a long, exposed distance up to *Der Fuhrer*, who is waiting behind his desk up on the stage. A stern bust of Hitler has been placed on the desktop facing outwards, so that even if he himself is smiling, his sculpted image will always be glaring across the desk to intimidate his rival. In the event, Mussolini confounds all these preparations simultaneously by appearing from a door on the stage behind Hitler's chair. From this advantageous position Mussolini immediately establishes complete dominance, towering over Hitler, slapping him on the back in a familiar and patronising way, and casually striking a match on the back of the bust (which is now pointing harmlessly away from him) in order to light a cigar and blow smoke in Hitler's face. This power struggle between the two dictators, conducted largely on the basis of spatial advantage, illustrates the kind of jockeying for position that goes on between people throughout their lives. In everyday life the greater part of it occurs spontaneously and unconsciously, but it is useful for actors to recognize the major principles (even if they are sometimes applied primarily to upstaging co-performers).

PERSONAL SPACE

For any interaction between two people there is an optimum degree of distance between them which strikes the balance between warmth and threat. Within about eighteen inches of our body is an intimate zone reserved for lovers, spouses, children and close family members. At this distance we can touch, kiss, smell body odours, and see pores and blemishes in the skin of the other person. Most of our conversations with friends and acquaintances are conducted at a distance of between eighteen inches and four feet, while more formal social and business interactions occur at a distance of four to nine feet. Still more formal occasions, such as conversations with important people and public addresses, employ distances of more than nine feet (Sommer 1959).

Observe a line of people waiting for service at a bank or post office and they behave as though there is an invisible 'bubble' surrounding each person that gives rise to even spacing between them. Each individual respects the personal space of those nearby. The same thing is seen on a beach when each newly arriving family selects an area of sand that is as far removed from other sunbathers as possible. Similarly, in a men's urinal the convention is to choose a place as far away from other men as possible, except perhaps in the case of close friends; to do otherwise creates suspicion. If we feel that our space is being violated, we attempt to compensate, usually by backing away. If physical withdrawal is not possible, as in a crowded tube train or lift, we control intimacy by other means such as turning our back or avoiding eye contact. If conversation occurs at all in such conditions it is usually restricted to safe topics such as the weather or the time, or non-threatening, jocular observations about the interior decor. Intrusive questions like 'Where do you live?' or 'Are you married?' are unacceptable under conditions of enforced physical intimacy.

There are noticeable cultural differences in the use of social space (Marsh 1988). Mediterranean people, Latin Americans and Arabs prefer closer proximity and more touching than North Americans, while the English are more stand-offish still. Since proximity independently signifies liking, we are apt to misunderstand someone from another culture as being over-familiar or strangely cold on the basis of their attempts to attain what to them is a comfortable distance. Sex differences also have to be considered: women tend to get closer to intimate friends and further away from non-intimate acquaintances than men, who are less affected by the nature of the relationship when it comes to selecting their ideal distance from another person. Social distance is to some extent reflected in physical distance. Ordinary people tend to stay further away from the Queen, the President, or their boss, than they do from a social equal. As a consequence, we regard people who get uncomfortably close as being pushy and presumptious, while those who back away from us are viewed as haughty, self-opinionated snobs. How to maintain optimal distances from other people is an important element of the therapy known as 'social skills training'.

The concept of 'intimacy regulation' can be applied to interpretations on stage. A good example of a comic application is the scene in Gilbert and Sullivan's *Patience* in which the pretentious poet Bunthorne addresses himself to the attractive young milkmaid of the title role, while at the same time his middle-aged, unattractive, but devoted fan, Jane, is in oppressive pursuit of him. The script has Jane 'supporting' Bunthorne by repeating after him any hostile remark that he directs to Patience (to his increasing annoyance) and the scene is very funny if she crowds him physically as much as she intrudes verbally. In this instance, the simple brief to violate Bunthorne's personal space as much as possible is virtually the only stage direction the actress playing Jane needs to keep in mind. Thereafter, wherever he goes she is always there, and always too close, to his progressive irritation and revulsion. The scene traditionally ends with Jane echoing the finger-snap gesture which Bunthorne uses to dismiss Patience, following which Bunthorne makes a sudden sprint to escape proximity from Jane, and she immediately dashes off after him.

MOTIVATION AND MOVEMENT

Motivation is the key to characterisation. Drama teachers exhort actors to ask themselves (as characters): What is it that I really want? What is the outcome I am seeking? They may further ask themselves what are the primary obstacles that stand in the way of these goals, be they material (e.g. lack of money), internal (e.g. Hamlet's conscience) or other characters with conflicting motives. Keeping these things in mind is bound to help an actor perform a role with conviction and sincerity. This approach corresponds with a particular method used by psychologists to classify personality – that based on their dominant needs (Chapter 4). For some people, achievement is all-important, hence ambitiousness is their striking trait (cf. Lady Macbeth); for others it is power (Hitler), sexual conquest (Casanova), love (Sweet Charity), atonement (Lord Jim) or protection (Blanche in A Streetcar Named Desire). The presumption is that most of the character's behaviour is directed toward fulfilling his or her primary need; understand that and their actions are immediately explicable.

Whether or not the motive be pervasive or transient, stage movements generally have to appear motivated. However, motivation does not always have to be goal-directed – it may simply be expressive. Goldovski (1968) calls these two types of motivation 'reasons' and 'urges'. Reasons are cognitive: for example, going to the door to open or close it, or to eavesdrop near it. In such cases the audience should be aware of the thought processes underlying the move. The exception, as we will see later, concerns reasons that are purely technical, such as 'dressing the stage' or adjusting sightlines. In this case the move is made to suit the director and every attempt is made to disguise the true reason. Urges are emotional: for example, moving under the impetus of stress or joy, an actor may happen to end up near the door. Urges do not dictate any particular direction, the body moves simply because it has to – it is so excited. The task for the actor in this case is to convince the audience of the strength and sincerity of the feeling which propels the move. Sometimes it is hard to distinguish urges from reasons as, for example, when a character is motivated by disgust to move away from another character. In this case the direction is unimportant provided it increases the distance from the other.

There is some disagreement as to whether operatic acting should be more expressive than acting in straight plays. Goldovski (1968) argues that the presence of music in opera makes for heightened emotional tension and that 'theatrical interpretation of energetic orchestral passages demands stage movement possessing a comparable degree of emotional and muscular forcefulness'. This is sometimes true, especially in large-scale scenes such as the Grand March in Aida or the stormy opening of Otello. But opera is not the same as ballet, and sometimes greater emotional power is achieved by 'planting' a character solidly against a tempestuous musical background. This allows the music to provide the emotional expression rather than the actor's limbs, and it is likely to do this more effectively than the traditional 'weeping, wailing and gnashing of teeth'.

To summarise, actors may move either in such a way as to betray some thought or intent, or they may move in a less goal-directed way in order to express an emotion. In the case of opera, the expressive function of movement is often better handled by the music; additional emoting on the part of the performer may sometimes be counter-productive, pushing the drama 'over the top', so that it becomes melodrama in the worst sense of the term.

INFORMATIVE VERSUS AFFECTIVE PRESENTATION OF LINES

Just as movements on the stage may be classified according to whether they are goal-directed (reasons) or expressive (urges), so Goldovski (1968) points out that the actor's lines can be delivered as either informative or affective. It is particularly useful to analyse operatic lyrics in terms of this distinction since it helps to make sense of the many word repetitions in opera. Some of the possibilities are as follows:

1. *Informative-informative.* The line is repeated louder the second time because it apparently was not heard or did not sink in the first time. The repeat is therefore an attempt to get a more satisfactory reaction out of the addressee.

2. *Informative-affective.* In this case a point of information is first presented in a straightforward, documentary way by the singer, following which the realisation strikes home and the full emotional import of what he has just said is *felt* on the repeat.

3. *Affective-informative.* This is the reverse of the case above, in which the passionate outburst comes first, then a cooler, more controlled statement is delivered, as though the character has managed to regain composure.

4. *Affective-affective.* Here sheer obsessional passion causes the singer to repeat the same thing over again. 'I love him! I love him!' can be used simply for emotional emphasis.

Goldovski applies this analysis to Santuzza's aria ('Mother you know the story') from *Cavalleria Rusticana,* and once having analysed it in these terms it is difficult to see how else the composer's intention could be understood. The informative-affective sequence is the most common, but all the other forms are identifiable on the basis of the particular set of words that Mascagni has chosen to repeat and the style of music which accompanies the two presentations. The reader may be interested to study this aria in these terms, classifying the pairs of repeated phrases according to the four patterns described above.

APPROACH-AVOIDANCE CONFLICT

It is possible, through certain stage orientations, to portray mixed feelings with respect to another character. The best known way of doing this is to deploy the 'cold downstage shoulder' while directing attention back across it to the other party (Figure 6.2).

Suppose the character who is the focus of attention (A) is located downstage right and the object of his mixed feelings (B) is at centre stage. A then turns away from B so that his left shoulder is downstage, functioning as a kind of physical barrier to B (avoidance), while at the same time A's head is turned across that shoulder towards B (approach). This combination of physical avoidance and mental approach may mean many things in dramatic terms, for example:

- You are not my social equal and I find you vaguely repulsive, but I will nevertheless listen to what you have to say because it may be in my interest to do so.

- I'm a virtuous girl/married woman but carry on and you just might persuade me.

- I've made up my mind to leave you forever but I still have some feelings for you.

This particular orientation is a favourite one among actors or singers whenever dramatically appropriate because of its practical spin-off. It enables the downstage performer to project outwards towards the audience while at the same time acknowledging the presence of the upstage performer. Thus it comprises one of

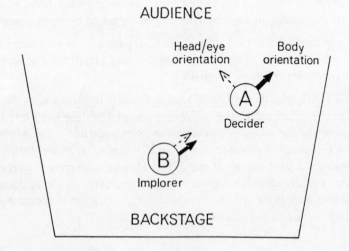

Figure 6.2: The 'cold downstage shoulder' as a technique for expressing mixed feelings. Although geographically upstaged by B, A's position is socially (and dramatically) dominant. B is characteristically seen as seeking a favour of A, while A is considering whether to respond to the request. The practical advantage is that both can easily project out

several techniques for 'cheating out' so as to avoid being 'upstaged' when disadvantageously positioned.

POWER OF THE PAUSE

In some circumstances the total absence of speech and movement has the greatest impact upon an audience. No performer or director should underestimate the dramatic value of silences, pauses or immobility. Paradoxically, such 'non-events' may create great tension and excitement. In waiting for the Godfather to make a decision, the right kind of pause carries enormous threat, reinforcing his power and generating anticipation, as the audience tries to predict which way he is going to 'jump'. The device is equally effective in opera; Wagner and the verismo composers knew well that a 'hush before the storm' could be very compelling. Although movement is contained at these junctures, a certain tension still needs to be conveyed.

Drama teachers often preach relaxation on stage, but this should not be interpreted to mean limpness or languidness either of body or voice. The more still and quiet the verbal or musical passage, the more menace or emotional life needs to be infused into the voice, and the body should be poised for action like a loaded spring – ready to react. The relaxation that enhances performance amounts to the elimination of irrelevant emotions and nervous fidgets, which amount to 'urges' that are out of character.

SPATIAL REFERENCES

The scenery on stage and the positions of the characters give clear spatial references to the performers. Much of their movement is necessarily directed towards these objects. But there are geographical reference points that cannot be seen by the audience. Although they exist only as ideas, it is nevertheless essential to alot them a specific theoretical location. Once they are located, it is then possible for the performer to demonstrate an attitude to these concepts, which may involve moving *towards* them (e.g. addressing, embracing or attacking) or *away from* them (e.g. fear, hatred).

When Aida comes to sing her famous aria 'Ritorna vincitor', agonising over her conflict between love and patriotism, she must first determine reference points for three concepts that are not visible on stage at that time. There is Ethiopia (to which she feels loyalty), Radames (for whom she feels love) and the gods (to whom she appeals for pity and support). If Radames has previously exited to the right, then in order to avoid ambiguity, Ethiopia should take the left. The gods are traditionally located overhead and downstage above the audience, approximately at the source of the follow-spot. (It is no accident that the highest tier of an auditorium is referred to as 'the gods'. Even though the seats are among the cheapest in the house, this is where deities are presumed to reside.) Other phrases in Aida's aria are introvert – they amount to talking to herself. Readers might pause to ask themselves where they would locate their own 'self' for the purpose of addressing that entity, and they would probably come up with a position somewhere just in front of their face. So it is that when actors talk to themselves the implicit reference point is somewhere in the variable triangle formed by eyes (brain) chest (heart) and hands (manipulators) which are often stretched imploringly out front. This is how Hamlet might ask himself the question 'To be or not to be?' or Aida might say to herself 'Return victorious? How could I say such a thing?'

It is an obvious matter of technique that, unless there is some very good reason, a performer will not select a reference point for any idea that is directly behind him, since he could not refer to it without upstaging himself. A possible exception might be an oppressive spectre that is conceived as a weight driving down upon his shoulders from behind. In this instance, the last thing he would want to do is turn to confront the monster that pursues him. We usually try to keep Satan behind us.

These spatial references motivate action in a manner that is somewhere between reasons and urges. Not only do they provide directions for movement and gestures but normally they involve a positive or negative attitude toward each idea or some more subtle feeling about it.

SYMBOLIC REPRESENTATION OF CHARACTERS

Sometimes an absent character to whom a performer wishes to relate may be spatially located by an associated object. For example, when Renato, in Verdi's *A Masked Ball,* sings his aria 'Eri tu', his violent outburst of jealousy and determination to wreak vengeance is broken by an interlude in which he spots a handkerchief on the floor that has been dropped by his wife Amelia. As the music becomes soft, warm and nostalgic he slowly picks up the handkerchief, presses it to his chest and sings 'O dolcezze perdute o memorie…' At this point the handkerchief has become a temporary spatial reference for Amelia, or more specifically, his previous love for her. She herself is just next door, having been sent to take farewell of their child before being killed in retribution. Thus, while he can address love to her memory as represented by the handkerchief, he cannot do this in her actual direction because his feeling for her has now turned to hatred.

The characters in a drama may acquire their own symbolic space by a process of association. If they gravitate towards a particular area of the stage often enough this becomes their psychological area and the audience will automatically identify it with them. This happens inevitably when a part of the set or its furnishings has direct connection with the social role or status of the character, for example a king can be represented by his throne or a secretary by her typewriter. In the film *One Flew Over the Cuckoo's Nest*, the authoritarian Ward Controller, Nurse Ratchett, spends so much time in her glass-encased nurse's station, from which she dispenses compulsory medication as well as a bitter attitude, that this becomes her psychological space with all its vicious overtones. References to her in her absence are then effectively addressed to her 'cage'.

FOCUS OF ATTENTION

Much of the actor's trade and the skill of a director is concerned with manipulation of the attention of the audience (Arnold 1990). It is the job of the actor to ensure that the director's wishes concerning where the audience's attention is to be focused are fulfilled. This means that the actor will sometimes move in such a way as to draw attention and will sometimes seek to be inconspicuous (often by absence of movement). Since a moving figure attracts the eye of an audience away from a static one, it is usual for actors to move only on (or shortly before) their own lines. Similarly, performers to whom the audience is supposed to attend cross downstage of others, and when turning do so in a downstage direction (so that their face passes the audience rather than the scenery). Hence much of what is called 'stagecraft' concerns the appropriate sharing of audience attention by means of movement.

The director is also concerned with *picturization* on stage. This means creating patterns on stage (or film frames in the movies) which satisfy the basic principles of artistic balance. If the proscenium arch is taken as equivalent to the frame of a painting, the deployment of characters within it should be satisfying to the viewer at any given time. This means that most movements have to be counterbalanced in some way. Often the non-focal performers will adjust their position inconspicuously after the focal (speaking) performer has initiated the move. The balance of the stage picture is thus restored so that there is even weight on the two sides and the performers are neither geometrically spaced nor masking one another.

Note the distinction between artistic and geometric composition. In painting a picture an artist will normally displace the focus of attention slightly away from the centre (usually to the left). Perspective lines in foreground objects are then used to draw the eye of the viewer towards that focal centre. The same effect is sought on stage both in the design of scenery and backdrops and the positioning of performers. A group of actors downstage on each side and looking back towards the main action is a favourite technique for directing audience attention; this is called *triangulation.*

Because the artistic centre of a painting is usually displaced left, it is widely agreed that stage right commands audience attention more easily than stage left, so this is where important entrances and action are often made to occur. Why this should be so is not entirely clear. One idea is that the left field of the viewer is more compelling because in Western countries we are used to reading from left to right and hence scan from left to right by habit. Another explanation is that we process spatial configurations with the right side of the brain which receives visual input from the left side, hence form and movement are registered more powerfully in the left visual field (which means stage right).

Directors can manipulate attention by many other means. One is *relative size* – important actors may be magnified by reducing the scale of the background set, props or adjacent performers, for example, to make the lead appear god-like. Or the reverse may be organized, for example, a burning bush may be made larger than Moses in order to emphasize his human frailty.

Lighting is not just for visibility; it is also an important way of focusing attention. Most obviously the lead can be picked out by a moveable spotlight (a 'follow-spot') or the 'live' area of a stage can be reduced by blacking out the background areas (in this way lighting is often used as a substitute for scenery.) It is possible to emphasize facial expressions (by front light) or eliminate them in favour of silhouette and shape (back lighting). Shock effects can be achieved by sudden reversals of light and dark and agitation can be created by change and movement of light and colour (stroboscopes, mirror balls, etc.). Neon lights flashing outside a hotel bedroom can induce excitement and emergencies are emphasized by the flashing red and blue lights of police/fire/ambulance services. Threat may be induced by storm clouds building on a cyclorama, perhaps culminating in thunder and lightning.

Colour is a major means of mood management, whether it is used in lighting, set or costume. A major part of the designer's task is to ensure that colours are properly co-ordinated and convey the right feeling. The emotional impact of various colours is widely agreed and supported by studies of physiological responses to differently coloured environments (Wilson 1966, Varley 1980, Gardano 1986). Some of the common associations of primary colours are listed in Table 6.2.

Table 6.2 Some Common Associations of Colours

Red	Heat, danger, blood, anger, excitement, activity, Christmas, nightclubs and prostitution.
Yellow	Sun, summer, joy, hilarity, health, daytime.
Blue	Cold, wet, gloomy, respectability, fear, moonlight, winter.
Green	Natural, outdoor, refreshing, peace, quiet, ghastly (in food and faces), Irish.
Purple	Passion, pomposity, royal, sinful, deep, desperate.
White	Snow, clean, pure, frank, virtuous, virginal.
Black	Mournful, death, night (dark), empty, ominous, villainous.

Sound is an equally important attention-focusing device. Principals are given acoustically advantageous locations on stage, or selective amplification can be used. It is common in cabaret to increase the sound level towards the end of a song in order to generate a climax. There is, however, a limit to credibility, not to mention the discomfort and damage to the ears that can be caused by over-amplification. Sound effects can also be used to create moods, for example, crickets (tropical), birds (springtime), cows (rural), traffic (urban).

Finally, *costume* is an important aspect of any performance. A lead singer can be emphasized by dressing him in white, which stands out among darker costumes of the others and catches the light more effectively (e.g. Elvis Presley's famous gold-studded white suit). Colour associations can be used to emphasize character. For example, the whore wears a low-cut black or purple dress, while the virginal woman is in high-necked white. A king is clad in purple and gold robes, the beggar in gray/brown, and so on.

Some of the above principles may seem obvious, but their importance cannot be over-estimated. Much of the emotional power and artistic satisfaction that is gained from a good performance, whether on stage or film, is due to the contribution of the director, designer and lighting team in successfully orchestrating audience attention and general 'atmospherics'.

BODY LANGUAGE OF DANCE

The principles of posture, gesture and use of space outlined above can be applied directly to the interpretation of dance movements. Dance may be thought of as the artistic extension of postural self-expression, although in practice it also pays homage to social rules and conventions. In fact, one of the interesting things about dance, in most of its various forms, is that freedom is juxtaposed with, or indeed emerges from, a framework of strong discipline (cf. technical acting). This is clear with classical ballet, but Martha Graham, whom some describe as the goddess of contemporary dance and who was quoted as saying that 'every dance is a fever chart, a graph of the heart', also recognised that years of hard work and preparation were necessary before 'spontaneity' could effectively be displayed (see her film, *A Dancer's World*). Some of dance training is concerned with the development of body suppleness and sheer physical fitness, but the language of posture and gesture also has to be acquired.

Central to the choreography of Martha Graham, among others, is contraction and expansion and particularly the progression from one to the other. When the body is curled up in a ball, with limbs contracted, a feeling of misery, oppression and submission is conveyed. But as psychological confidence and joy are developed, gestures become more open and body space is increased. Finally, territory is expanded triumphantly as movement around the stage becomes faster and freer. By such means the growth of dominance, self-esteem and freedom is displayed.

The body language of dance also features exaggerations of gender signals (Hanna 1988). Male dancers tend to use more abrupt, athletic movements, with more direct body orientation and upward, expansive gestures of the limbs (arms and legs fully outstretched). Women are more graceful and rounded in their movements, with beauty and suppleness being emphasized more than strength and vigour. Since many dance sequences are barely disguised courtship rituals it is no surprise to observe that the female partner tends to display more often and that the man initiates more body contact and joint manoeuvres (Table 6.3). Eibl-Eibesfeldt (1989) notes that the dancing of women in all cultures involves a kind of tease, with sexually suggestive gyrations and brief flashes of erotic stimuli (e.g. the whirling of the skirt in the French can-can, which provides brief glimpses of the posterior, and the Middle Eastern belly dance).

Table 6.3 Some of the gender-typical signals that are seen in male and female dance styles (modified from Hanna 1988)

MALES	FEMALES
SPACE	
Control greater territory. Move in others' or common territory. Accorded greater bodily space	Yield space to dominants when approached or passed. Approached more closely by both sexes
More vertical movement	More horizontal movement
Initiate directional changes in group interaction	React to directional changes
TIME	
Dominant – does not wait	'Women-in-waiting'
Begins actions	Responds to actions
CARRIAGE STYLE	
Allowed more movement and relaxed body comportment	More circumspect and constrained body comportment (clothing – skirts and heels also constrict action)
Options of firm stride and width in stance and sitting; use of ankle to knee cross in sitting	Narrow stance and sitting with legs together; thighs may cross in sitting, but feet are still close
Pelvis rolled slightly back in walk on flat shoe	Walk has pelvic anterior roll and mincing step on high heels

Table 6.3 Some of the gender-typical signals that are seen in male and female dance styles (modified from Hanna 1988) (continued)

GAZE

More direct gaze while speaking/listening	Submissive watching and averting of gaze
Prolonged gaze indicates sexual attraction	Prolonged eye contact with aversion indicates sexual attraction

GESTURE

Larger, more sweeping gestures Arm and hand held as solid unit	Smaller gestures. Fingers, wrist and forearm articulate more
Use less facial expression	Use more facial expression and smile
Less likely to return smile when smiled at	More likely to return smile smiled at

TOUCH

Touch non-familial women more often; encompass women, hold shoulder, lock arms	Touch non-familial men less often
Shake hands with men (ritual bracketing or coming together)	Embrace women
Touch each other and themselves less	Touch each other and themselves more (grooming)

QUALITY OF MOVEMENT

Unemotional, reserved	Emotional, expressive
Body expands in energy when meeting authority	Body expands and contracts in energy when confronting persons of significance

It may seem strange to describe male dancing as hyper-masculine, since dancing itself is regarded as an effeminate pursuit and male ballet dancers are often stereotyped as being homosexual. Indeed, gender signals are often mixed, but they may gain power by contrast effects, in much the same way that a woman's femininity may be emphasized by dressing in a man's suit or pyjamas.

When anthropologist Desmond Morris was commissioned by a British newspaper to observe and report on the body language of Michael Jackson in concert, he likened him to the 'Cock of the Rock'. This is 'a bizarrely ornamented South American bird in which the male is brightly coloured and the female a drab brown. The males dance to the females on specially cleared arenas on the jungle floor. These dances are great social occasions with males stretching and twisting, performing their special display, staged amid a crescendo of sharp cries' (*Mail on Sunday*, 17 July 1988). Morris noted that the screams of Jackson's audience were in response not to song phrases, but to fancy footwork in which his exceptional skill and suppleness was exhibited. Morris further observed that Jackson's gestures were 'macho' in several aspects:

- The extreme vigour and athleticism of his performance
- Stiffly spread legs, planted defiantly
- Pelvic thrusting and blatant crotch-grabbing
- Raised fist, scowl and snarl.

Jackson might be considered 'androgynous' in the sense that plastic surgery, gaudy costuming and the exhibitionistic act of dancing itself are often viewed as feminine, but the body language of his gestures makes copious use of high-volume male gender signals. Furthermore, his colourful dress and dancing are only considered effeminate in the context of Western industrial society today. In most species of fish, birds and mammals it is the males who are more highly decorated and perform vigourous courtship dances. In tribal societies, the warriors spend days preparing costumes and make-up before going into battle. Male plumage is also apparent in our own recent history – for example, Elizabethan courtiers, Restoration dandies, cavaliers and the Victorian military.

Not all gestures in dance are gender differentiated, however; some are common to both sexes – especially when their meaning is culturally determined. For example, a hand on the heart occurring in a ballet sequence means sincerity regardless of whether it is performed by a male or female. Similarly, pointing a finger is used for emphasis and pressing the palms together in an upright position is a gesture of blessing. Attitudes and emotions such as joy, anger, fear, attraction and disgust also have unisex non-verbal signals (Chapter 5).

We have noted that the mirroring of gestures is an indicator of mutual warmth and understanding. When couples dance together in courtship (e.g. in a discotheque) there is an opportunity to discover if they are suited by noting the ease with which physical synchrony can be achieved. Many folk dances involve a ritual whereby partners are exchanged in a set sequence before returning to the original partner. This provides an opportunity for contact with many different people so that rapport can be assessed.

Of course, moving in harmony may also be a way of consolidating or demonstrating group unity (as can community singing). Group dances usually require the assimilation of certain social rules and hence confirm and display group membership. As noted in Chapter 2, dance may also be used for trance-induction, either for individual or social purposes, the constant beat and repetitive movement progressively pacing and taking over electrical brain rhythms.

Dance has many individual and social functions, but above all it is an expression of emotion through bodily movement and a celebration of physical mastery and cultivation. In today's 'civilized' society, the urge to dance (and sing) is all too often contained and the act viewed as degenerate and dangerous outside of a few socially sanctioned contexts. It takes people like Isadora Duncan to remind us that the Ancient Greeks (such as Plato) described an uneducated person as 'danceless'.

CHAPTER 7

COMEDY AND COMEDIANS

There are many types of comedy: *satire*, which attacks manners, morals, ideas and social institutions with wit and sarcasm; *farce*, which pokes fun at life by inventing absurd situations and exaggerated characters; and *burlesque*, which ridicules other works through caricature and parody. There are also *black* or *sick* comedies, which are in such bad taste that the audience may have difficulty in deciding whether to take offence, throw up or laugh boisterously (Styan 1975). 'Comedy' comes from the Greek word *komoidia,* and refers to the light-hearted dramatic form that developed, historically, in parallel with tragedy. Usually it was set in the 'here and now' and it frequently lampooned its dramatic sibling (Glover 1990).

The distinction between tragedy and comedy remains today (Kerr 1967). Tragedy evokes profound passions such as foreboding, anguish and horror, while comedy focuses on fun, joy and confusion. Tragedy deals with events that are sad and disastrous, such as death and cruelty, while comedy deals with happy life events such as romance, marriage and the outwitting or humiliation of petty villains. In tragedy, mankind is exalted with the highlighting of courage and commitment in the face of insuperable odds, whereas comedy traditionally belittles man by pointing up his selfishness, stupidity and weakness. The two are sometimes intermingled or alternated within the same play or opera. Shakespeare used comic scenes to ease tension and give the audience a short respite before piling on the ultimate excitement, horror or grief. The Falstaff scenes in *Henry IV* and the gate porter scene in *Macbeth* are well-known examples of this device. Many other works that are primarily tragic use humour in early scenes in order to magnify the eventual tragedy. Puccini's *La Bohème* and the Oscar-winning film *One Flew Over the Cuckoo's Nest* use humour early on so that we get to like and identify with the characters before disaster overtakes them. *Melodrama*, which enjoyed great fashionability in the early Victorian era, almost reverses this formula, making sensational appeal to sad and sympathetic emotions before moving towards a happy ending.

A few decades ago, melodrama went through a period of being played entirely for laughs. As the formula became familiar it became increasingly difficult to suspend disbelief, and at the same time, the emotions it aroused were so powerful that embarrassment was created and it was found easier to 'take the mickey' out of the dramatic form and conventions than deliver them as they were originally intended. (The same often happens with hard-core pornography; humour is used to defuse the shock.) Although melodrama is again being presented with sincerity, it illustrates the fine line between tragedy and comedy, both in theatre and in real life.

Tragedy readily turns to comedy if things go wrong. Everyone can think of their own examples. A tenor friend was once singing the death scene from *La Bohème* in a provincial theatre which, because of its low budget, had supplied a hospital bed on casters for Mimi to die on. As Rodolfo fell to his knees against the side of the bed to express his anguish and pay his last respects, the whole bed, Mimi and all, shot off towards the wings as though making a bid for the operating theatre. The tears of sorrow welling in the eyes of the audience were swiftly transformed into gales of helpless laughter, leaving little chance of reconstructing the tragic atmosphere before the curtain. Equally ludicrous must have been the occasion when an under-rehearsed firing squad shot Tosca instead of Cavaradossi in an ill-fated San Francisco production.

Clearly, the misfortune of others, particularly those with grandiose pretensions, is a primary source of amusement to us. We enjoy seeing others brought down to our own level. If a disabled child or a tramp slips on a banana peel we do not find it funny, but we laugh uproariously if it is a pompous bishop, self-important mayor or tyrannical old headmaster (Gutman and Priest 1969; Cantor and Zillman 1973). Tragic opera takes itself seriously and so rides for a fall.

ORIGINS OF HUMOUR

Over the past few decades, psychologists have done much research on the reasons why people smile and laugh (Chapman and Foot 1976; McGhee and Goldstein 1983; Durant and Miller 1988). Although mysteries remain, some answers have begun to emerge.

Comparisons with other species, especially apes, reveal that smiling and laughing are not different degrees of the same thing, but are derived from separate, almost opposite, evolutionary paths. Smiling seems to have developed from a rather nervous, submissive stretching of the lips wide across the teeth, a facial expression that in chimpanzees signifies an attempt to appease a social superior; the teeth are closed together and therefore not prepared for biting.

In humans too, smiling is a major way in which harmlessness and acquiescence are communicated, which goes some way towards explaining why women smile more than men. Analysis of newspaper photographs show that the men, mostly politicians and top businessmen, are usually serious-faced, while women are nearly always pictured smiling (even when attending their husband's murder trial or visiting them in hospital). Likewise, anyone familiar with the Clint Eastwood 'Spaghetti Westerns' knows that the men, who are always striving to look tougher than each other, seldom smile (except occasionally sadistically), while the women frequently have to 'appease' in this way (Duncan and Fiske 1977).

Laughter is different entirely. It stems from the more aggressive, threatening kind of teeth-baring seen in chimpanzees and other apes, which amounts to a demonstration of readiness to bite. This gesture, along with the glottal, percussive, expiration sound that often accompanies it ('ah-ah-ah') occurs mainly in group situations, when the support of others can be counted upon. Similar observations in humans (De la Cruz 1981) have led psychologists to conclude that two of the main functions of laughter are to express hostility and to affirm group solidarity. Since males are typically more aggressive than females, and more given to the formation of same-sex gangs, they might be expected to laugh more. Research shows that men initiate laughter more (though women tend to join in by way of social conformity) and that humour is more central to males' communication patterns than that of females (Cox, Read and Van Auken 1990; Johnson 1990).

Studies of laughter in children (McGhee 1979) reveal another important component: that of fear or tension. Children laugh when some kind of anxiety has been aroused, followed by a realization that there is no danger after all, or when there is a mixture of anxiety and security. Typical situations which evoke laughter in young children include peek-a-boo games, being tickled in vulnerable parts of the body, playing on a swing, running into cold water and being chased by an adult who pretends to be a monster but is known really to be harmless. In all of these instances, a degree of danger is involved, but within a safe context in which the child recognizes that it is all 'just in fun' (Rothbart 1973). Tension-relief laughter, as this may be called, seems to derive from crying, beginning as the modification that occurs when the infant recognizes its mother and danger is dissipated (Morris 1977).

An adult example of tension relief laughter is seen in this description of a near-fatal flying accident:

> A certain fighter pilot, returning to his base following a successful mission, buzzed his field at almost 400 miles an hour and misjudged a very slight rise in the ground. His aircraft hit it and went cartwheeling across the field into a hangar. The pilot, who was thrown free, was later found sitting up against a wall, laughing. (Bond 1952, pp.28–29)

In this instance the laughter appears to have been provoked by the sudden realization of safety. It has been suggested that laughter may have originated as a pre-linguistic signal to fellow humans that danger has passed. The gasp for air instinctively taken before confronting danger is released in a rhythmic vocalization connoting safety to one's clan-mates, while at the same time bodily tension is relaxed (Grumet 1989). This would imply that laughter is more an expression of triumph than threat.

Most laughter-provoking situations are also social. They involve relationships with, or at least require the presence of, other people. Even tickling needs to be done by somebody else to make us laugh. Thus, while laughter may have elements of aggression, superiority, fear or anxiety, it is also intimately bound up with social communication. As the child grows up it becomes progressively a means of affirming group membership by endorsing the common values of the group. We laugh to indicate to other people that we share the same perception, whether it be a permissive stance with respect to unusual or illicit sex, an intellectual rapport, or a feeling of superiority over some national or religious group. The individual who does not laugh when the group laughs renders him or herself an outcast (see the description of social contagion in Chapter 3).

THE TWO-COMPONENT THEORY OF HUMOUR

Much of what has been said so far can be summarized by saying that humour arises out of a judicious mixture of warmth and security on the one hand, and hostility or fear on the other (Figure 7.1). In evolutionary terms, humour combines the tendency to appeasement (smiling) with dominance (laughing), and developmental studies reveal that children laugh when anxiety and security cues appear in close proximity. Hence humour requires both the arousal of tensions and their release (simultaneously or in quick succession). Authority is suddenly humanized, a taboo is trivialized or fear is turned to triumph (see Table 7.1).

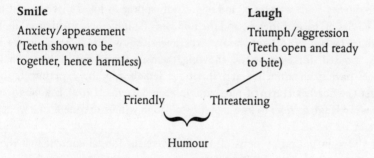

Smile

Anxiety/appeasement
(Teeth shown to be
together, hence harmless)

Laugh

Triumph/aggression
(Teeth open and ready
to bite)

Friendly   Threatening

Humour

Figure 7.1 The two-component theory of the origins of humour

Table 7.1 The sequential or simultaneous juxtaposition of cues that are frequently involved in humour

Danger	Safety
Arousal	Relief from tension
Taboo	Trivialization
Anxiety	Triumph
Authority	Humanization

The tension-release principle is most obvious in jokes that sequentially build arousal before dispelling it. 'Did you hear about the honeymoon couple who couldn't tell the difference between Vaseline and putty?' (pause) 'All their windows fell out'. All kinds of ghastly and embarrassing possibilities are contemplated by the audience before the punchline defuses all anxiety. But as with 'white-knuckle rides' at the fairground, humour more often entails a simultaneous mixture of threat and safety cues. The more tension that is aroused the funnier the joke is likely to seem. Schurcliff (1968) demonstrated such a relationship experimentally, showing that practical jokes were rated as funnier if a high level of anxiety was first aroused.

Freud (1905) pointed out that most jokes can be analyzed into two major components, the *libidinous material* (typically sexual and aggressive) that powers the reaction, and the formal structure, or *technique*, that provides the social excuse for stimulating taboo feelings. He believed that humour serves as a safety-valve for repressed sex and aggression – jokes permit us to share unacceptable tendencies with other people in a slightly oblique way; not all our cards are put on the table face up. It is always possible to blame the audience for taking up an innuendo (as do some music hall comedians) and we can express hostility towards other people or groups in the form of a joke and then accuse them of having no sense of humour when they take offence.

Evidence that libido underlies much humour comes from various sources. One is the frequency with which sex and aggression appear in jokes that are told in private circles of trusted friends, and the routines of nightclub comedians (Janus, Janus and Vincent 1986). Laboratory experiments show that if an audience is sexually aroused, for example by showing them erotic movies or (for a male audience) having an attractive and flirtatious female run the experiment, the enjoyment of nearly all types of humour is increased (Levine 1969). Eskimos even use the word laugh to refer to love-making; to 'laugh with' someone is to have sex with them.

Jokes vary in the proportions of libidinous versus formal content that they contain. Some jokes are blatantly sexual or aggressive and are called 'crude', 'sick', 'blue' or 'black'. Nevertheless, they are capable of giving rise to a great deal of mirth under certain conditions, particularly when people are among close friends or social barriers are already partly down, such as when those present are very permissive, having a stag night or drinking alcohol. In these circumstances, such jokes are likely to provoke full-bodied 'belly-laughing', because both arousal and safety signals are at high volume. At the other extreme are jokes in which the technique is dominant. In the case of many jokes, including some puns and incongruity jokes, there may be no libidinous content at all. Outright laughter is not the most usual reaction to such jokes. Something more like abstract intellectual appreciation (mental 'tickling') is more typical. Pure puns are likely to evoke a groan rather than any expression of enjoyment.

The strictly Freudian theory of humour focuses on sex and hostility as providing the motive power, but other sources of tension, such as embarrassment, fear, grief and curiosity, may also power a joke. Purely intellectual, or 'cognitive' factors are also important. Some theories of humour (see Pollio and Talley 1991) concentrate on the construction of jokes (the excuse) rather than the emotional content that makes them pleasurable. Common elements such as surprise, incongruity or ambiguity are identified, the idea being that it is the sudden reversal of a progressive build-up of uncertainty that provides the enjoyment of humour. This does describe the structure of some jokes, but much of the pleasure we gain from humour still derives from expressing forbidden feelings and being reassured that other people have similar desires and frustrations to ourselves.

FUNCTIONS OF HUMOUR

The main functions of humour, both personal and social, have been summarized by Ziv (1984) as follows:

1. Airing social taboos

Humour provides a safety valve for the expression of taboo thoughts, especially those relating to sex and aggression. These are natural needs and tendencies that have to be socially regulated, but total suppression is unrealistic. In the same way that watching or participating in a boxing match provides a socially acceptable outlet for aggressive impulses, so humour is an arena for the controlled release of impulses that are potentially threatening to civilized society.

2. Social criticism

Satire is a form of humour in which social and political institutions and individuals in the public eye are ridiculed and humanized. This may be simply a means of releasing tension, and hence supportive of the *status quo,* or it may lead to change in the system (Paletz 1990).

Since frustration is one of the main causes of aggression it is not surprising that those who frustrate our aims and pleasures are the prime targets of humour (e.g. judges, police, government officials, parents, teachers, or indeed anyone in authority). The humorous pleasure obtained from a joke can be enhanced by raising the social power of the victim (e.g. guitar-player changed to bank manager) and his degree of alienation from the audience (Cantor and Zillman 1973). Outright aggression towards people in power whom we fear and despise is not permissible, so humour gives indirect satisfaction.

Interestingly, the PC (political correctness) movement has raised certain previously disadvantaged groups to the status of 'sacred cows' that society protects. This means, paradoxically, that 'alternative' comedians such as Andrew Dice Clay

('The Dice Man') fill their routine with attacks upon women, blacks, homosexuals and disabled people.

3. Consolidation of group membership

The social function of humour is seen in its development. The smile is the earliest positive communication from infant to parent, appearing about two weeks after birth and meaning, primarily, 'I feel good'. But it also has a component of *recognition*, first to human faces and voices in general, then after eight weeks becoming selective, with infants smiling only at their own parents, and not strangers.

In young children smiling and laughing are both associated with contentment and enjoyment and tend to accompany play, and they mostly occur in a social context. Humour thus becomes an important basis of social cohesion – a private language of the in-group. When an audience laughs at the jokes of Bernard Manning or 'The Dice Man' they are asserting common values (or prejudices), sharing attitudes or, as one journalist put it, 'validating their hostilities'. Recognition that other people think the same way as ourselves and share our problems and experiences is a major source of humorous pleasure. At the same time, the victimization aspect of humour (whether the target is an individual such as Joan Collins or Dan Quayle, or a group such as mothers-in-law) is one reason why it can easily become offensive.

Humour may also be a way of bringing group members back into line with the norms of the group. For example, a group of hippies might laugh at one of their group who turns up clean-shaven. In this case, the laughter directed at him is a form of social sanction. At the extreme, a group member may be totally rejected (excommunicated) by ridicule and mockery, a process that is seen at its cruellest among children in a school playground.

4. Defence against fear and anxiety

By laughing at things which frighten us we bring them under control and render them less menacing. Typical is Woody Allen's comment, 'It's not that I'm afraid to die, I just don't want to be there when it happens' (Dorinson 1986). Gallows humour, 'black' humour and jokes about disasters (such as those circulating shortly after the space shuttle blew up on a televised mission) operate as a kind of defence mechanism. Self-disparagement, a form of humour that is the speciality of certain comedians such as Woody Allen, may be adaptive in the same way (for the joke teller as well as the audience).

5. Intellectual play

As noted, humour may also be primarily cognitive. Intellectual humour gives us momentary freedom from the tyranny of logical thought. It allows us to escape the bounds of reality and indulge our capacity for originality and creativity. The humour of Spike Milligan, for example, features a childlike, slightly schizoid, fresh perspective on the world. Any analysis which ignores this most advanced and 'human' function of humour is bound to be limited.

Table 7.2. The way in which various national groups stereotype each other in humour with respect to the stupid versus clever (canny, successful) dimension (from Davies 1986)

Country in which jokes are told	Allegedly stupid groups	Allegedly canny groups
England	Irish	Scots
Wales	Irish	Cardis
Scotland	Irish	Aberdonians
Ireland	Kerrymen	Scots
United States	Poles	New England Yankees
Canada	Newfies/Ukrainians	Scots/Nova Scotians
Mexico	Yucatecos	Regiomontanos
France	Belgians	Scots/Auvergnats
Low Countries	Belgians	Dutch
Germany	Ostfriedlanders	Swabians
Sweden	Norwegians	Scots
Finland	Karelians	Laihians
Greece	Pontians	Scots
Bulgaria	Sopi	Gabrovonians
India	Sardarjis (Sikhs)	Gujaratis
South Africa	Van Der Merwe (Boers)	Scots
Australia	Irish	Scots
New Zealand	Irish, Maori	Scots

(For most of these countries one can also add the Jews to the list of canny groups)

AUDIENCE INVOLVEMENT

The extent to which we enjoy a joke depends on who we are and how easily we can identify with the characters who triumph, as opposed to those cast as victims (Table 7.2). Jewish people laugh at Jewish jokes in which the Jew is portrayed as a clever manipulator of words or situations. They may also laugh at jokes illustrating minor weaknesses of character if told by other Jews – a kind of gentle self-mockery. They are not likely to be amused when 'gas-chamber' jokes are told by a Teutonic blond with known Fascist sympathies (Davies 1986, Saper 1991). Jokes directed at other ethnic groups (e.g. Poles in the US or Irish in Britain) are also likely to be perceived as unfunny disparagement by the target groups themselves.

Sex differences in preferences among different types of humour are quite marked (Love and Deckers 1989, Barrick, Hutchinson and Deckers 1990, Butland and Ivy 1990, Johnson 1992). Generally speaking, males are more responsive to sexual and aggressive humour, while women are more appreciative of nonsensical and defensive forms of humour. Not surprisingly, women are less favourable towards 'sexist' jokes in which women are disparaged and men are unimpressed by jokes which point up their chauvinism or expose their ego-insecurities.

Reactions of women to sexist jokes of the kind typified by seaside postcards that focus on women as sex-objects, may also depend upon the physical attributes of the woman herself. Wilson and Brazendale (1973) found that, at the time of their research, women rated by men as unattractive enjoyed jokes in which the female character was depicted as a passive recipient of male interest and attention, while women rated as attractive were more amused by jokes in which the woman took the sexual initiative or symbolically 'castrated' male characters. Apparently, the unattractive women, feeling deprived of male attention in real life, were deriving some kind of fantasy gratification from the male-predatory postcards, whereas the attractive women, being fed up with crude male advances of the type depicted, derived greater satisfaction from the female-dominant cartoons.

'Psychodynamic' processes of this kind are often involved in humour appreciation. Another demonstration is that of O'Neill, Greenberg and Fisher (1992) who set out to test the Freudian theory that jokes allow temporary satisfaction of usually unacceptable impulses. Anal jokes were presented to a group of women who were also tested for 'anality' of personality (obstinacy, orderliness and parsimony). Results supported the prediction that women scoring higher on the anal traits would find anal jokes funnier. In other words, the more taboo the subject matter the more power it has to fuel humour based upon it.

The motivational/emotional power of humour depends upon its relevance to the preoccupations, desires and fantasies of the audience. This means that recognition (topicality) is important in humourous material as well as its capacity to touch upon widespread pleasures, anxieties and frustrations. Men like sexual and hostile humour more than women on average because they are biologically more lustful and competitive. But variations on traits such as sex drive within sex will also predict humour preferences. It is no surprise that female comedians such as Phyllis Diller, Whoopi Goldberg and Victoria Wood feature references to women's issues such as PMT, diets, tampons, gynaecological examinations and male chauvinism, or that domestic comedies dealing with the resolution of family problems (e.g. *I Love Lucy, Roseanne*) are enjoyed mainly by women (see Cantor 1991).

Whereas sexuality and aggression are central themes in Western humour, primitive people joke mostly about the immediate physical environment and the Chinese typically joke about social relationships (Holland 1972). Analysis of a series of jokes exchanged among black Americans in the Southern US in the 1960s revealed that 72 per cent were about race relations (Prange and Vitols, 1963). No doubt this tells us something about the major concerns of these cultural groups at the time of the research.

Grumet (1989) performed a content analysis of *Henny Youngman's 500 All-Time Greatest One-Liners* (Youngman 1981) which was supposedly based on half a century of experience as a 'stand-up' comedian as to which jokes were most successful with his (American) audiences. Ten major themes were discerned (Table 7.3), each relating to some common human problem. The majority of jokes incorporated more than one of these themes, and many contained three, four or five of the basic ingredients.

Table 7.3 Ten major themes observed in the jokes of the stand-up comedian Henny Youngman (adapted from Grumet 1989)

Rank	Primary psychodynamic theme	%
1	Aggression	20.2
2	Misfortune e.g. physical injury	15.6
3	Ineptitude e.g. stupidity	11.8
4	Family conflict	11.0
5	Social unacceptability e.g. ugliness	9.6
6	Interpersonal estrangement e.g. racial or ethnic differences	9.2
7	Criminal behaviour or untruthfulness	7.0
8	Sexuality	6.2
9	Money or property	6.0
10	Orality e.g. excessive eating or drinking	3.4

Some examples:

> A man brags about his new hearing aid: 'It's the most expensive kind I've ever had'. His friend asks, 'What kind is it?' He says, 'Half past four'! (Themes 2, 9, 3)

> My doctor put his hand on my wallet and said, 'Cough'. (Themes 7,9,2,10)

> I've been married for fifty years and I'm still in love with the same woman. If my wife ever finds out, she'll kill me. (Themes 4,8,1,2,7)

(Grumet 1989, p.102)

It appears that the most successful jokes are those that touch on many concerns simultaneously, thus expanding the potential audience involvement as regards the range of people in whom some degree of tension is aroused before all anxieties are abruptly discharged with a tight, economic punchline.

It may be useful at this point to offer a detailed analysis of a particular joke. Take the cartoon of a puny, acne-stricken man, head wreathed in the remnants of a bouquet, standing before a slamming door, saying, 'Maybe some other time, Miss Quirk'. Why and to whom is this funny? Its emotional arousal derives from the fact that dating is a highly emotive aspect of life for both men and women. Men fear rejection from women they approach and women are frequently pestered by undesirable men. The cartoon thus deals with a common, tension-provoking experience and reassures all parties that they are not alone in the preoccupation.

Next there is the aggression/superiority component. In a sense, both parties gain a sort of victory. She has done to him what many a woman would secretly like to do to some of her suitors – made it abundantly clear that she detests him and that he hasn't got a chance. Yet in a kind of way, he has struck back, with an impertinent retort that puts a brave face on it and gains some sort of last laugh. This surprising rejoinder from a pathetic little man who should by rights be devastated, constitutes the formal aspect of the joke, but it is the content concerning the social and sexual struggle that provides the emotional power.

Various identifications might enhance our pleasure in this joke. We could think of ourselves as the woman with the courage to treat unwanted suitors so forthrightly, or as the weak man who retains sufficient composure to make a resilient crack in such adversity. Alternatively, we might bask in superiority over both characters, slapping our own back over the fact that we are relatively successful in the mating game and do not have to suffer such indignities. Perhaps we see all of these little triumphs simultaneously, and thus derive some pleasure from each.

This example gives an idea of the complexity of analysis required to explain the effect of a single, rather simple, joke on various audiences. The truth is probably more complex still. No such analysis can do total justice to this or any other joke, and in fact, the very act of analysis tends to diminish the joke. Nevertheless, processes of the kind described are no doubt involved in the experience of humour. The reader is left to apply these principles of humour to well-known comic scenes in drama and opera, for example, Falstaff's ducking in the Thames at the hands of the merry wives of Windsor, or the Mikado's description of punishments appropriate to various social nuisances.

HUMOUR AND THE BRAIN

The ability to 'get' a joke seems to depend upon an intact right hemisphere of the brain (Shields 1991). Studies of patients with serious right-side stroke injury show that they have difficulty in appreciating metaphorical aspects of language and in grasping the overall shape of a story. They frequently 'miss the point' of narratives and jokes because the structural part of their language functioning is deficient (Gardner 1981). For example, they are given the stem of a joke as follows:

> A parade was going down the street and two cousins were talking on the balcony. Said one: 'Here comes the parade and Aunt Helen will miss it'. 'She's upstairs waving her hair', said the other.

The patient is then asked to choose a punchline from a set of four, the correct one being 'Mercy, can't we afford a flag?'. Patients with damage to the right side of the brain often choose a non-sequitur like: 'I wonder what's for dinner?' Asked to explain this choice, they say it's because a joke should end with a surprise.

Further evidence for right hemisphere involvement in humour comes from the finding that individuals who are fast at solving visually displayed mental rotation problems (a right hemisphere function) show enhanced humour appreciation, rating jokes as funnier (Johnson 1990). Apparently, appreciation of humour depends upon the capacity to see relationships and comprehend patterns. These non-literal aspects of language are made possible by the differentiation of the two hemispheres of the human brain and the complex interplay between them. Humour may be powered by emotional needs such as sex, aggression and fear of death, but it is also very much a cerebral and human capacity.

The reflexes involved in the outward display of laughter are not well under-stood. There are contractions of the facial muscles, also the diaphragm and abdominal muscles, so that the whole body shakes. Blood vessels dilate, a staccato, cough-like sound is produced and there may even be a loss of control of bodily secretions (e.g. tears or urination). Grumet (1989) describes this general reaction as an 'epileptoid catharsis', claiming that instinctive drive energies from the limbic system (the emotional brain centres) are temporarily emancipated from cortical (particularly prefrontal) control, thus releasing tension in a socially acceptable way. The mechanism is symbolically triggered by humour and results in a reduction of anxiety, possibly even a euphoric state equivalent to being 'sated by a good meal, sexual activity or opoid use'. In psychological terms, the latter effects, including the enjoyment of humour, are due to a precipitous drop in the excitation of the sympathetic nervous system. The punchline is the comedian's mechanism for triggering this sudden decline in emotional arousal.

THERAPEUTIC EFFECTS OF HUMOUR

There is no doubt that we feel the better for a good laugh: this is why most people seek out humour, reading funny stories and cartoons, going to the theatre and watching TV comedies. Experimentally, it has been shown that exposure to humorous material has the capacity to mitigate unpleasant emotional states like anger, anxiety or discomfort (Hudak *et al.* 1991) and Cousins (1979) has given a most affecting personal account of how humour was used to help him through a painful period of hospitalization for ankylosing spondylitis.

In Grumet's view (1989), laughter is therapeutic because it releases instinctive forces that are normally held in containment by the frontal lobes of the brain, which have evolved in response to the demands of modern civilization. Humour is a symbolic means of circumventing these inhibitions, with the joke teller inviting the audience to join him in a safe collective release of repressed energies. The laugh reflex dissipates nervous energy and tames our incorrigible emotions. If we take things seriously we have to hold in check our anger, lust, dread, stresses and conflicts. Laughing is a magical, if temporary and partial, solution to our problems that is virtually essential to survival in modern times.

Attempts have been made to harness humour therapeutically in clinical settings (Haig 1986). This seems a reasonable way to proceed, since an inability to laugh at oneself and the world is one of the most striking symptoms of mental illnesses such as depression and schizophrenia. Some decades ago, a psychologist from New York's Bellevue Hospital, Dr Murray Banks, made a record called *What to do Until the Psychiatrist Comes*, intended as a home cure for depression and anxiety. Since laughter is physiologically incompatible with the state of the autonomic nervous system that prevails in fear and anxiety (the stress reaction), Banks reckoned that making neurotic people laugh should produce a temporary cure at least. With all the skill of a professional comedian he set about telling stories drawn from his clinical experience which made light of the problems presented to him. The result was highly successful: many people in a near-suicidal state of depression were unable to resist his humour and reported feeling a great deal better.

More recently psychologists have begun to conduct properly controlled trials to examine the power of humour to alleviate emotional distress. Several studies have confirmed that humour is an effective coping strategy for handling adversity, the use of humour being associated with lower levels of loneliness and depression and higher self-esteem (Nezu *et al.* 1988, Overhulser 1992). It is even possible to measure the beneficial effects of humour in terms of immune system resources (Martin and Dobbin 1988, Lefcourt, Davidson-Katz and Kueneman 1990, Labott *et al.* 1990). These studies show an increase in salivary immunoglobulin A levels following video presentation of humourous material, compared with sad-video or no-video controls. Thus humour has the power to reduce pain, helps us to cope with stresses and apparently even increases our resistance to disease.

THE ROLE OF COMEDIANS

Superficially, comedians are just entertainers, spreading a little fun about them. But their social function goes beyond that; they serve an educational function as well, exposing our selfishness and folly and rescuing us from an over-serious view of life.

The earliest societies recognized the importance of clowns as philosophers and social commentators. In medieval times the fool or jester served as 'conscience to the king' (Sanders 1978): 'Jibing, cajoling and sometimes berating him, the jester used humour as a levelling force to give perspective to the king's decisions'. The fool was licensed to break society's polite codes and say the unsayable, thus allowing for a form of release when reverence of authority became stifling.

This use of wit raised the court jester almost to the role of advisor. As Jack Point says in Gilbert and Sullivan's *Yeoman of the Guard*:

> When offered to the world in merry guise
> Unpleasant truths are swallowed with a will
> He who'd make his fellow creatures wise ·
> Should always gild the philosophic pill.

It is easy to imagine an American President reading and being influenced by *National Lampoon* or a British Prime Minister taking heed of the attitudes expressed in the puppet satire, *Spitting Image*. Political commentary is commonly offered by comedians. For example, in Woody Allen's *Bananas* there is a scene in which US paratroops are about to be dropped into a Central American 'banana' republic. One says to the next, 'Which side are we fighting for today – El Presidente or the Revolution?'. The other replies: 'This time the CIA's taking no chances – half of us are fighting for El Presidente and half for the Revolution'.

As if to restore balance, comedians such as Woody Allen are often highly self-effacing, trading on their own inferiority and thus making us feel good. They thus seem to operate on a continuum from *fools*, who make us feel superior, to the barbed *wits* who draw attention to our folly – making us feel inferior. Court jesters walked a tight-rope such that an ill-timed joke or one that hit too close to home could result in dismissal or even execution. The element of foolishness may be partly necessary to balance or defuse the wit, thus saving the clown from social anger.

Today we do not execute jesters who overstep the mark but we do come close. Charlie Chaplin was persecuted and driven from the United States because he was suspected of communist sympathies. Lenny Bruce was arrested for obscenity three times (and once convicted) before he committed suicide in 1965. His liberal use of four-letter words may have been part of the reason, but his political subversion was probably more important (Paletz 1990). Benny Hill's show was cancelled by the TV network that produced it despite high viewing figures and great success in the US. His use of 'seaside' and 'schoolboy' humour, together with scantily clad, attractive young women ('Hill's Angels') was deemed 'sexist' in the late 1980s even though it arguably undermined the dignity of men to a degree that was at least equivalent. He died of a heart attack not long after.

Modern comedians, like the medieval court jesters, often represent our desire to be eccentric and rebellious, to knock down sacred cows. They are irresponsible and lawless, refusing to be over-awed and bullied by authorities or 'the system'. Inevitably 'the system' occasionally strikes back, imposing censorship or punishment upon them. According to MacDonald (1969) humour is 'like guerrilla warfare. Success (and perhaps survival) depends on travelling light, striking unexpectedly and getting away fast' (p.160).

But not all comedians are politically subversive. Some, like Bob Hope, can be seen as authority-supporting (Paletz 1990). Hope may direct jibes at presidents or government institutions but, as he said on the CBS *Morning Show* (15 January 1987), 'I never go deep. I just prick 'em a little. I never draw blood.' His jibes are inoffensive to the extent that Hope will play golf with the President the following day. Most of his jokes target impersonal, apolitical issues such as bureaucracy and waste. For example:

> Did you read that the astronauts' spacesuits cost two million dollars each? When did NASA hire Gucci?

> Like everyone else I've paid my income taxes, and I'd like to congratulate our cameramen for their trick photography. You'd never know I'm not wearing a shirt.

Bob Hope would never really seek to damage the political and economic system that had served him so well over the years. He is the benign court jester who reinforces the power of the king by giving vent to minor annoyances and unifying the court with laughter.

MOTIVATION OF COMEDIANS

The story is told of a Frenchman who went to a psychiatrist in a distressed condition and said 'Doctor, I'm terribly miserable and depressed. Can you give me some pills or something that would help?'. The psychiatrist replied: 'You don't want pills; go and see Grock (the famous clown). He'll cheer you up and make you feel better'. 'I am Grock,' replied the unhappy man.

Although comedians make other people laugh they often seem to be very unhappy people themselves: lonely, isolated and failing to see the funny side of their own condition. The image of the unhappy clown occurs frequently in history and literature (Pierrot, Rigoletto, I Pagliacci, Jack Point) and there are many instances among modern comedians. Spike Milligan is a well-known manic-depressive, intermittently requiring medical help. Tony Hancock apparently committed suicide in an Australian hotel room after years of alcoholism and depression. Lenny Bruce and John Belushi are also believed to have killed themselves deliberately. At his trial for tax evasion (at which he was acquitted) Ken Dodd was revealed as a sad, miserly man in private life, hoarding large sums of cash in his attic just to prove to himself that he was a star. John Cleese and Woody Allen have both sought psychotherapy and apparently have a rather morbid perspective on the world when not being professionally funny.

Of course, many cases of apparently happy and stable comedians could also be cited, and there is scant evidence for a higher than average rate of depression in comedians. Rotton (1992) found entertainers as a group died at an earlier age than those in comparable professions, but this finding was not specific to comedians, nor was it possible to be sure that stress or suicide had anything to do with the early demise of entertainers. The best evidence for psychopathology in humorists is the report of Janus (1975) that 85 per cent of his sample of male comedians had sought psycho-therapeutic treatment at some time in their lives. Though no control figures for other professions were given, this does seem high. Fisher and Fisher (1981), however, did not find clinically significant neuroticism in their Rorschach protocols of comedians.

If we were to accept for the moment that many comedians (though by no means all) are depression-prone, are there any special stresses within the profession that might account for this? We could speculate that keeping material up to date and effective and being funny at all times of the day or night in response to public expectation would make for a stressful life-style. Perhaps more importantly we might point to the fact that comedians often make capital out of their own peculiarities and deficiencies (e.g. Oliver Hardy's fatness, Woody Allen's unattractiveness, Jack Benny's meanness and the gender ambiguity of Frankie Howerd). If they were to internalize and dwell upon these traits which they use as 'stock in trade' their self-esteem might well be jeopardized. Alternatively, it may be just a contrast effect – we take particular note of depression when it strikes comedians because it seems so paradoxical; as dispensers of fun they should not themselves be prone to misery. Research is needed to settle this issue.

Another possible link between depression and comedy is that people who are unhappy to begin with might gravitate towards the role of clown, for example, becoming humorists as a mechanism for coping with their own depression and using it to make others laugh as a secondary development. This was the hypothesis investigated by Fisher and Fisher (1981) who studied comedians in an attempt to discover what inspired them to 'make fools of themselves'. Their conclusion was that comedians were concerned with 'the denial of threat' on their own behalf primarily, the spin-off being that other people (their audiences) also gain help in coping with life's catastrophes. The Fishers traced this tendency in comedians to a lack of nurturance and security in childhood, resulting in the development of comedy as a strategy for detoxifying painful and tragic events. Rorschach Inkblot testing revealed a great deal of 'nice monster' imagery, 'beings or things that seem to be bad, ugly or sinister but are not really so'. If the use of humour as a coping strategy is successful then clinical depression or stress should not be manifest; however, the adaptive mechanism must be presumed to break down occasionally.

Approval-seeking is another possible motivation of comedians. Woody Allen gave 'exhibitionism and narcissism' and 'the need to form relationships and be accepted' as two of his reasons for becoming a comedian (Lax 1975). Art Buchwald had a difficult childhood, spent partly in an orphanage. 'I learned quickly that when I made others laugh they liked me' (Buchwald 1967). Dustin Hoffmann said much the same, claiming that comedy was used as a means of gaining attention in the family within which he was an insignificant member. He also found that jokes were effective in defusing his father's anger when he had done something wrong (Bates 1986). W.C. Fields, in a rare moment of seriousness, said he was drawn towards comedy because 'the pleasure which I cause them tells me that, at least for a short moment, they love me' (Monti 1973). These reports are consistent in saying that humour is adopted as a way of opening up human relationships by individuals who are sensitive to the possibility that they might otherwise go unloved. Apparently, Jack Benny could not stand taking a vacation in Cuba because people there did not recognize him and he was just another anonymous figure (Fein 1976).

It could be argued that everybody wants to be loved and that businessmen make money for the same motive. Against that is the fact that so many comedians seem to lead isolated, miserly lives and have difficulty forming satisfactory relationships. We mentioned Tony Hancock, who died alone in a hotel bedroom. Two British comedians, Benny Hill and Frankie Howerd, who died within a day or so of each other in 1992, both lived alone (it was a few days before Hill's body was found). Kenneth Williams, while saying that he was gay by nature, claimed to have avoided all relationships, both serious and carnal. The only person he ever loved was his mother (Williams 1985). He was, however, strikingly narcissistic. George Melly, in a *Sunday Times* review of Williams' autobiography *Just Williams* notes that although 'living through almost 60 years of turbulent history and profound social change, he records no thoughts on anything unrelated to himself'. The alienation of great clowns is graphically described by Thomas Mann in *The Confessions of Felix Krull*: 'world-renouncing monks of unreason, cavorting hybrids, part human and part insane art'.

Not all comedians are unmarried. Fisher and Fisher (1981) report that 75 per cent of their sample had married and 20 per cent had been divorced. Woody Allen and John Cleese have each been married several times, and a certain amount of torment is revealed in their work. Allen's main theme is that of a physically unappealing 'schlemiel' striving to attract women by his wit (which is exactly what he succeeds in doing in real life). Cleese repeatedly portrays an uptight, authoritarian, Englishman, crippled by his concern for respectability but harbouring a deep desire to break loose (become an American or an Italian) and indulge his sexual, Bohemian desires. It is hard to escape the impression that the frustration and anger displayed by Cleese in his comic roles connects with his own background and personality (Margolis 1992). Both these great comedians have sought help from psychotherapists but they also seem to be engaged upon a programme of self-treatment (equivalent to dramatherapy) in their comic creativity. Whether or not this is a successful coping mechanism is difficult to assess, but it does seem inevitable and research suggests that humour can be effective in this way (Overhulser 1992).

Finally, it should be noted that not all comedians make play of their weakness, desperation and torment. Some are strikingly dominant, assertive, even sadistic. They bully their 'straight men' and audiences and give vent to prejudices and resentments in a way that would horrify people in real life (and offends many as entertainment). Phil Silvers as Sergeant Bilko tyrannized his platoon, while Rowan Atkinson as Blackadder and Rik Mayall as Alan B'Stard MP in *The New Statesman* are psychologically and physically cruel to those about them to an extent that makes the viewer cringe. Mayall claims that by playing parts like B'stard he purges himself of the qualities he most dislikes about himself. 'There's a bit of Alan in all of us', he said in a *TV Times* interview (January 1989) 'and I am getting rid of my bit by acting him'.

Andrew Dice Clay is an outstanding example of a stand-up comedian who hits out at everyone including his audience. With attacks on stutterers, hunchbacks and midgets with their 'pumpkin heads and little bug legs', and old people in walkers who waste his time on public transport, he is the perfect inversion of all that is politically correct. Another prime target is women, whom he describes as 'dishrag whores who ought to shut up, fix dinner and service their men when needed'. A well-endowed woman in the front row is typically told to 'stand the fuck up and show your fucking tits'. Such an act, being highly dangerous, usually rouses great fervour in his (admittedly self-selected) audiences. Whatever The Dice Man's personal problems, he is neither submissive nor depressed. Most extraordinarily, his charisma is such that he has a considerable following from among the groups he attacks (women, blacks, etc.).

Such humour may release tensions by giving a mouthpiece to repressed aggression but it is not acceptable to everybody. A Scottish 'alternative' comedian performing in Canada for the first time got as far as saying 'Good evening, moosefuckers' before he was laid unconscious by a disgruntled patriot from the audience.

CHAPTER 8

THE POWER OF MUSIC

Music plays an important part in the lives of most of us, providing us with pleasure, emotional solace and inspiration. When people are asked to list their hobbies and interests, some kind of musical enthusiasm is usually declared, making it the most popular of all avocations (Roe 1985, Coslin 1980). In one study of American university students (Toohey 1982) 28 per cent reported listening to music for over five hours per day. Music even features prominently among people's primary values: alongside family and sex, and usually above religion, sport and travel (Cameron and Fleming 1975). So important is musical appreciation that items concerning it appear in standard tests of marital compatibility. It is not surprising, therefore, that psychologists have devoted considerable attention to understanding how music has the power to affect us so profoundly.

An extreme form of emotional response to music has been called a 'thrill'. Goldstein (1980) describes a typical thrill as 'a slight shudder, chill, or tingling sensation, usually localized at the back of the neck and fleeting'. A more intense thrill 'lasts longer, and may spread from the point of origin, up over the scalp, forward over the face, downward along the spine, and forward over the chest, abdomen, thighs and legs. It may be accompanied by visible gooseflesh (piloerection), especially on the arms. Incipient weeping may occur, and sighing, together with a feeling of a lump in the throat' (p.127). He investigated the stimuli that most often elicit thrills and found that they had in common 'a confrontation with something of extraordinary beauty or profound and moving significance'. Music was top of his list of thrill-provokers, being cited by 96 per cent of his survey respondents.

Goldstein played passages of music to ten subjects, asking them to report the occurrence of thrills. The pattern was fairly reliable for the same subject listening to the same piece of music. He then injected his subjects with naloxone and found that in three of his subjects the thrills were significantly diminished. Since naloxone is chemically an opiate-antagonist, Goldstein concluded that endorphin-release within the brain may be involved in the experience of thrills obtained from music. In other words, music has power to give pleasure in a manner parallel to euphoriant drugs. The psychological mechanisms which mediate this effect are the subject of this chapter.

Of course, there are various types of music and the principles that apply to classical music and jazz are not necessarily the same as those relating to rap and rock. Generally speaking, modern music features hypnotic dance rhythms more than harmony and puts more weight on image than high-level musicianship. Nevertheless, there is a great deal of overlap. Nigel Kennedy is a classical violinist for whom a 'yobbo' image was important to success, and Freddie Mercury, of the pop group Queen, was a talented composer. The Italian tenor Pavarotti sings in classic operatic style, yet made *Top of the Pops* because his physique, beard and handkerchief make him memorable, and his recording of the aria 'Nessun dorma' was used to introduce a televised World Cup football series.

Image is important for musical performance of all types. However, extra-musical factors like charisma and group hysteria were discussed in Chapter 3, and attention-getting devices were dealt with in Chapter 6. This chapter, therefore, focuses on the emotional effects that derive from purely musical sources.

EVOLUTIONARY THEORIES

There have been various speculations concerning the evolutionary origins of musical performance and appreciation, which have been described in detail by Nadel (1971). What follows is a summary of his account of the better-known theories, together with the criticisms that have been levelled at them.

Sexual selection (Darwin)

Darwin (1883) observed that among most species of birds the males are not only more handsome and brightly coloured than the females, but also more given to song. This is especially so during the mating season, when they flaunt their plumage and sing passionately. Therefore, he supposed that music and song originated as a form of courtship display.

This analogy has some appeal in that singing is frequently used in human courtship. ('If music be the food of love, play on' *Twelfth Night*.) Moreover, anthropologists have noted that in nearly all human societies it is males who design and construct musical instruments and compose most of the music. In fact, cross-culturally speaking, the manufacture of musical instruments is nearly as closely identified with masculinity as the development and use of weapons in warfare (Daly and Wilson 1979). Most love songs take a young woman as their subject and, in Italy at least, the serenade is a well-recognized seduction device.

Weaknesses in this 'tweet-tweet' theory of musical evolution are equally apparent. While it is true that in many species of birds it is only the male that sings (and hormonal control can be demonstrated by the fact that females will sing if injected with male hormones; see Nottebohm 1981), there are other types of bird in which the female also sings. In the case of the bay wrens of Panama, the female not only enters into a duet with the male, but is actually more assertive in initiating it and more responsive in making reply. Anyway, birds are fairly remote relatives of humans in the evolutionary tree, and the courtship theory does not explain why the vast majority of mammals and primates do not produce anything much resembling music or song. (A possible exception is the gibbon which engages in a kind of courtship duet and which, interestingly, is one of the few pair-bonding primates.) Another problem with the theory is that, although men do create more music than women in human society, music-making is by no means an exclusively male occupation. Women compose music, play instruments and sing to an extent that embarrasses the male courtship theory. While it may be argued that some female pop singers are there more to be looked at than listened to, there are as many adulated women opera singers who are better listened to than looked at. Certainly, the female singing voice can be beautiful in its own right.

Finally, it has been pointed out that in tribal peoples around the world, religious and battle songs and lullabies are just as common as love songs. All things considered, the Darwinian suggestion that singing arose as a courtship ritual, while intriguing and consistent with many observations, does not explain all aspects of musical behaviour and experience.

Emotional speech (Spencer)

A second theory of the origins of music, and especially of singing, is that attributed to the Victorian sociologist Herbert Spencer. Spencer (1885) noted that when we get excited the pitch of our speech rises, the intervals become more marked and regular, and the words tend to be stretched in duration. This modification of speech under conditions of high emotional arousal Spencer thought was the basis of singing and perhaps music in general. Imagine how, in ordinary life, a woman might say casually, 'I hope you win' to her husband as he sets off for a Saturday afternoon game of tennis. Next, imagine how a queen in a Shakespearean play would say to her liege, as he departs for battle 'Return victorious'. This time, by comparison with the everyday event, the words would be formulated more precisely and rhythmically, and they would be intoned in a louder voice, with higher pitch. The result would be that the statement would carry more conviction and emotional intensity.

This transformation is taken a step further again when Aida sings 'Ritorna Vincitor' to her hero Radames in Verdi's opera. In musical context, the words are stretched even longer in duration, and they are louder and higher still. Thus, moving from conversational idiom to grand opera, words acquire a progressively magnified emotional significance. This is one reason why modern operas that attempt to set to music everyday, mundane comments like 'Mind if I use your telephone?' often seem ridiculous.

Critics of the emotional speech theory argue that free-range speech allows for more discrimination among different emotions than does singing in accordance with a formalised melody. Therefore, they say, it is hard to see what is gained by the imposition of musical convention, with all its limitations. Proponents of the emotional speech theory (who, incidentally, include illustrious philosophers such as Wagner and Rousseau), might reply that emotional power is gained even though discrimination of detail is lost. The vocal line of a Puccini aria may not be subtle, but it is more emotionally expressive than a spoken line could ever be. As with Darwin's theory, there is probably some truth in Spencer's account of the development of singing, although it does not amount to the full story.

Work calls (Bücher)

In his book *Work and Rhythm* (1919), economist Karl Bücher maintained that song and music developed out of the rhythmical bursts of vocal and instrumental sound used by early people to facilitate work in concerted labour. Thus, we have sea-shanties, rowing songs, chain-gang songs, Maori hakas and military marches. Many of these work co-ordination songs have been taken up in grand opera, for example, the Anvil Chorus in *Il Trovatore* and the Sailor's chorus in *The Flying Dutchman*.

This 'yo-ho, heave-ho' theory, as it has been called, also seems limited. Anthropological studies show that primitive songs are not particularly marked by simple, clear rhythms. Furthermore, they seldom arise out of the work itself, but are more often composed about it, apparently as an afterthought. Very often, too, they are used not to increase work output so much as to exert some magical influence on the product of labour. Again, this theory describes certain aspects of music, and the manner in which it is sometimes used, but does not provide a comprehensive account of its origins.

Long-distance communications (Stumpf)

When we call to another person over a distance, our voice not only increases in intensity but is raised in pitch, and the tone is sustained and stabilized. According to Karl Stumpf (1898), this is how singing arose (a notion in some ways similar to the emotional speech theory). Critics point out that there is little evidence that primitive people use music for this purpose, nor are the cries that animals address to each other over long distances especially musical in quality. Drum-signals are well-known as a means of long-distance communication (the 'bush telegraph') but they are based mainly on rhythm and the number of beats. The pitch factor that is so central to the Western concept of music is much less significant.

It is true that the high pitch and protracted phrase of opera did function to assist projection throughout a large auditorium in the pre-amplification days. However, there are other forms of singing (such as Crosby-type crooning into a microphone) that are recognisably musical without depending on distance projection.

Supernatural language (Nadel)

Nadel himself (1971) maintains that all art is the transference of human experience into an out-of-the-ordinary form. Therefore, he says, the essential meaning of music is to be found in its artificial, 'supernatural' attributes. In Nadel's view, music does not derive from any necessity of everyday life; it is a 'gift from the gods' – a special mystical language.

In primitive cultures, he observes, the most widespread use of music is in connection with ritual customs. Medicine men and priests wear special robes, emblems, masks and suchlike in order to partake of 'the other world' – that of the supernatural (Chapter 2). So too, the speaking voice must assume a special vesture, 'an out-of-the-ordinary tone to parallel the loftier rites'. This 'abnormal-isation' of human vocalisation Nadel says is the origin of song. Since the tone-speech of song is held to be the language of gods and demons, it must be adopted by mortals who desire to invoke them.

Magical incantations frequently have foreign or meaningless words. Presum-ably this is because it is easier to associate out-of-the-ordinary experiences with supernatural powers. This may be one of the reasons why some Catholics rebelled against the vernacular mass and why many people hold that foreign language opera is superior to that performed in their own tongue.

Nadel notes that music is like a religious experience in its power to create ecstacy and intoxication. Indeed, both pursuits can produce extremely emotional, occasionally transcendental effects. But which is the cause and which the effect is difficult to tell. Music may transport us by creating mystical feelings, but on the other hand, religious ceremonies might leave us cold if it were not for their use of music.

Like the previous theories, Nadel's idea is attractive in its power to account for certain aspects of music, particularly its ability to convey noble and mystical sentiments, and its frequent use in association with religious and magical rituals. However, it is less comfortable in accounting for some of the lighter applications of music, such as love songs and dances. It is even more hard put to explain why music can be applied equally well for sacrilegious purposes such as the dirty songs so beloved of students and rugby clubs.

Each of the above theories contains a germ of truth, but none is capable of providing a complete explanation of what is clearly a complex phenomenon. They have in common the assumption that music derives from primitive song, with musical instruments being an extension of our vocal apparatus, yet even this is probably an over-simplification. The well-springs of our responsiveness to music are many and varied, and they go deeper into our psychobiological nature than the above theories suggest.

THE BIOSOCIAL NATURE OF MUSIC

Some of the basic psychobiological processes involved in music were mentioned in Chapter 2. Physiological rhythms can be paced by musical beat: for example, if heart rate is accelerated by exercise, lullabies will slow the pulse faster than either jazz or no music at all (Eibl-Eibesfeld 1989). Lullabies from diverse cultures share melodic and rhythmic forms that imitate the slow breathing of someone falling asleep. Faster and louder music has been shown to increase heart rate and hence induce a feeling of excitement. Repetitive rhythm can induce trance-like states, sometimes ecstasy (Rouget 1985). This may be because neural circuits resonate in such a way as to produce changes in brain chemistry or electrical conditions akin to epileptic convulsions (Neher 1962). The alteration in brainstate in turn liberates unusual behaviour, be it religious, sexually promiscuous or violent. Hence music is used in connection with religious rituals, sex orgies and war dances.

Breathlessness can be built into music, particularly vocal music, to evoke excitement (or failing lung capacity in the case of operatic heroines dying of consumption). Syncopation can be used by a composer to simulate panting or a heart that is missing beats, and 'snatched' entries make a singer sound short of breath and emotionally desperate. An example is seen in Act II of *La Traviata* when Violetta pleads to Germont, 'Ah consider... how I love him... with a passion... all transcending... I have no-one... to be near me... etc.'. Each phrase is preceded by a quickly gulped intake of air which is audible in the orchestral silence that falls on the first beat of each bar. The converse is also true. Music which slows progressively, has a relaxing effect, as do vocal phrases which allow plenty of time for the singer to breathe. An example is the end of Rodolfo's aria in Act I of *La Bohème* when the tenor sings 'Now that I've told you my story... pray tell me yours...' and so forth. The successive phrases become slower and ample space is left between them for full and easy breathing. The result is that a feeling of calm is restored which, after his early exuberance, is necessary to bridge the gap into Mimi's account of herself.

Cross-cultural patterns have been observed in melodies. People can accurately categorize songs of different types (hunting, war, mourning, lullaby and love songs) that come from diverse cultures (Eggebrecht 1983). Similarly, spectrographic sound analysis (Fig 8.1) shows considerable consistency across culture for these various types of music. Mourning songs, for example, are typically slow and soft, with regular rhythm and downward inflexions in the melody, whereas joyful songs are faster, louder, have irregular rhythms and a tonal course that is first up and then down (Table 8.1).

Another universal characteristic of music across different cultures concerns the mathematics of the internal beat. Epstein (1988) has shown that a beat is maintained with utmost precision even across intervals lasting several minutes, and that when a tempo changes between movements or within the same piece, it nearly always does so by a simple ratio (e.g. 1:2, 2:3, 3:4 or *vice versa*). This applies both to Western classical music and music of various tribal societies. Other universal

Joyful

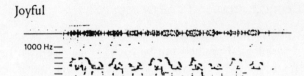

Sad

Source: Eggebrecht 1983

Figure 8.1: An example of sound spectrograph recordings comparing joyful and sad pygmy music. Similar differences are observed in cultures around the world

Table 8.1 Typical characteristics of music evoking particular emotions, as derived from cross-cultural studies

	Joy	*Sadness*	*Excitement*
Frequency	High	Low	Varied
Melodic variation	Strong	Slight	Strong
Tonal course	Moderate, first up, then down	Downward	Strongly up, then down
Tonal colour	Many overtones	Less overtones	Barely any overtones
Tempo	Rapid	Slow	Medium
Volume	Loud	Soft	Highly varied
Rhythm	Irregular	Regular	Very irregular

Source: modified from Eibl-Eibesfeld 1989

features of music such as the use of the pentatonal scale and playing with overtones have been described by Leonard Bernstein (1976).

It has to be conceded, however, that the effect of music also depends upon encoding processes that vary with time and culture. A certain background or experience is usually necessary for full enjoyment of a musical work, and in this sense it has parallels to language learning (Jackendorff and Lehrdahl 1982). Music has a 'deep structure' rather like the rules of grammar that underlie speech and writing and which are culturally variable and depend upon learning (Dowling and Harwood 1986, Gaver and Mandler 1987).

Just as each species of bird has its own song pattern (and indeed there are regional dialects within species) so music is used by humans to express and consolidate group identity. Anthems, hymns and football songs are examples of the way in which singing and music is used for social bonding. Important cultural records such as genealogies and migration routes are also stored and communicated as ritual chants (Malm 1977). This is because rhythm, like rhyme-schemes, enhances memory and is therefore particularly important for historical record-keeping in preliterate societies.

LEVELS OF ASSOCIATION

An important way in which music engages our emotions is through associations with other sounds or ideas that are emotive. Indeed, music may even present what ethologists call 'supernormal stimuli', simplified and exaggerated versions of signals that are evocative in the normal course of events. This will become clear in the discussion of three types of association that follows.

Direct sound associations (imitations)

At the most basic, primitive level, music has the power to engage our emotions by simulation of sounds from our environment that have instinctive interest for us. Such sounds include bird-songs, footsteps, animal roars, falling rain, babbling brooks, thunder, cries of anguish, breathless sobbing and an excited heartbeat. We do not necessarily have to learn to respond to these sounds; their arousal potential may be partly built into our nervous system as a result of their importance to our survival throughout evolutionary history. An innate readiness to react emotionally to particular stimuli in our environment has been confirmed by psychophysiological work showing that we have brain cells and circuits preprogrammed to respond to significant stimulus configurations such as the human face or the cry of a distressed infant (e.g. see Desmione *et al.* 1984, Furnald 1992, Lumsden and Wilson 1983, pp.65–73).

Consider how a storm is usually represented in music. The most celebrated musical storm sequences, such as those in Verdi's *Rigoletto* and Rossini's *William Tell*, show several common features. They build to a climax and fade away again, just as a storm does (albeit much more quickly). They make copious use of timpani rolls and cymbal crashes, which are reminiscent in timbre to bursts of thunder. They include passages of powerful syncopation against a previously well-established beat, as though the heart is 'missing a beat' out of fear and excitement. They are likely to include rumbling low tones (like the sound of distant thunder) and chromatic whining sounds (like wind in the eaves or trees).

Direct representation of a storm in music is a fairly straightforward case, but the elements of the storm may be used in other contexts to arouse fear and excitement without the listener being aware of the noises of nature to which the musical sound is alluding. The sound of a timpani boom can be used as a musical exclamation regardless of whether the listener is aware of any connection with the sound of thunder. Similarly, a pastoral scene may derive emotional tranquility from a warbling flute line regardless of whether an audience consciously associates that sound with the song of contented birds on a sunny spring morning. In such cases, the effect the music is having on our emotions depends upon the reminiscence of sounds from our environment that play upon our mood through instinctive connections.

Cross-modal associations (analogies)

A second, more complex, form of association by which music gains effect is that of metaphorical (usually spatial or visual) representation. Examples include the love duet that 'soars into the sky', a patriotic march that is 'firm, noble and uplifting', a depressed piece of music that is 'slow and laborious and full of dark colours', or a joyful piece that is 'young, sprightly, light and warm'.

Clynes (1986) argues that music and emotion both connect in a pre-programmed biological way to spatio-temporal forms so that they have their own stable 'shape', an idea that has some empirical support (De Vries 1991). However, in most instances, there is no simple or necessary biological connection between the musical sound and the emotion evoked. Rather, a kind of coding or language is used, which depends upon shared understanding between composer and audience. Some of the spatial analogies are fairly obvious (like high versus low notes), but others are more subtle, such as the understanding that major keys are 'bright and open' while minor keys are somehow 'mournful and mysterious' (Hevner 1935).

A good illustration of the use of metaphorical association is the scene in Wagner's *Siegfried* in which Mime tries to impart the experience of fear to the innocent young hero, Siegfried. Beside all the verbal allusions to forests at night, foul winds and ferocious animals, the fearful effect is built out of chromatic sound that is progressively threatening because it is unrelenting (maintaining an insistent rhythm), getting closer and closer (increasing in volume) and refusing to reveal its identity or offer any kind of reassurance (avoiding key resolution).

Cross-modal association may explain some instances of absolute pitch – the ability to identify a key or pitch 'out of the blue' by ear alone and without reference to other, recently heard notes or keys (see Chapter 9). A small proportion of people are known to experience what is called 'coloured-hearing *synesthesia*' (Marks 1975) – a consistent tendency to visualize a particular colour when presented with sound of a certain frequency. If, for example, middle C always evokes the visual sensation of black and F sharp is always purple, then it is easy for such an individual to name a note and display absolute pitch. Such idiosyncratic colour-matching schemes are quite rare, however, and do not account for a very high proportion of people who have perfect pitch. Most people do not automatically link tones with particular colours, but if pressed to make such an association they usually describe low notes in terms of dark, spectrally mixed colours, like brown, while high notes are linked with bright and 'pure' wavelengths such as electric blue. Analogous thinking is probably involved in this judgement; presumably some concept such as purity, focus or incisiveness is used to mediate between the auditory and visual sensations.

But metaphors are elusive and variable, and the colour blue is also associated with coldness and depression – hence the term 'blues', referring to 'cool' jazz which expresses heartbreak. It is this richness of human metaphorical thinking that is one source of our appreciation of music.

Conditioned associations (learning)

The third major basis of the emotional appeal of music is that of associations between previous hearing of musical segments and the things that were happening at the time they were heard. A long-term effect of this kind, with which concert singers are familiar, is that of *nostalgia*. An audience of elderly people who may have difficulty remembering what they did earlier that day, and who may be deadened to most current experiences, are frequently moved to tears by the powerful emotions evoked by songs from their heyday. This is due not so much to the intrinsic quality of the songs themselves as to the romantic, joyful and sad memories that are revived by them.

These memories are not necessarily evoked consciously. Following the Pavlovian model of 'classical conditioning', the emotion appropriate to important life experiences can be transferred in an automatic and irrational way to the associated stimulus (the musical phrase), just as the whirring sound of a dentist's drill can produce an immediate approximation to all the fear and pain that has ever been experienced in his surgery. It is not so much conscious recall that is involved in the feeling of nostalgia as an immediate 'short circuit' between what psychologists call a 'conditioned stimulus' (in this case the music) and a 'conditioned response' (the emotion experienced).

Not all of these associations are as long-term as those of real-life nostalgia. Many composers build a kind of nostalgia into the course of a music drama, such that a theme which appears relatively neutral in an early scene has acquired profound emotional significance by the time it re-emerges towards the end.

Examples include 'I'll see you again' in Noel Coward's *Bitter Sweet*, 'I have a song to sing O' in *The Yeoman of the Guard* and Mimi's deathbed recognition of the bonnet that Rodolfo had bought for her during their joyous Christmas courtship in *La Bohème*.

In the eighteenth century the overtures to operas were independent pieces of orchestration used as curtain-raisers – a signal that people should take their seats and settle down because the show was about to begin. Whatever the merits of the overture to *The Marriage of Figaro* as a composition in its own right, it has no connection with the music of the opera itself. The same applies to the *Barber of Seville* overture, which Rossini understandably judged to be so popular that he carried it over from use in two previous operas. Later composers such as Verdi and Wagner, who had developed a more sophisticated sense of theatre, made their overtures an integral part of the evening's drama, using them to familiarise the audience with central musical themes, or (especially by shorter preludes) to set the musical colour of the scene that was to follow. The fact that the prelude to *La Traviata* anticipates the tragic ending of Violetta's life was aptly applied by Zeffirelli in his film of the opera as a point of departure from which the body of the drama became Violetta's flashback. This was in no way alien to Verdi's intention; it was correctly exploiting the possibilities of the modern film medium to highlight an idea implicit in the musical construction of the opera.

Perhaps the most concerted application of classical conditioning in music drama is seen in the *leitmotifs* of Wagner, most notably in his epic *Ring Cycle*. Wagner's technique was to provide characters, objects, emotions and ideas with key musical phrases that would constantly occur in association with them through-out the four-part work. As Debussy put it, each character, when he appeared on stage, would 'present his musical calling card'. But this is true not only of characters but also concepts, like Siegfried's sword, spring and salvation. Add to this primary coding the many forms in which the *leitmotifs* could occur (major versus minor keys, different instruments, various speeds, rhythms, chord inversions, etc.), plus Wagner's ingenious ability to combine and interweave them, and it becomes almost possible, at the emotional level at least, to follow the drama by absorption in the music alone. Wagner was not the first composer to use *leitmotifs* but he developed the method to its highest level.

True to his belief that in opera the drama is primary, Wagner seldom wrote music for its own sake; he always used it to amplify the feelings of his characters. This aim was achieved by coding and identifying the major components of the drama and then exploring the relationships among them musically as much, or perhaps more than, verbally. His success in doing so depends on the ability of the listener to form the necessary associations between musical themes and emotional experiences.

TONES AND TENSION

Another aspect of music that has been researched by psychologists is that of its formal structure: for example, the psycho-physical relationships underlying scales, melodies and harmony (Spender 1983). Although musical structure varies from one culture to another, most systems incorporate the concept of *tonality*. This refers to our need to make sense out of a musical piece by identifying a central 'key' note, called the *tonic*, around which the tune and harmonies revolve and without which it could not end satisfactorily. If the piece did not 'come down to earth' at this point we would be left with an uncomfortable sense of incompleteness.

In Western music, the fifth note in the eight-note scale (e.g. G in the scale of C) is the second most important note and is called the *dominant*. This note also has considerable tension-reducing properties. In playing the scale upwards from the tonic, the dominant gives the impression of being a moderately stable resting place before one proceeds with the final three notes. The most tension-producing note in the Western scale is the seventh (B in the scale of C major). This is called the *leading note*, because it cries out for the resolution that only the eighth (key) note can provide. The fourth note also produces a degree of tension, straining as it does for resolution either to the dominant above or the third below.

One of the basic principles of musical composition is that of setting up tensions which are eventually discharged. The progress from leading note to tonic is prototypic, but a great deal of musical structure is intended to prolong the period of tension before resolution is arrived at. Just as sexual satisfaction may be enhanced by teasing (ranging from extended foreplay to various sadomasochistic practices), so can musical pleasure be heightened by delay of gratification. It is no accident that certain musical pieces are described as orgasmic in their impact; they are usually constructed so as to tease the listener to distraction before mounting to an unmistakable climax of excitement which gives way quickly to a resolution of major key-note chords.

Such well-known musical forms as the *appoggiatura,* the *turn,* the *trill* and the *deceptive cadence,* can be thought of as devices for delaying the achievement of a musical goal. As with riding a roller-coaster, we can enjoy a certain amount of anxiety provided the outcome is assured. Music, then, may be understood as a system for generating tensions which we obtain pleasure from having relieved.

In a study of the musical elements responsible for various emotional reactions, Sloboda (1991) had 83 people report on the occurrence of physical experiences while listening to music. Shivers down the spine, laughter, tears and lumps in the throat were reported by over 80 per cent of the subjects. Structural analysis of the particular musical passages that most frequently evoked these responses showed that tears were most often produced by melodic appoggiaturas, and to a lesser extent by movements through the cycle of fifths (see discussion of 'key relationships' below) to the tonic. Shivers were most frequently evoked by sudden changes in harmony and a racing heart was linked to acceleration and syncopation.

Such findings support the theory that music has emotional impact partly through violating and confirming expectations.

MELODIC STRUCTURE

The completion theory of music is supported by analysis of commonly occuring melodic patterns. Rosner and Meyer (1982) describe two recognisable types of tune which they call 'gap-fill melodies' and 'changing-note melodies'.

Gap-fill melodies are usually comprised of a large upward jump in pitch followed by a sequence of closer intervals that 'fill' the gap by presenting most of the notes previously skipped over. A well-known example of such a tune is 'Somewhere Over the Rainbow', where the word 'somewhere' introduces an initial octave gap which is filled by the next section of the tune. A common variant on this pattern is its reversal, an initial downward plunge followed by upward rising intervals inside the bounds of the gap. The *changing-note melody* is one in which the major structural tones form a pattern moving from tonic, to the leading note, to the second, and back to the tonic. In the key of C this would be C,B,D,C. Such a pattern can be seen in a great many classics, but a widely known example is the First World War favourite, 'Mademoiselle from Armentiers'. A common variant on this formula begins with the third E,D,F,E (or E,F,D,E) but the pattern is always harmonised by a chord progression moving from the tonic to the dominant, and then from dominant back to tonic. This structure may not be obvious because melodies are usually built up hierarchically, and the underlying patterns may only be identified by a process of reductive analysis. An example of such a breakdown of a Mozart melody by Rosner and Meyer is shown in Figure 8.2. Only at the most reductive level (line c) does the changing-note sequence become apparent.

Source: Rosner and Meyer 1982

Figure 8.2: Reductive analysis of part of Mozart's Oboe Quartet in F major (K370). The top line is the complete melody as written by Mozart. At the first level of reduction (a) the melody is comprised of rising and falling scale patterns. On the next level (b), rising and falling thirds create complementary dyads. An 'archetypal' changing-note pattern (F,G,E,F) appears at the third level (c)

Rosner and Meyer do not pretend that these two categories of tune exhaust the possibilities of melodic structure. Rather, they use them to illustrate the fact that powerful conventions can be identified, even though they may be specific to Western music. Each of them can be interpreted psychologically as creating a tension which is then resolved. The gap-fill melody creates a gulf which we enjoy hearing bridged, thus satisfying our desire for 'closure', while the changing-note sequence amounts to a departure from, and subsequent return to, the 'safe base' of the tonic.

At a more 'macro' level, the form of the sonata can also be analysed in terms of the creation and dispelling of tension. According to Kamien (1980), sonatas typically begin with a phase called 'exposition' which imparts psychological stability. It then goes through a period of 'development' in which conflict and heightened tension are introduced. Finally, it ends with a 'recapitulation' or 'coda' which provides emotional resolution of the preceding turmoil.

CONSONANCE AND DISSONANCE

When two notes are sounded simultaneously, some combine easily and harmoniously to produce *consonant* chords, while others seem to clash with an unpleasant sound that we call *dissonance*. In the case of simple, pure tones, the prediction of consonance and dissonance is fairly straightforward. Frequencies that are so close together as to sound virtually identical are consonant together, as are those that are so widely spaced that they produce no aural conflict. Dissonance occurs when the notes are discriminable but so close together that they seem to compete and interfere (the worst point being a 4% difference in frequency, which is just less than a semitone).

Musical instruments and voices produce complex tones, which rather complicates the whole matter of consonance. When a note is sounded on a musical instrument, a whole set of overtones or 'partials' is set up in addition to the 'fundamental' note. When the frequency of a pair of notes is related as a simple mathematical ratio (comprising small integer numbers), the partials show a high degree of coincidence, with the result that the two notes are heard as merging harmoniously with one another. When the two notes are related by a complex ratio (requiring numbers of seven or more), the partials will interact in such a way as to produce an unpleasant roughness or 'beat'.

The simplest ratio between two notes is 2:1, which we call an *octave*. Since this consists of doubling the fundamental frequency, it corresponds exactly with the first partial of the lower note and naturally enough sounds very harmonious (so harmonious, in fact, that we regard it as the same note and denote it with the same alphabetical letter). The octave is regarded as consonant in all cultures, and is of such universal appeal that even laboratory rats have been demonstrated to recognize it, responses conditioned to a particular frequency generalizing to the same note removed by an octave (Blackwell and Schlosberg 1943).

The intervals that are most commonly used in Western music have fairly simple mathematical relationships between their frequencies and therefore sound consonant. The fifth has a ratio of 2:3, the fourth 3:4, the sixth 3:5, the major third 4:5, and the minor third 5:6. All of these are relatively harmonious chords, compared with, say, the semitone (a pair of notes that are adjacent on a piano keyboard) or the tritone (three whole notes or six semitones apart), which can only be expressed as ratios of double figure numbers and which tend to sound rather jarring (see Figure 8.3).

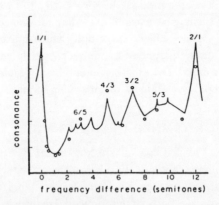

Source: Kameoka and Kuriyagawa 1969

Figure 8.3: The consonance of pairs of complex tones as theoretically calculated from degree of shared harmonies (line) and determined empirically by listener judgements (circles)

However, musical harmony depends upon cultural learning as well as physical consonance, and the acceptability of various intervals and chord patterns changes over time. A few centuries ago, the fourth was regarded as highly consonant, while the third was perceived as somewhat dissonant and seldom used by composers. Today, we hear the third as highly consonant, while the fourth begs for some kind of resolution, one possibility for which is movement to the third. This can be tested by playing middle C together with the F above it on the piano, and noting the relaxation of tension that is experienced when the F is shifted down to E. It is curious that in today's music the third is usually perceived as more harmonious than the fourth, even though the latter is more consonant in physical terms. At least this is true for higher frequencies; for lower notes and instruments the third is rather too close for comfort and tends to sound 'muddy'. Most composers therefore use thirds sparingly in the bass section.

Another cultural shift in musical perception concerns the tritone which divides the scale in half. The interval between C and F sharp was regarded as highly objectionable in medieval times. Dubbing it *diabolus in musica* (the devil in music), church musicians of the time were at pains to avoid it. However, modern musicians have no such abhorrence for the tritone. Although it sounds dissonant in itself, falling as it does halfway between the fourth and fifth and involving complex frequency ratios, it is readily resolved by shifting both notes either a semitone further apart or a semitone closer together, thus producing an interesting sequence of chords.

This again highlights the principle that tension must first be aroused before pleasure can be gained in relief from it. It is not possible really to enjoy consonance without the interspersion of a certain amount of dissonance to build excitement. The history of musical taste and composition has been one of increasing the proportion of dissonance (measured in physical terms) relative to consonance, thus yielding progressively greater thrills. Or, like the drug addict, the modern listener perhaps requires more of the stimulus to produce the same effect.

In taking the complexity of music one step further than his predecessors, each composer depends upon the cultural learning that has been contributed by previous composers. People growing up with Mozart hear Wagner as highly dissonant; those who are comfortable with Wagner may still hear Berg as dissonant and so on. In the twelve-tone music of Schoenberg we appear to have reached the limits of complexity, but who knows what is yet to be invented?

THE GOLDEN SECTION

The ancient Greeks, at least from the time of Pythagoras, were aware of the principle of consonance and dissonance and the mathematical basis of it. Perhaps by analogy, they tried to apply the idea of perfect ratios to visual art and architecture. Plato believed there was great artistic value in the *Golden Section*, which is a relationship between two lines such that the ratio between the shorter and longer line is equal to the ratio between the longer line and the sum of the two. Even though the effectiveness of this principle is doubtful in the sphere of the visual arts, there have been attempts to refer it back to music. Howat (1984) has shown how the composer Debussy incorporated this numerical principle into much of his work (for example in the bar structure of his movements). Apparently, Debussy believed that this secret mathematical device would lend additional beauty to his compositions. Although there can be no doubting Debussy's success as a composer, few who enjoy his work could consciously recognise these 'golden sections' in the listening and there is really no good reason to suppose that this structure enhanced the quality of his music through the unconscious response of his audience. The mathematical ratios that underlie consonance and dissonance affect our experience of the sound much more directly and physically than the Platonic ideal possibly could, so in the absence of better evidence we must presume that the latter does not contribute to musical pleasure.

KEY RELATIONSHIPS

A kind of deep structure that probably does have an emotional impact upon the listener is that of key relationships. Certain composers appear to have coded closely related ideas and feelings with adjacent keys.

First, it may be necessary to explain how keys are related to one another. We have noted that the Western scale is built out of two groups of four notes, each separated by intervals following the pattern of tone-tone-semitone. The top half of any scale can be used to form the base of a new scale that begins from (and takes its name from) the *dominant* of the previous scale. The simplest example is going from the key of C (all white notes on the piano) to G (the dominant of the scale of C). In order to keep the same pattern of intervals, the scale starting from G has to incorporate one black note (the F sharp). If this process is repeated (going

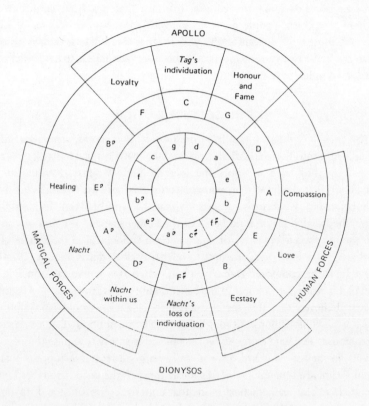

Source: Drummond 1980

Figure 8.4: Drummond's analysis of key associations in Wagner's Tristan and Isolde. The circle shows musical keys arranged in accordance with their similarity. Capitals represent major keys and small letters their minor equivalents. Outer layers show nature of material in the opera for which each key is used

from the key of G to D) then a second sharp has to be included in the scale and so on. Hence creating scales from the top half of the previous one can be thought of as twisting keys in a *sharpening* direction. But it is also possible to create new scales by taking the bottom half of the previous scale and using it to form the top of another. In this case, the new scale begins from the *subdominant* of the previous scale and involves *flattening* it. Each new scale includes one more flat in it.

Because the Western equal-temperament scale has only five black notes, the processes of sharpening and flattening can be performed only six times before they converge on the same scale (which can be either F sharp or G flat). Hence, if keys are arranged according to the proportion of notes they use in common they form a closed circle (Figure 8.4). Scales which are closely related are side by side on this circle while those that are more distant are located opposite one another.

Some operatic composers, such as Gluck, Weber and Wagner appear to have used keys to represent emotions in a fairly logical fashion. For example, if C = salvation, G = love, D = passion, A = anxiety and E = loss, the psychological proximity of the feelings is matched by the key relationships. Loss is far removed from salvation, but love is a cross between salvation and passion, passion seems well-placed between love and anxiety, and so on. Emotions can thus be mixed out of keys in the same way that purple can be mixed from red and blue.

Figure 8.4 shows Drummond's analysis of Wagner's opera *Tristan and Isolde*, as regards the relationships between keys and themes. The main axis (top to bottom) is that between the Apollonian virtues surrounding day (Tag) and the Dionysian forces surrounding night (Nacht). The opera explores the psychological connection between love and death, both of which involve a transformation of consciousness away from self-control and identity. Love moves away from commonsense (daylight) in a human and exhilarating direction (sharpening on the key circle) whereas night departs in a magical but rather chilling direction (flattening) before they ultimately converge in a simultaneous consummation of love and death.

We cannot be sure that Wagner himself was fully conscious of this structure when he set out to write *Tristan and Isolde*, but from what we know of the grandiose scale of his conceptions he almost certainly did plan something of the kind. He always wrote his own lyrics and claimed that he had the music in his head as he constructed them. It was also explicit in his prose writings that musical key changes should be used to underline departures of thought and feeling. Few members of an audience would consciously glean this underlying musical structure from listening to the opera, but nevertheless it may be one of the reasons so many people find the work so profoundly moving.

OPTIMAL UNCERTAINTY

A theory of musical appreciation which has some experimental backing is that of *optimal uncertainty* (Berlyne 1971). According to this idea, a pattern of notes or chords that is totally predictable will be dull and uninteresting, and one that is totally unpredictable will also be boring (or perhaps disturbing if it is too intrusive). Musical pleasure is gained at the intermediate point where our brain is engaged in discovering structure and generating hypotheses about what sounds will occur next, but yet is not overtaxed. According to this theory, the purely cognitive thrill of making sense out of a sound sequence is a major source of pleasure in musical listening, to be put beside that of the resolution of dissonant chords.

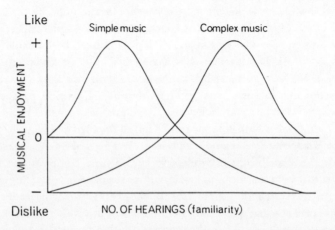

Figure 8.5: Hypothetical relationship between musical appreciation, familiarity and complexity. Maximum enjoyment is obtained when 'uncertainty' is optimised (music that is neither too meaningless nor too predictable)

This theory accounts for some of the striking things about musical taste, such as the movement towards complexity that occurs over history and within the musical learning experience of any individual, and the fact that most people enjoy a piece of music increasingly each time they hear it repeated, up to the point where it becomes over-familiar and hence boring. It explains why complex compositions can be heard more times than simple works before the overfamiliarity effect leads to a diminution of pleasure (Figure 8.5). It also accounts for the personality correlates of musical preference: sensation-seeking people are more tolerant of complexity in music than are conservatives (Glasgow *et al.* 1985; Little and Zuckerman 1986 – see Figure 8.6).

The optimal uncertainty in music comes primarily from the fact that composers deal with variations on culturally learned themes, particularly 'archetypal' se-

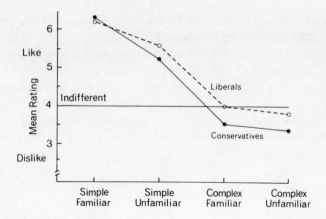

Source: Glasgow *et al.* 1985

Figure 8.6: Mean ratings of four categories of music for subjects classified as liberal or conservative on a personality test. Conservatives showed a stronger dislike of musical selections pre-chosen as complex in terms of melody and harmony

quences of notes and chords such as those identified by Rosner and Meyer (1982). Analysis of Western music at any one period of history reveals great similarity in the note patterns used by various composers, and these recognizable 'rules' form the familiar order from which the composer's new work departs. Without this semblance of structure, the level of uncertainty would be excessive and the listening experience would be tedious or stressful rather than interesting and pleasurable.

The element of predictability in musical sequences makes it possible to program computers to write melodies that vary in uncertainty and complexity as measured in information theory terms. These computer-generated melodies can then be used to study the role of uncertainty in the arousal value and enjoyment of music. For example, Konečni (1982) have shown that if people are insulted to the point where they become angry, their preference will shift away from complex melodies to simple ones. If complex music is inflicted upon them, especially at loud volume, their anger is likely to be increased, whereas quietly played, simple music soothes away their anger more than silence. Similarly, music will enhance performance on boring 'vigilance' tasks but is likely to interfere with tasks demanding more continuous attention (Davies *et al.* 1973).

These studies can be regarded as a direct demonstration of the power of music to influence our emotions, as well as the important role that is played by information load in creating this effect. They suggest that in everyday life, people use music to optimise their arousal and mood, tuning in to loud and demanding music when they are bored, and switching to placid, easy pieces when environmental conditions are stressful (as, for example, in tuning the car radio when driving home from work during rush hour).

Clearly, the enjoyment of music depends upon many diverse factors. Some are a natural consequence of the physics of sound and the characteristics of our acoustic processing system, some are inherent in our instinctive make-up, and others depend upon learning, experience and conditions prevailing in the social environment. Any attempt to understand the remarkable impact that music exerts upon our emotions and intellect that does not take account of all these factors is bound to be incomplete.

CHAPTER 9

MUSICAL ABILITY AND TRAINING

It is possible to enjoy music without knowing much about it or being able to play an instrument. Equally, a highly skilled musician may become bored and disinterested. Music appreciation is not the same as aptitude, although the two often go together. Nor is musical talent the same as general intelligence as measured by standard IQ tests. There is a slight tendency for a high IQ to go with musical ability, but musical talent also has a considerable degree of independence from other mental abilities. Exceptional musical ability appears quite mysteriously. Sometimes it is displayed by children with deficient verbal and social skills – the so-called 'autistic' or 'idiot-savant' syndromes (Howe 1991). Others, of genius-level IQ are apparently 'tone-deaf'. Reported correlations between IQ and musical ability vary enormously, but are typically in the region of .3 (Shuter-Dyson and Gabriel 1981). This means that the overlap between musical ability and general intelligence is fairly low. A high IQ is not a necessary prerequisite of musical talent.

MEASUREMENT OF MUSICAL ABILITY

Various tests of musical ability have been devised over the years, both for research purposes and for selection to music colleges. Most of these tests accept the principle that musical ability itself has to be subdivided into a number of components which are separately scored.

Fairly typical are the *Seashore Measures of Musical Talent* (Seashore *et al.* 1960), which are commercially available in standardized form. These take about one hour to administer and comprise six tests as follows:

1. *Pitch.* 50 pairs of tones are presented with frequency differences ranging from 17–2 cps. Is the second tone higher or lower than the first?

2. *Loudness.* 50 pairs of tones, with intensity differences ranging from 4 to .5 decibels. Is the second tone stronger or weaker than the first?

3. *Rhythm.* 30 pairs of rhythmic patterns. Are they the same or different?

4. *Time.* 50 pairs of tones varying in duration from .3 to .05 secs. Is the second tone longer or shorter than the first?

5. *Timbre*. 50 pairs of tones, each made up of a fundamental and first five harmonies. Are the two tones the same or different?

6. *Tonal memory*. 30 pairs of tonal sequences (10 each of 3, 4 and 5 tones). Which note is different?

Like most tests of its kind, the Seashore shows acceptable reliability (repeated testing of the same people produces similar scores) but no more than moderate validity (prediction of progress within a music college). These tests do discriminate musically experienced people (e.g. professionals) from the non-musical but this may be an effect due to training rather than natural aptitude. They are notoriously bad at assessing the more creative aspects of musical talent, such as composition, skill and appreciation of complex music. Although six scores are provided, they show some degree of overlap (correlations ranging between .2 and .5) and the total score is often found to be the best predictor of musical performance. Of the various sub-tests, pitch and tonal memory correlate most highly with singing and instrumental skills. Rhythm shows some validity, but loudness and time seem to be of little use.

As predictors of progress in a musical course (say learning a particular instrument) tests like the Seashore are little better than general IQ or previous scholastic achievement. Indeed, they often come out worse when it comes to direct comparison. They may, however, contribute to overall predictions by adding slightly different, more specialized information.

Seashore-type tests measure only the basic aural skills – what might be called the perceptual processing of musical stimuli. Attempts have been made to measure skills related to the *performance* (output) side of music-making (e.g. Thompson 1987). At the most basic level, these comprise tests of eye–hand co-ordination and motor speed and accuracy. As the skills assessed proceed through rhythm-matching and sight-reading they ultimately converge with tests of attainment, where it could be said that they become criterion measures rather than predictors.

Another approach to the measurement of musical aptitude is that of testing *appreciation* of classic form, sometimes called 'musical literacy'. For example, Gordon (1970) had subjects state their preference between two versions of a specially composed musical phrase, one of which was 'better' than the other according to the consensus of professional musicians. Not surprisingly, perform-ance on this kind of test is more affected by musical training and experience than the basic listening skills tapped by Seashore-type tests.

Other researchers (e.g. Chalmers 1978, Manturzewska 1978) have been concerned to measure *interest* in music relative to other pleasures and activities and *preferences* among different musical styles. This is based on the premise that motivation may be just as important to progress in musical training as ability. Such tests may also help in vocational decisions and choices among different instruments and styles of music. Measures of interest and preference range from questionnaires to the rating of music samples (e.g. Glasgow *et al.* 1985).

GROUP DIFFERENCES

Any list of the greatest composers in history seems to be comprised mostly of men. This is so despite the fact that for some centuries a higher proportion of women than men learned to play a musical instrument. Women have written many successful ballads (going back to Victorian times) but few symphonies, operas or musical comedies of any stature. Does this mean that males have superior musical ability? This question is complex and not easily answered.

Tests such as the Seashore do not reveal any striking sex differences. Girls actually show more interest in auditory stimuli from an early age, whereas boys are more interested in visual stimuli. Also, a higher proportion of boys have difficulty in learning to sing (Davies and Roberts 1975). Another clearly established difference is that women are more sensitive to sound in that they report a tone as being 'too loud' at a lower decibel level than men (McGuinness 1972), which might account for many domestic disputes about the ideal sound level for the TV or stereo.

Whatever the reasons for the compositional genius shown by certain men, it cannot be traced to average sex differences in basic musical skills. More likely, it is related to the greater right hemisphere specialization of male brains (see below) and to certain personality characteristics like persistence and megalomania that testosterone seems to promote. Both for genetic and anatomic reasons males show more extremes of ability in most areas, and are hence over-represented in both the learning disabled and genius categories (Wilson 1989). Thus the finding that more boys than girls are 'tone-deaf' may be the other side of the coin of the exceptional musical talent shown by men such as Bach and Beethoven.

As far as performance ability is concerned some degree of 'androgyny' seems to be optimal (Kemp 1982). Compared with the general population, male musicians appear to be more feminine and females more masculine. Perhaps this is because music partakes both of traditionally male skills (e.g. mathematical ability and competitiveness) and female virtues (sensitivity and expressiveness), so that a combination of the two is ideal.

People of African origin are often said to have a natural rhythmic ability. Certainly their contribution to jazz is undeniable and they seem to excel in modern dance (e.g. Michael Jackson). However, no superiority is detectable on tests like the Seashore. If anything, American blacks score slightly lower than whites on all the Seashore scales, though rhythm is the subtest on which they are least likely to be disadvantaged (Shuter-Dyson and Gabriel 1981). This could mean either that race differences in rhythmic aptitude do not exist, or that Seashore-type tests are inappropriate for assessing them. At present there is insufficient evidence to say. And even if differences were found they might just as well be due to cultural traditions and experience as any innate factors (Suhor 1986).

Blind people are sometimes said to develop exceptional listening skills to compensate for lack of sight. Certain blind singers and pianists are cited in support of this theory. If so, this should appear as improved performance on standard aural tests. But again, no consistent superiority is found for blind people using tests like the Seashore. One study gives them a slight edge on pitch memory, while another found them to be disadvantaged on rhythm. Thus, despite the high level of talent shown by certain blind performers, there is no real evidence that blindness as such confers any significant musical advantage. Differences due to musical training are far more significant than the differences between normal-sighted and blind people (Shuter-Dyson and Gabriel 1981).

TALENT VERSUS TRAINING

One of the most important questions in relation to music education is that of the origins of musical talent. To what extent does musicality emerge spontaneously from the nature of a child and to what extent can it be developed by experience and training?

The case of Mozart has been cited as supporting both arguments. Some claim that the exceptional ability displayed by Mozart, as both performer and composer, which was apparent by the age of four, could only be accounted for by the unfolding of inborn genius. Environmentalists point out, however, that his father Leopold was a music teacher who, perhaps frustrated in his own ambitions, devoted himself to promoting the career of his son. Wolfgang was apparently given little opportunity to play normally with other children but was immersed in music from infancy and exploited by his father like a circus freak. Since Leopold Mozart was not beyond minor duplicity (e.g. lying about the ages of his children on publicity material) he probably underestimated the help given to the compositions attributed to his young son. No doubt Mozart was born a genius, but he was also given a helping hand by being raised in a 'hothouse' environment.

Certainly, musical ability appears very early in life, emerging first as melodic babbling around the same time that spoken language is developing. Moog (1976), studying the order in which singing skills develop in children, found that most babies would begin by picking up the sound of simple, memorable words like 'ding-dong'. Then would come rhythmic skills, and finally the pitch of tunes. By the age of four, 76 per cent of children could sing one line of a song more or less correctly, but a small proportion continued to have difficulty in learning a tune. The acquisition of harmonic skills, such as accurately distinguishing consonance and dissonance, comes rather later (around the age of seven or eight). Certain aspects of rhythm, harmony and general appreciation of music continue to develop into the teenage years (see Table 9.1). But as with most abilities, there are individual differences in the age at which these skills are mastered, some children progressing through these stages more quickly than others (especially when given formal training).

Great musicians often distinguish themselves at a very early age – Mozart, Haydn, Beethoven, Mendelssohn, Sullivan and Britten had all begun composing before they were teenagers. But for every child prodigy there is an equally

Table 9.1 The ages at which children typically acquire various musical skills

Ages	
0–1	Reacts to sounds
1–2	Spontaneous music making
2–3	Begins to reproduce phrases of songs heard
3–4	Conceives general plan of a melody; absolute pitch may develop if learns an instrument
4–5	Can discriminate register of pitches; can tap back simple rhythms
5–6	Understands louder/softer; can discriminate 'same' from 'different' in easy tonal or rhythm patterns.
6–7	Improved singing in tune; tonal music perceived better than atonal
7–8	Appreciates consonance vs dissonance
9–10	Rhythmic perception improves; melodic memory improves; two-part melodies perceived; sense of cadence
10–11	Harmonic sense becoming established. Some appreciation for finer points of music
12–17	Increase in appreciation, cognitively and in emotional response.

Source: Shuter-Dyson and Gabriel 1981

impressive late-starter. Glück spent the first 12 years of his life in a totally unmusical environment and only displayed his talent when sent to school. Wagner set out to be a playwright and only in his teens did he buy a book on composition with a view to adding music to his dramas. George Gershwin and Leonard Bernstein were raised in homes without a piano and received virtually no support from their families before growing up to become two of America's most outstanding pianists and composers.

Sosniak (1990) confirmed that early environmental support is not essential for the emergence of musical talent. She interviewed 24 exceptionally able American concert pianists, as well as their parents, and found that they did not necessarily come from musical homes. In half of the homes the parent had either no musical involvement or only a passive (listening) interest in music prior to the time their child began learning the piano. However, the parents were supportive, and it appeared that the first teacher had an important role in generating enthusiasm for piano playing. It did not seem to matter whether the teacher was highly rated in terms of musical ability, provided they were warm and encouraging, hence making the lessons pleasurable and rewarding.

Sloboda and Howe (1991) interviewed parents and students (aged 10–18) at a specialist British music school in an attempt to discover the background circumstances that predict musical achievement. Although many of the students had emerged from strongly musical families and had received a great deal of supervision and encouragement, those that were most highly accomplished according to their teachers seemed to have come from less musically active families. The outstandingly talented teenagers had actually had fewer lessons as children and had not practised any more than less accomplished students. Thus, it seems that while family support may help a musical career, it is certainly not an essential requirement: natural talent seems to play a large part in musical excellence. A proportion of those students coming from musical families may have taken up study of music because of family pressure rather than natural talent or love of the art. The fact that outstanding musicians do not necessarily practise more than mediocre ones does not prove that practice is useless. Rather, it suggests that naturally talented musicians can work less hard than others to achieve the same level of expertise.

Twin studies are the best-known way of demonstrating genetic influences on any attribute and these lend some support to the idea that music ability is hereditary. Identical twins are more similar than fraternal twins on scores derived from tests such as the Seashore, but results are variable and usually account for less than half of the variance (Stafford 1970, Rowley 1988). Although heritability might be higher if actual musical accomplishment (or even musical genius) was measured, rather than basic Seashore-type skills which are themselves of dubious validity, it does seem that there is plenty of room for experience and training to be functional in the development of musical ability.

The value of training is indicated in a study by Coon and Carey (1989) which divided twin samples into groups with and without music lessons. In the untutored sample, the identical twins were more alike than fraternal twins in musical performance. However, when twins received music lessons (always, both twins went) the identical twins were no more alike. What this study reveals is that natural talent and spontaneous interest contribute to musical ability but that formal training may override this source of variance, at least up to moderate levels of musical performance. This is consistent with the work of Doxey and Wright (1990) showing that when musical ability is assessed at age 4–6 years environmental factors such as parental attitude, the presence of musical instruments in the home and having siblings who are taking music lessons are positively associated.

However, spontaneous and internal factors may be more important for high-level performance. Sloboda (1990) reviews evidence concerning the conditions which favour the emergence of musical excellence. Looking at studies of both idiot-savants with exceptional ability to reproduce musical structures on a piano after hearing them only once, and self-taught distinguished jazz musicians such as Louis Armstrong, he concluded that formal training is unnecessary for the development of musical talent and may even be harmful if it takes the fun out of music. What does seem to be important is that the child has casual and frequent exposure to the musical forms of the culture from an early age, the opportunity to freely explore a musical medium over an extended time-span and resources for involvement in music (including time, access to instruments and financial and social support). Sloboda emphasizes that an absence of threat, anxiety and demand in the context of music is essential. Motivation should be intrinsic (coming from within) rather than external (bribes, browbeating, etc.). Exceptional musicians are not necessarily put into formal training at an early age, but they nearly all report having experienced intense positive emotional or aesthetic states ('peak experiences') in response to music, from their earliest listening days onwards.

Although Seashore thought that the abilities measured by his test were largely fixed by heredity, there is no doubt that concentrated coaching on them can improve the scores of children and adults to some extent. How permanent the advantages of this training are, and whether it has spin-off in real musical aptitude, is less certain. It may be that much of the improvement is due to a better understanding of what is meant by concepts such as pitch rather than any true gain in musicianship (Shuter-Dyson and Gabriel 1981).

The assumption that lessons with a specialist teacher help in learning to play an instrument like the piano or violin is so widespread that few empirical studies have been undertaken to evaluate it. Those that have (e.g. Coon and Carey 1989, Morrongiello 1992) do demonstrate that children with training have an edge over their untrained peers on various music perception tasks as well as performance skills. For example, training accelerates the development of sensitivity to the diatonic (seven-note) scale structure and memory for detailed information in melodies. It also increases the likelihood that absolute pitch will be acquired (see below). There is considerable agreement among teachers that the years between five and nine are particularly propitious for music training, this being the earliest age at which a child can profit from verbal instructions, master rhythmic, melodic and harmonic skills and acquire an understanding of notation (Shuter-Dyson and Gabriel 1981). However, the contribution of formal training to the emergence of exceptional (original and creative) music-making is less clear. The work of Sloboda suggests that lessons can stoltify creativity by inhibiting enjoyment, and Bamberger (1982) has described the frequent breakdown in the performance of child prodigies as their internally developed representations confront outer rules and traditional musical systems. In other words, musical competence and genius do not necessarily follow the same developmental paths.

Early training in singing songs can produce short-term improvement, but it is unclear to what extent the advantage so gained is carried forward into adulthood. Training may largely accelerate progress towards the same ceiling of ability, although some gains are likely to be permanent, such as control over the vocal apparatus, familiarity with culturally typical intervals and melodies and a general appreciation of music as an art form. How essential singing lessons are to the development of vocal prowess is open to question because it is difficult to untangle the effects of maturation and experience from those due specifically to the contribution of the teacher. Certain singing teachers gain great reputations, but a kind of circularity often develops; the teacher's reputation helps them attract good students who proceed to enhance that reputation further. Also, a kind of *folie à deux* is sometimes developed between teacher and student, whereby the student is convinced that progress is being made mainly because the teacher says so on an intermittent reinforcement basis. There may also be a 'Svengali effect', whereby the student can perform brilliantly in the teacher's studio but is unable to transfer the skill to outside situations where the teacher's encouragement is not available. No doubt some singing teachers do good for some students, but others are detrimental, instilling unrealistic ideas, spurious techniques and practice regimes that fatigue the voice (perhaps leading to permanent damage to the vocal cord).

The great difficulty in assessing the value of various courses of musical training is that of separating cause and effect. Talented people find their way into training and there is then a tendency to attribute their talent to that training. Usually, however, there will be a degree of interaction between the two, with a musical education helping the student to reach full potential. There is also the advantage that teachers and music colleges provide the stimulation of an environment that lives and breathes music and offers practical knowledge such as what type of instrument to buy and how to clean it, as well as professional hints like where to find jobs and auditions.

One slight danger is that the musical establishment induces conformity which stoltifies highly original talent. They may even be unable to recognize great creativity because their standards of excellence are backward-looking. After all, Verdi, the most celebrated composer that Italy has ever produced, was declined admission to the Milan Conservatoire on grounds of insufficient talent.

ABSOLUTE PITCH

The ability to identify notes and keys apparently without reference to pre-viously heard notes or to produce a specified note on demand is a special aspect of musical ability that is not yet well understood. The more 'musical' a person is the more likely they are to possess absolute pitch, but it is not clear whether the higher incidence among professional musicians is due to experience and learning or to selective entry into the profession of individuals of exceptional natural ability. About one in four conductors have absolute pitch, compared with about one in four hundred singers (Alexander 1971). This difference could be due to the fact that conductors are selected largely for musical ability while singers are selected more for the sound of their voice, but the age at which musical training begins is probably more important. Certainly, it is possible to be a great musician without absolute pitch – Tchaikovsky and Wagner were among some of the world's greatest composers who apparently did not have this facility (*New York Times*, 23 Dec 1990).

While absolute pitch is sometimes useful for a singer, there are other times when it can interfere with performance (Ward and Burns 1982). A singer who has learned a song in a particular key and then has to sing it to the accompaniment of a piano pitched down a semitone (as many are, especially when they get older and can no longer take the same degree of tension in tuning) is not normally thrown to any extent because he sings with relative pitch anyway. But the singer with absolute pitch may be caught in unpleasant conflict between the key in which the song was learned and that heard in the accompaniment, with the result that he or she may mix the two, sing sharp, or perform in a generally unsettled way. Pianists with absolute pitch may also be thrown by the discrepancy between what they see and what they hear. The accompanist Gerald Moore expressed great relief when the facility of absolute pitch he had had from childhood faded over the years.

Two examples serve to illustrate the possible advantages and disadvantages of absolute pitch. When soprano Kirsten Flagstad suffered a serious ear ailment that rendered her virtually deaf, for over a year she was able to carry on singing major Wagnerian roles at the Metropolitan Opera using only her own absolute pitch and visual contact with the conductor. On the other hand, a prominent mezzo-soprano with absolute pitch singing a difficult piece with unaccompanied choir fell apart completely when the choir drifted flat (as they frequently do) because she was unable to follow their shifting key (*New York Times, op cit.*).

Absolute pitch is more useful to an instrumentalist or conductor than to a singer. Alexander (1971) maintains that conductors are often regarded as the 'natural enemy' of an orchestra and have to work hard to gain the respect of the players. If judged opinionated without sufficient cause the orchestra may set traps to humiliate them. For example, at the beginning of Act III of *Tosca* there is a passage in which the horns blow in unison. Should they conspire to play a semi-tone low, the subsequent entry of the basses sounds awful. The conductor with absolute pitch (e.g. Solti, Muti, Maazel, Abbado or Levine) is able to correct the horns before this happens, but others are liable to make fools of themselves by accusing the basses of being too high.

The origin of absolute pitch is not well understood. In Chapter 8 it was suggested that colour-tone synesthesia might explain the ability in a few instances. Among the composers who reported seeing colours on hearing music are Liszt, Schriabin, Rimsky-Korsakov and Messiaen. But synesthesia is rarer than absolute pitch itself and so cannot explain all cases. One or two individuals have a permanent ringing in their ears (tinnitus) of a fixed tone, providing them with an internal 'tuning fork' against which to compare all other pitches; but this is also rare and is probably better described as 'pseudo-absolute pitch' (Ward and Burns 1982).

Some musicians with absolute pitch maintain that particular keys induce particular moods or 'colours'. For example, they will say that D major is 'martial and brilliant', G minor is 'grief-laden', C major is 'noble, open and affirmative', D minor 'stormy', D flat major 'warm', and so on. But while compositional practice may have followed conventions of this kind, sound frequencies cannot be the basis of this because pitch standards have changed over the years. In other words, D major cannot sound brilliant because a keynote of 290 Hz inherently suggests this. Bach, Haydn, Beethoven and others who established that association in their compositions were actually writing to a different D. Up until about 1820, pitch was variable but typically at least a semitone lower than today's standard of A = 440 Hz. (The situation is similar to that of astrological sun-signs, where the stellar constellations have all shifted along one since the personality characteristics corresponding to them were described.) The associations between key and mood are no doubt real to those with absolute pitch who experience them, but they must be derived from learning rather than any intrinsic property of the sound frequencies involved.

Absolute pitch may be a form of long-term tonal memory. Investigating this idea, Siegel (1972) concluded that people with absolute pitch have stored a number of limited points in the pitch continuum in long-term memory and use these as references for identifying other tones. Some instrumental players can spontaneously sing an A, which they use for tuning their instruments, but any other note would have to be worked out in terms of an interval from this.

To what extent can absolute pitch be acquired? In some cases it is so powerful and manifested so early in life that it seems to be constitutional, but such individuals are probably exceptional. It seems that most people who display absolute pitch have acquired it very early in life, probably at a particular age of 'readiness' similar to that of language learning. Research with Royal College of Music students by Sergeant (1969) found a very striking connection between the occurrence of absolute pitch and early musical training. Of those taking up music lessons between the age of two and four, 93 per cent showed absolute pitch, while none of those who started after the age of 14 showed the ability. Sergeant also found that absolute pitch was better for instruments with which the student was familiar, and those that had been studied first. Where a student had changed instruments, their pitch-naming remained superior for the earlier-learned instrument, which again suggests the importance of early learning experiences.

Although early training seemed very important it was not the only factor. Some children who started lessons early never acquired absolute pitch and others only became aware of the ability in their late teens. Furthermore, pitch-naming ability is seldom as 'absolute' or 'perfect' as the names imply. People show degrees of the ability and many who have it maintain it tenuously. Fatigue, illness and a long absence from music often disrupt pitch-naming and as people get older their internal pitch tends to get higher. In middle-age it is often transposed a semi-tone, and later on by as much as a full tone (Vernon 1977).

While the most striking forms of absolute pitch seem to be inborn or learned in childhood, it is possible to improve pitch-naming performance well into adulthood. The most successful training methods seem to be those based on the idea of focusing on fixed reference points rather than giving equal attention to all the notes along the scale (Cuddy 1971). Brady (1970) describes a method by which he taught himself absolute pitch at the age of 32. He programmed his computer to produce tones of various pitches in the chromatic scale, with high proportions of the note C. Practising for half an hour per day, he consciously worked on retaining just that one pitch. After two months he could identify C with little error, but the other notes were beginning to acquire a particular 'colour' and he found himself identifying the pitch of sounds in his environment. The refrigerator hummed in B and his child's toy produced an A.

Thus, it does seem to be possible to develop some degree of absolute pitch in later years, particularly by use of standard reference points. Which points are best to use probably depends upon the musician's common experience. Singers might use C because the white note scale is often a starting point for vocal exercises, whereas instrumentalists might use A (the usual tuning standard) and pianists might prefer something like the F major triad. But whether or not absolute pitch is an important skill to acquire remains open to argument. At best it is a mixed blessing (see above) and there is little evidence that it connects with other musical traits, such as the ability to improvise or make judgements of relative pitch (Ward and Burns 1982).

MUSIC AND THE BRAIN

In most right-handed persons the left hemisphere of the brain is dominant, dealing with verbal, analytic and executive functions, while the right hemisphere has a more visual, spatial, holistic and intuitive mode of operation, and is more heavily involved with emotion and joke perception (Chapter 7). Music perception, composition and performance depend heavily on pattern processing, and so are widely held to be right hemisphere activities.

Many patients suffering verbal aphasias due to left hemisphere damage show no impairment of musical appreciation or ability. Gott (1973) describes a patient whose left hemisphere had been completely removed due to a malignant tumour. Asked the meaning of the word 'spangled' she proceeded to give a complete rendition of 'God Bless America', ending with the comment 'Now that is what it is'. Apparently she liked to sing and could do so quite well, usually with appropriate words, and could use this mode of expression to communicate where normal speech was not available to her. Similarly, the observation that many stammerers show no impediment when singing, which has been used as an approach to management of the disability, confirms the separation of speech and music as left and right hemisphere functions respectively. Today it is possible with positron emission (PET) brain-scanning to observe the difference directly. When listening to music most people show more activity in the right side of the brain, whereas speech processing indicates greater energy consumption on the left.

It would be oversimplification, however, to say that the left hemisphere is not involved in musical processing. Some aphasic patients do show impairment of musical ability, especially those aspects of music that come close to the symbolic function of language, such as the naming of chords and remembering lyrics (Marin 1982). A case in point is that of a 40-year-old professional violinist who suffered a left-hemisphere cerebral 'accident' (as evidenced by the pattern of body paralysis and verbal difficulty). Although his pitch discrimination remained intact, he lost his absolute pitch ability and, while he could still play and sing music correctly, he could no longer recognize or identify a work, its composer or its style (Wertheim and Botez 1961). Thus it seems that certain linguistic aspects of music require an intact left hemisphere, even though the configurational aspects of music (such as melody and harmony) are more strongly localized to the right.

There is also some evidence that the lateralization of musical processing is more clear-cut for musically unsophisticated people than it is for the musically trained (Gordon 1983). This somewhat surprising discovery can best be explained by supposing that professional musicians, as a result of long years of study and immersion in their art, progressively bring their dominant (left) hemisphere to bear upon musical analysis and performance, in addition to whatever is happening on the right. Eventually, their whole brain is involved in their music, not just the right hemisphere, as is more the case with the general population. A kind of parallel can be seen in the multi-lingual person whose later-acquired languages have been found to spill over into right hemisphere territory more than the primary language which remains localized to the left.

Because the right ear is connected primarily to the left side of the brain, and *vice versa,* it is possible to compare the musical abilities of the two sides of the brain by presenting stimuli to the two ears separately. Other experiments present different sounds to the two ears through headphones simultaneously and ask the subject to assess them. This is called a *dichotic listening* task. Studies using these methods confirm that musical training results in a shift towards a right-ear (hence left-brain) advantage, and that this is due to the trained musicians making greater use of analytical strategies for performing the tasks (Bever and Chiarello 1974; Burton *et al.* 1989).

It seems that what musical training and experience contributes is a language-like system for coding and describing the auditory sensations that are basic to music. This assists with remembering, discussing and performing music but it would not necessarily enhance appreciation of it at the emotional level of pure enjoyment. The latter probably depends more on the global pattern-processing, 'intuitive' functions of the right hemisphere in both musically trained and naive listeners.

After a detailed review of brain lateralization experiments, Shuter-Dyson and Gabriel (1981) conclude that the main value of these studies to the music educator is to point out the fact that 'music is simultaneously synthetic and analytic. There are two modes of perception and performance and, on the face of it, the need is to train the student not only to operate successfully in these two modes but to gain practice (and pleasure) in frequently switching between them'.

There are indications that men and women differ with respect to degree of brain assymetry. In particular, the right hemisphere of the human male brain seems to be more specialized for spatial functioning than the right side of the female brain, which duplicates the functions of the left side to a greater extent (Kolb and Whishaw 1980). This accounts for many otherwise puzzling facts, such as the marked advantage of males in spatial IQ tests, the slight superiority of women on verbal and memory tests, and the greater vulnerability of males to constitutional and traumatic brain damage (the anatomical location of brain injury being more critical in determining its psychological effects in the case of men than women). It might also help to account for the fact that, although women have written many celebrated novels over the last few centuries, they have not distinguished themselves as composers. Hassler (1990) has shown that the finding of greater cerebral assymetry in males holds true even when the comparison is between male and female composers and instrumental musicians. However, the theory linking gender with degree of lateralization remains controversial at present, and it is probable that social and motivational factors, such as opportunity and determination also contribute to the differential accomplishments of men and women in the field of music. Certainly, there is so much overlap between men and women in abilities of all kinds that no-one should be deterred from pursuing a musical career purely on the basis of gender.

BIOFEEDBACK

One of the ways in which music influences our emotions is by pacing our physiological rhythms such as heartbeat and electrical brain waves (Chapter 8). The power of rhythmic presentation of stimuli to induce semihypnotic states, even coma or seizure, is well-known. But while music can influence our body rhythms, it seems probable that it is in some sense also derived from them. The musical beat may gain effect partly by simulating body rhythms.

Since the discovery that these 'automatic' body processes can be brought under greater conscious control by transducing them in such a way as to permit auditory or visual feedback, experiments have been conducted on the possibility that brain waves can be directly harnessed as a creative force. If a professional composer sits at a piano wearing earphones that provide him with a sound equivalent of his own brain waves, he can use this as a base for inspiration while his fingers 'wander idly over the noisy keys'. This set-up is interesting because the composer's own thoughts and feelings are responsible for the electrical output of his brain, and these will be affected by what he is hearing and playing as well as any other ideas that spontaneously occur to him in the process. The unique reciprocation involved may prove to be a source of new musical styles and ideas, apart from being a fascinating experience to the musician.

In a more clinical application of EEG auditory feedback, attempts have been made to see whether non-verbal patients, such as autistic children, can communicate advanced 'right-hemispheric' conceptions via an output of 'brain music'. The idea is that if the individual's disability is specific to speech production, or verbal output in general (including writing), then providing him with an independent 'mouthpiece' might just reveal a wondrous world of hitherto untapped imagination. There may be some people who, devoid of any facility with conventional language, can nevertheless speak quite eloquently via the medium of music (Chapter 12). As with the idea of using brain waves to assist professional composers, developments with this clinical procedure have not so far been staggering. But the idea is new, so the individuals whose creativity would be most enhanced may not yet have been identified, and long-term learning and experience may yield greater rewards. Although we do not yet know what will come of it, biofeedback represents an exciting new area of interface between psychology and the performing arts.

MIDI TECHNOLOGY

Another form of feedback that shows promise as a clinical and teaching device is the Musical Instrument Digital Interface (MIDI) system (Salmon and Newmark 1989). This is a development of the Moog Synthesizer which enables a musical performance to be digitally coded by computer so that detailed analyses of it can be made subsequently. Variables stored by the computer include the duration, pitch, loudness and timbre of notes and the time intervals between them.

One of the most obvious applications is the editing of performances, since it permits errors to be corrected as well as other 'clean up' operations (parallel to word processing). But its capacity to describe individual differences in performance skills in statistical terms gives it enormous scope as a research and remedial aid. Ordinary sound recording gives an exact record of a musical performance, and some simple operations such as slowing down the playback are possible. The advantage of MIDI is that numerical scores can be produced on subtle aspects of the performance such as the degree of overlap in the sounding of adjacent notes played legato. Salmon and Newark show how individual differences in scores such as this can be related to the skill and experience of the pianist. Hence it becomes possible to analyse what makes a good performance. A beginning has also been made in using the technique to monitor progress in overcoming problems due to overuse injury.

MIDI, therefore, offers a method for detailed analysis of both playing strengths and weaknesses which should in the future prove useful to teachers and clinicians helping performers to optimize their performance and overcome their difficulties.

CHAPTER 10

PERSONALITY AND STRESS IN PERFORMERS

Performers are, by definition, in the public eye. Often they are considered to be godlike creatures; just to see them, touch them or obtain their signature can be a thrilling experience for their devoted 'fans'. There is great speculation as to what they are like in person, and their lifestyle, love affairs, marriages and divorces are examined by the media and the public with fascination, envy and awe. What sort of people are they really and what special stresses do they have to cope with? We saw in Chapter 7 that comedians often seem to be lonely and depressed people in their private lives and the possible reasons for this were discussed. Now we consider the question of whether other types of performers (actors, singers, musicians and dancers) also have special problems of adjustment.

Some people, including many professional psychoanalysts, believe that performers are social misfits – immature, exhibitionist people who have never grown up properly, or neurotics engaged in a programme of self-treatment. Others would say that they begin as normal, even attractive and talented people, but end up disturbed because of the unique stresses imposed upon them by their occupation and lifestyle. Still others regard them as fortunate, well-balanced people who only appear neurotic because of the extent of self-disclosure and media attention they receive. In this view, the personal problems of performers are no greater than anyone else's, but they are highlighted because it makes them more interesting. Finally, it is possible to argue that their behaviour appears eccentric because they are relatively free of the social constraints that inhibit self-expression in more conservative occupations such as politician or clergyman. We begin this chapter by looking in more detail at some of the hypotheses concerning the nature and special problems of performers.

EXHIBITIONISM

One psychoanalytic theory about performers is that they have an immature need to 'show off' in front of other people. Deprived of sufficient attention and praise by parents and others in childhood they have an undischarged need for social approval that is manifested in performance. Stage appearances are thus an extension of the desire for attention that is seen in the child who says 'Daddy, look at me' before diving into a swimming pool: in both cases it is applause that is demanded. A parallel may be seen in certain cats that chew their tail well into adulthood, often denuding it completely of hair. Ethologists (and vets) maintain that this represents an undischarged sucking instinct, due perhaps to insufficient experience of the mother's nipple. Instincts that are denied consummation in early life may become insistent throughout life.

It is no doubt true that many performers had difficult childhoods, in which they apparently had to strive for attention and affection. For example, Bates (1986) describes the background of Dustin Hoffman, who was skinny and tiny as a child, wore corrective teeth braces for eight years and had an older brother who was very clever and good at sport, to whom he felt inferior. His family had moved house six times by the time he was 12, so he frequently found himself 'the new boy' in schools and neighbourhoods. He had to cope with taunts about his physical appearance from other children who said that his big nose and darting eyes made him look like a rat. The implication, endorsed by himself, is that he became an actor in order to cope with these childhood problems and gain some much-needed social recognition. It is easy to find such examples of performers with an unhappy childhood who seem to fit this pattern. However, it might be equally easy to find people with similar experiences who grew up to be engineers or accountants, so this sort of case-history material falls short of being scientific.

There is some research that seems to confirm that performers are characteristically exhibitionistic in personality. Friedman *et al.* (1980) have produced a questionnaire to measure non-verbal emotional expressiveness, which, for shorthand, they call the 'charisma test'. This is described as measuring the ability to 'transmit emotion and thrill and excite others' and it uses items such as 'When I hear good dance music I can hardly keep still', 'I can easily express emotion over the telephone' and 'I show that I like someone by hugging or touching that person'. Scores on this test were found to be positively related to theatrical experience of various sorts as well as lecturing and holding political office. They were also related to an absence of stage fright and the ability to convey emotions on videotaped tests of non-verbal acting skill. As regards personality, the 'charisma' test correlated .52 with Extroversion, .45 with Dominance and .42 with Affiliation, but the highest correlation of all was .60 with Exhibitionism as measured by the Jackson Personal Record Form. It thus seems that emotional expressiveness (charisma), acting ability and exhibitionism have much in common as personality characteristics.

Although performers do seem to be exhibitionistic this does not prove that lack of attention and approval in early childhood is the cause. It would be equally logical to argue that the exhibitionism developed as a result of reinforcement for theatrical behaviour in childhood. In other words, performers may have learned very early in their lives that outgoing behaviour brings the reward of applause from parents and others and so it becomes enhanced and habitual. This social learning hypothesis is virtually the reverse of the psychoanalytic (deprivation) idea.

It is difficult to think of a way of testing between these rival hypotheses, but in any case, there is reason to think that both might be wrong. Modern behavioural genetics, using twin comparisons, permits personality variance to be partialled into three main sources: genetic, shared family environment, and other environmental effects. Parenting style, insofar as it is consistent within the family, falls into the second category, and yet this apparently has no important influence on the development of personality. Personality seems to be determined about 50 per cent by genetic factors and 50 per cent by environmental processes that are not common to the members of a family (Rowe 1989). The latter may include pre-natal hormone effects on the brain and serial birth position. The whole matter is complicated by the fact that children often see their siblings as receiving more praise and attention than themselves even though parental treatment is even-handed. Thus perceptions of social deprivation or reward could still affect a child's future tendency towards exhibitionism regardless of the actual behaviour of the parents. The only conclusion that is possible is that performers do seem to be exhibitionistic but the origins of this exhibitionism are unclear.

IDENTITY CONFUSION

Another analytic idea, referring particularly to actors, is that performance is part of a search for identity. Again, presumably because of childhood experiences (such as Dustin Hoffman's moving house so many times) the actor becomes confused as to who he really is, and so playing a role in a play or film provides (albeit temporarily) a clearer sense of self. Peter Sellers once said in an interview that he never knew who he was till he put on a false moustache, strange accent or funny walk. A study which was interpreted as supporting such a theory is that of Henry and Sims (1970). These authors investigated self-image problems in professional actors using 'depth' interviews, a projective test called the *Thematic Apperception Test*, and a self-rating 'identity diffusion' questionnaire. Their conclu-sion was that, compared with various control groups such as housewives and executives, the actors had more confusion or 'diffuseness' in their sense of identity. When the actors were retested some weeks into the rehearsal period of a new play, it was found that their identity confusion had lessened somewhat. The researchers presumed this was because the role they were working on in the play was providing them with the clear identity that was lacking as a result of 'role disjunctive' experience in early life. Because actors have failed to develop a strong sense of self in childhood, Henry and Sims argue, their life becomes 'a quest, a search for the one life style appropriate to them... The role experimentation so begun, and subsequently institutionalized in acting, becomes the modus vivendi that has meaning for them' (p.62).

This idea of the actor searching for clear identity sounds plausible at first. Unfortunately, an equally persuasive case has been made for the opposite idea – that acting *creates* role confusion rather than operating as a method for coping with it. According to this theory, the experience of adopting so many different roles leads to a breakdown in the sense of self, so actors *come* to wonder who they really are. Girodo (1984) details the difficulty that is faced by undercover agents, for example in drug enforcement, who have to immerse themselves completely in the values and lifestyle of the criminal subculture they are investigating. Their role-playing has to be convincing, for their very life is at stake, and they assume the new identity so powerfully that they are likely to have problems rediscovering their original selves. Girodo calls this 're-entry strain' and it is occasionally so powerful that schizophrenia is the result. So it may be with actors. 'To be applauded every night for certain character traits, values and attitudes makes it nigh on irresistible not to carry them over to some extent in private life. However, it is not only the applause but the "living oneself into the part" for weeks on end that makes the separation of stage and home life extremely difficult' (Rule 1973). At the extreme, this loss of identity may be appropriately described as 'possession' (see Chapter 2).

The public often conspires to consolidate the identity confusion of performers by treating them as though they really are the people they portray on stage or film. Sometimes they impose upon them a simplified persona which they are required to represent in real life, and insofar as this differs from their true self it may entirely overwhelm them. James Dean was expected to play the delinquent, confused kid, Marilyn Monroe the simpering, dizzy blonde, John Wayne the tough guy and Maria Callas the egocentric prima donna. Sometimes these pressures seem to lead to the detriment, or even death, of the performer (Conrad 1987).

Hammond and Edelmann (1991b) undertook to study the effects of acting upon self-perceptions by having two actors complete Repertory Grids (a technique for measuring self-image) on repeated occasions across periods of performing and resting. They observed that one actor (female) was greatly influenced by the roles she played, while the other (male) maintained stability of his self-concept. Thus it seems probable that there are considerable individual differences in the extent to which role-playing permeates the performer's own self. Although they did not have sufficient numbers in their sample to be sure, Hammond and Edelmann supposed that the nature of the role played (deeply dramatic vs light comedy), the length of time immersed in it, and the type of training (imaginative vs technical) might be important in influencing the likelihood of identity shifts. The other big factor, of course, is whether the role played differs substantially from the original self or is very much the same. In the latter case, no disturbance of self-concept is risked.

It seems, therefore, that performers sometimes suffer identity problems, but these are more likely to result from over-identification with the characters being played than disorientation arising out of childhood experiences.

PERFORMANCE AS SELF-TREATMENT

It is frequently suggested by psychoanalysts and critics that performers are neurotics engaged in a programme of self-treatment – this is implicit in the idea that performing a role can serve to stabilize an insecure self-concept. Role-playing might also be used to bolster self-esteem. For example, the roles of Sylvester Stallone (Rocky and Rambo) feature a 'small', barely articulate, man becoming a hero, and it is tempting to relate this to a personal escape from feelings of inadequacy.

In Chapter 7 we explored the theory that comedians are stigmatized, depressed individuals endeavouring to cheer themselves up by being funny. Woody Allen, John Cleese and Andrew Dice Clay were cited as examples of writer/performers who seem to be indulging in a form of public psychodrama, their personal frustrations and insecurities being aired for all to laugh or cringe at. If theatre and humour are cathartic to an audience, then surely performers themselves can partake of the benefit equally, or more so. Fisher and Fisher (1981) examined this idea in a study of actors and comedians that used methods ranging from historical anecdotes and interviews to Rorschach Inkblots and personality questionnaires. Their conclusions were encapsulated in the catchy title of their book, *Pretend the World is Funny and Forever*: comedians were said to specialize in the denial of threat, while actors were concerned with repressing the idea of mortality by extending historical time backwards into the past and forward into the future. These two forms of denial were presumed to originate in the personal fears of the performer, while helping others to allay anxieties into the bargain: 'Each has an influential social role that helps people to cope with catastrophe and the discontinuities resulting from death' (Fisher and Fisher 1981 p.218).

Although the Fishers' study did include some objective measures and control groups, it emerges as a rather uncomfortable blend of psychoanalytic theory with empirical data. For example, the score used to establish 'time continuity' in actors included any reference to history (e.g. Richard III, Roman toga, Victorian dress, 18th century chair) or the future (Buck Rogers, Star Wars, hypermodern) in responses to the Rorschach Inkblots. Yet it should come as no surprise that, compared with non-theatrical people, actors make frequent reference to such concepts which reflect the time setting of so many dramatic works. Against this, the authors' interpretation sounds grandiose: 'We see in the actor's focus on this theme a conviction that one is part of a long-term, time-locked process which exceeds the duration of any single individual. To experience oneself as part of an historical continuity is to feel tied to something larger in magnitude than self. This would duplicate, at another level, the actor's fascination with fusion as it expresses itself in religious imagery...'. Psychological defences are no doubt involved in the theatrical experience (Chapter 1) but the Fishers appear to overinterpret their projective data. Other of their findings, although derived from student samples, are less open to criticism because they are based on objective personality tests. In particular, they found that performers tended to be exhibitionistic and impulsive relative to non-performers. This confirms the Friedman *et al.*, (1980) study and is consistent with other studies of the personality of actors to be described below.

Although the temptation to psychoanalyse performers, both as individuals and a group, is strong, there are reasons for being cautious in doing so. As an illustration, consider another psychoanalytic study of actors, that of Barr *et al.*, (1972). Again using a mixture of depth interviews, projective tests such as the Rorschach Inkblots and perhaps a certain amount of their own imagination, they concluded that professional actors were intellectually bright but had 'poorly integrated, largely hysteric and schizoid personalities. They were exhibitionistic and narcissistic, having much pent-up aggression. They were passive, vulnerable to stress, tended to be overtly anxious and had impaired body images. Their major defences were regression, projection, denial, isolation and reaction formation. Last, homosexuality was a major area of pathology. (p.17)' Although this description might tie in with self-report findings at some points, there are two reasons for reservations. One is that the methods used (depth interviews and projective tests) are notoriously low in reliability and validity. The other is that psychoanalysts tend to see immaturity and pathology wherever they look. Their interpretations are nearly always unflattering and they assign diagnostic labels to behaviours that might equally well be viewed as positive, adaptive and creative. However compelling, this kind of thinking needs to be regarded sceptically. Performers do have their problems and peculiarities but there is a danger that the jargon of psychoanalysis is used to disparage rather than describe.

ARE PERFORMERS EFFEMINATE?

A widely held stereotype of performers, especially dancers and singers, is that they have gender identity problems. In particular, theatrical males are regarded as likely to be homosexual or effeminate. This was one of the conclusions reached by Barr *et al.*, (1972) and some writers take it as so self-evident that they proceed straight to explanation before confirming the observation. For example, Lane (1959) says that 'not all actors have homosexual tendencies, but theatrical life has a strong attraction for the homosexual... he is in an environment where a love of fantasy and a delight in dressing up is approved' (p.50).

At a time when homosexual behaviour was illegal, some gay men may have sought refuge in the relatively tolerant environment of the theatre, but today at least they do not predominate to the extent that Lane describes. In fact, Neuringer (1989) was unable to find any over-representation of gays among actors compared with other occupations. He suggests that the reputation of the theatre as a gay stronghold is probably due to the greater openness, unconventionality and free expression of feelings and attitudes among actors (as with creative people in general) combined with an exaggerated media interest and readiness of the public to 'think the worst' of performers.

One of the problems with the research reviewed by Neuringer is that few studies are directly concerned with sex orientation – they infer homosexuality from personality scales of masculinity-femininity which really measure toughness versus emotional sensitivity. In this sense, ballet dancers are found to be more feminine in personality than controls and other types of performer (Bakker 1988; Marchant-Haycox and Wilson 1992). As a group, dancers seem to be tender-minded, dependent and emotionally sensitive compared with non-dancers of the same gender, and these traits are recognized as typically female. Actors, however, appear to have high levels of the male hormone testosterone compared with other occupational groups (Dabbs *et al.* 1990). Entertainers (including comedians) and football players seemed to be the most masculine of several groups tested as regards sex hormones – ministers of religion were lowest.

HORMONES AND THE VOICE

Whether or not singers are masculine or feminine in personality seems to depend partly on the depth of their voice. The timbre of the human voice is a product of anatomical processes that are guided by sex hormones. All children have soprano or contralto voices up until puberty, when male hormones released in the bloodstream of the teenage boy cause an expansion of the larynx and an increase in the length of the vocal cords. However, in some men, this lowering of the voice is arrested prematurely, probably as a result of a variation in the endocrine mechanism governing laryngeal expansion (Alexander 1971). The result is a 'freak' male voice that we call tenor. Even more unusual, in the normal course of events, is the virtual absence of any voice-deepening as the man passes puberty, yielding a voice called counter-tenor. The 'castrati', much prized in Italian church music a century or two ago, were adult male sopranos created by pre-pubertal castration. The counter-tenors of today are vocally equivalent, but do not necessarily have any obvious anatomical deficiency.

The precise hormonal processes responsible for these different voice categories are not well understood. Tissue sensitivity (the extent to which organs 'take up' the effect of hormones) is no doubt important, but high levels of circulating male hormone seem to be related to a lower pitched voice, and vice versa with respect to female hormones. Meuser and Nieschlag (1977) found that within a sample of male choristers the basses and baritones had a higher ratio of testosterone to oestradiol (male and female hormones respectively) than tenors.

If voice type is hormonally determined, then certain other somatic and temperamental characteristics might also be connected. Anyone familiar with the world of opera knows that certain stereotypes exist regarding the personality characteristics of singers with different kinds of voice and these were examined by Wilson (1984). A questionnaire was sent to all the professional opera singers that could be located in the London area, including all of the principals in the 1982/83 winter seasons at Covent Garden and the English National Opera. This

survey asked about age, physical build, lifestyle, experience, values and performance difficulties, before requesting self-ratings on various personality traits and
ratings of other people with whom they were familiar (one representative of each
voice type and one male and one female non-singer). Scores were then analysed
by voice type. Lower voiced singers were found to be taller than higher voiced
colleagues of the same sex (Table 10.1). This was most marked with women, the
mezzos being nearly three inches taller than sopranos, but baritones were about
one and a half inches taller than tenors. Lower voiced singers were also heavier,
but not as much as would be expected on the basis of their extra height.
Comparing the weight figures with British weight-for-height norms, sopranos
came out six pounds overweight (on average), mezzos one pound over, tenors 14
pounds over, and baritones 12 pounds over. Thus, with the exception of mezzos,

Table 10.1 Mean scores for four voice types on self-reported physical,
background and performance variables. Lower-voiced singers
are taller, more stable, and more given to sexual affairs
with fellow singers than higher-voiced singers

	Soprano	Mezzo/ Contralto	Tenor	Baritone/ Bass
Age	33.30	31.86	38.69	36.00
Experience (years)	11.49	9.15	15.54	13.38
Height (inches)	64.43	67.36**	70.00	71.43**
Weight (pounds)	135.42	140.86**	170.64	176.30**
Collar (inches)	14.00	14.50*	16.00	16.76*
Stage fright	2.05	1.93	1.92	1.62
Uneven performance	1.44	1.29	1.54	1.24
Self-opinion	1.02	.92	.92	.90
Enjoyment of applause	2.56	2.36	2.39	2.48
Argumentativeness	1.44	1.39	1.46	1.52
Sexual interest in co-singers	1.98	2.07	2.23	2.24
No. of affairs	1.54	1.57	1.46	1.95**
Determination to succeed	1.81	1.63	1.31	2.05**
Belief that talent is underrated	2.19	2.21	2.23	1.95
Missed cues	1.12	1.29	1.54	1.24

Source: Wilson 1984

* $p<.05$, ** $p<.01$ on a t-test for significance of difference compared with
same-sex singers of other voice-type. Where measurement units are not specified,
the item is scored on a scale ranging from 1 (lowest level) to 3 (highest level)

singers tend to be solidly built, though perhaps not the massive 'tanks' that they are popularly conceived to be. In accordance with stereotype, sopranos and tenors were stockier in build than their lower-voiced gender equivalent. Nevertheless, at five feet ten inches, these (largely successful) tenors could not be considered short.

Higher voices reported stage fright more often, were more variable in perform-ance from one occasion to the next, and more self-opinionated. Tenors more often missed cues because they were not on stage in time, yet they were also more likely to believe that their talents were underrated. These differences are consistent with opera folklore concerning the 'hysterical' tendencies of higher-voiced singers but, given the sample sizes available, they are not statistically reliable. Two other differences are both statistically significant and theoretically interesting. Baritones reported more backstage affairs with fellow artists than tenors; they were also more 'determined to succeed at all costs'. Since libido and ambition are traditionally male characteristics, these findings are consistent with the German finding of a higher male/female hormone ratio in deep-voiced men.

Asked to rank various aspects of life with respect to the value they assigned to them, most singers put 'opera' first in importance and 'family' second. Only sopranos rated family as marginally more important than opera. 'Other types of music' came third for both female groups, with 'sex' in fourth place; for men this order was reversed 'sex' coming third and 'music' fourth. 'Religion', 'travel' and 'sport' were lower in priority for all groups, though men put religion last while women thought sport was least important. These value patterns reveal traditional sex differences, men being relatively fond of sex and sport and women more

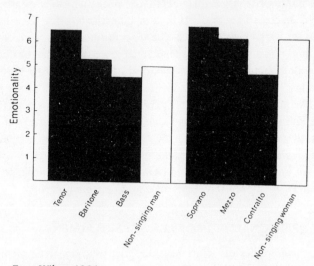

Source: From Wilson 1984

Figure 10.1: Mean ratings of emotionality of singers of six voice categories and male and female controls by 91 opera singers. (Within each sex higher-voiced singers tend to be more emotional.)

interested in family and religion. The greater interest in family of sopranos, relative to mezzos, might be taken as a further indication of constitutional femininity in higher-voiced women.

Personality self-ratings suggested that higher-voiced singers of both sexes were more emotional, unreliable, conceited, difficult and inconsiderate than lower-voiced singers. In support of the hormone hypothesis, higher-voiced singers also rated themselves directly as more feminine and lower in libido than lower-voiced singers, and baritones rated themselves as less faithful than tenors (consistent with their report of having more affairs with fellow artists). Ratings made by other singers concerning their friends in opera tended to support the self-rating evidence of 'hysteria' in tenors and sopranos. The relationship of emotionality to voice type, for example, is shown in Figure 10.1.

Comparisons with controls showed that non-singing people fell within the range of high- and low-voiced singers on many traits (e.g. emotionality), but compared with singers as a group, non-singers were less extrovert, less conceited and more intelligent, faithful and considerate. Thus the stereotype of the opera singer as exhibitionistic, arrogant, inconsiderate and often a bit 'thick', is confirmed in this study, while the finding of more masculine physical and mental traits in lower-voiced singers is consistent with the hormonal evidence.

The connection between voice type, body build and personality is probably due to pre-natal hormones. There is now much evidence that sex hormones circulating during embryonic development have power to influence sex orientation and gender-typical behaviour in adulthood, probably by affecting the way in which the hypothalamus and other brain structures develop (Ellis and Ames 1987). It should be no surprise, then, that depth of voice (which is clearly a sex differentiated characteristic) is involved in these interrelationships. Constitutional factors linking sex hormones with voice type are confirmed in the work of Lyster (1985). He found that a sample of 48 tenors had more sisters than brothers (52 against 36) while a sample of 61 basses had nearly twice as many brothers as sisters (77 against 46). His interpretation was that sex hormones in the parents influence the likelihood of male and female children. It is not clear why this should be so, but the finding with singers may relate to an earlier observation of Lyster that deep-sea divers produce twice as many daughters as sons. The suggestion is that the water pressure may have reduced the testes' ability to produce testosterone. Hormones in the mother are also likely to be influential; Grant (1990) reports that dominant mothers are more likely to produce sons than daughters.

PERSONALITY PROFILES OF PERFORMERS

As noted, most studies of actors have adopted psychoanalytic methods of dubious validity and there have been few empirical studies of actors' personality. Eysenck and Eysenck (1975) report that actors are generally inclined to be extrovert and emotional, while Fisher and Fisher (1981) found (mostly amateur) performers to be impulsive and exhibitionistic. Stacey and Goldberg (1953) found that professional actors were reflective, introvert and depressed compared with student actors, suggesting that experience may blunt the personality to some extent. Hammond and Edelmann (1991a) compared 51 working professional actors with 58 amateur actors and 52 controls using the Eysenck Personality Questionnaire, Rosenberg Self-Esteem Scale, Marlow-Crowne Social Desirability Scale, and scales of self-consciousness, self-monitoring, concern for appropriateness, shyness and sociability. Actors emerged as less shy and socially anxious than controls, and slightly more extravert and sociable. They were also more privately self-conscious and displayed greater sensitivity to the expressive behaviour of others than non-actors. Amateur actors were between non-actors and professionals on most of these attributes. There is little in these studies to support the highly negative (psychopathological) stereotype of actors 'discovered' by the psychoanalytic researchers. Hammond and Edelmann (1991a) did find that the psychoticism and neuroticism scores of actors were slightly higher than controls, but they were still well within normal (non-clinical) limits.

Empirical studies of musicians, singers and dancers are equally scarce. Kemp (1982) studied 688 student musicians and 202 professional musicians using Cattell's 16 PF test and reported that, compared with controls, both groups were inclined to be introverted (e.g. reserved, sober and self-sufficient) and anxious (emotionally unstable, apprehensive, tense). A tendency to emotional instability in musicians was also reported by Piparek (1981) who studied 24 members of the Vienna Symphony Orchestra. Using interviews and unspecified projective tests, he found that neuroticism scores were five per cent higher in musicians than other professions he had studied. Kemp (1980) compared the personalities of different instrumentalists, again using the 16 PF, in 625 music students aged 18 to 25. Brass players emerged as significantly more extroverted than other instrumentalists (more happy-go-lucky and group-dependent) and less sensitive (i.e. more tough-minded). Similar findings were reported by Davies (1978) who studied a Glasgow-based symphony orchestra using the Eysenck Personality Inventory. Brass players were the highest on extroversion and lowest on neuroticism, while string players were the highest on neuroticism. (However, females generally score higher on neuroticism than males, so the fact that there are more male brass players and female string players may partly account for the finding with respect to neuroticism).

Greater signs of psychological difficulty have been found for pop and jazz musicians. Using the EPQ, Wills and Cooper (1988) found neuroticism scores that were higher than any other professional group reported in the test manual (especially guitarists, with a mean of 16.90, and pianists at 14.72). Psychoticism scores also appeared quite high (especially guitarists at 4.90 and drummers 4.50). Wills and Cooper were unable to say whether their findings reflected the intrinsic personality of musicians or the stress of their occupation.

Ballet dancers also show signs of stress in their personality scores. Bakker (1988) studied ballet students aged between 11 and 16 years (all female), comparing them with non-dancing controls on a variety of standardized questionnaires. Dancers were lower in self-esteem than non-dancers, with a less favourable physical self-concept. They were also more introverted, anxious and achievement-oriented. These results were interpreted in terms of an interaction between self-selection on traits such as sensitivity and ambitiousness that would promote success in dancing and the stresses placed on young dancers by the exacting discipline that ballet requires. Since part of the dancer's job is giving expression to feelings, it was supposed that high emotionality would not necessarily be detrimental to performance; it might even be beneficial in some respects. The introversion of dancers could be connected with the fact that ballet is a solitary activity requiring a great deal of disciplined training. Other, more abandoned and sociable types of dancing are more likely to appeal to extroverts.

In a follow-up study two years later, Bakker (1991) tested the same group of ballet students to see whether their personality had changed as a result of their ballet education. He also looked for differences in personality between those who dropped out of ballet and those that continued on a professional career path. Results confirmed the dancers as more introverted, emotional, achievement-oriented and lower in self-esteem than controls, but there was little difference between those who continued and those that dropped ballet. Bakker therefore concluded that the personality traits typical of dancers are due primarily to self-selection. In other words, the ballet subculture attracts students of a particular personality type, even though selection and learning within that subculture might reinforce this stereotypic personality profile to some extent.

The most comprehensive study of the personality of performing artists to date is that of Marchant-Haycox and Wilson (1992). In order that different types of performers could be compared with each other as well as the general population, samples of actors, musicians, singers and dancers were tested with the Eysenck Personality Profiler, which provides a full spectrum of 21 personality traits. They also completed a checklist of psychosomatic problems so that levels of stress and the personality correlates of stress-proneness could be examined.

The expectation that different types of performer would be discriminable in personality was confirmed (Table 10.2). Although performing artists tended to be introvert and emotionally volatile as a group (compared with controls), this broad characterization obscures important differences among various categories of performing artist. Actors, for example, appeared relatively extravert and adventurous (being especially expressive, dogmatic, aggressive and irresponsible compared with controls). Dancers were the most emotionally unstable group (being particularly unhappy, anxious, hypochondriacal and lacking in self-esteem and autonomy). Musicians were relatively introvert and unadventurous, appearing resigned to the practicalities of a hard and unglamourous profession. Singers combined the

Table 10.2 Traits on which each type of performing artist gained the
most extreme score as regards difference from controls

Actors		Dancers		Musicians	
Expressive	1.01*	Unhappy	1.15	Inactive	.78
Reflective	.93	Anxious	1.04	Submissive	.73
Guilt-feelings	.83	Hypochondriacal	.90	(Unadventurous	.70)
Dogmatic	.68	Tenderminded	.82	Unambitious	.63
Aggressive	.66	Dependent	.76	Unsociable	.61
Irresponsible	.64	Inferiority feelings	.75	Empathic	.42
Impulsive	.45	Obsessive	.56	Controlled	.38
		Careful	.54		

Source: Marchant-Haycox and Wilson 1992

* z-score based on difference from control group divided by s.d. of control group
(i.e. actors were more than 1 s.d. higher in Expressiveness on average than
controls). Note: singers were between actors and the other two groups on all traits
except 'unadventurousness' (on which musicians were almost as high)

traits of the other three groups, as indeed their art draws upon those of the others
about equally.

Around one-third of actors, singers and dancers reported suffering from
performance anxiety at some time or another, and 47 per cent of musicians. All
groups of performers except actors suffered from shoulder-ache significantly more
than controls. Otherwise, there were no striking differences between performers
and controls, with the exception of depression, which seemed to afflict dancers
especially (47% reporting this symptom). Stress symptoms were predicted by
personality traits. For example, depression, panic and migraine were associated
with general emotionality (sometimes called 'neuroticism') and shoulder-ache went
with introversion. Perhaps not surprisingly, general adventurousness was associated with alcohol consumption and liver disease.

Marchant-Haycox and Wilson (1992) interpreted their results as reflecting
self-selection in choice of occupation combined with qualities required for survival
and advancement within the profession and reactions to the particular stresses
imposed by the performer's lifestyle.

SOURCES OF STRESS

Much of the stress exhibited by actors, singers, dancers and musicians is no
doubt related to the exacting, highly competitive nature of these professions. They
frequently have to work unsocial hours, are required to move about geographically

to stay in work, can seldom relax because they are under perpetual scrutiny from audiences, critics and producers, and are often poorly paid and treated by employers and public as itinerant vagabonds (Reciniello 1991). These professions are notoriously overcrowded; a high proportion of performers are out of work at any given moment and rejection at auditions is a frequent experience. This perpetual pressure is bound to engender a degree of insecurity (Phillips 1991).

In addition, there are several sources of direct physical stress. Shoulder-ache is no doubt connected with the 'overuse' syndrome, problems stemming from repetitive use of the same muscle groups during long hours of practice and performance that affect up to 50 per cent of instrumentalists (Fry 1986; Lockwood 1989) (see Table 10.3). Singers are constantly worried about contracting laryngitis or nodes on the vocal cord which may terminate their career. Dancers are entirely dependent upon their bodies as instruments and may have 'weight clauses' in their contracts that require perpetual dietary control (MacDonald 1991). Dietary restraint and the constant struggle to remain trim may well contribute to the high incidence of depression among dancers.

Table 10.3 Some of the typical overuse syndromes reported by Fry (1986)

Violinist's neck. Pain resulting from long hours of holding the instrument under the chin. Injuries to the muscles and tendons of the hand and forearm are also common in violinists.

Cellist's back. Low back pain associated with sitting with restricted movement for long periods.

Double bassist's spine. Backache is common in the early stages of a bass player's career. Usually controllable with spinal exercise and muscle building.

Clarinettist's and oboeist's thumb. Pain resulting from the load carried by the right thumb in playing.

Bassoonist's hands. Overuse injury due to constantly correcting the tilt and twist of the instrument upon its floor-spike.

Flautist's elbow. The right arm and spine are particularly susceptible in flautists and piccolo players.

Hornplayer's and trumpeter's hernia. A near blackout is often suffered on sustained high notes and the pressure aggravates conditions such as hernias and piles.

Percussionist's palsy. A relatively low risk group, but often suffer in neck, shoulder, hands and joints.

The musicians studied by Marchant-Haycox and Wilson (1992) were classical instrumentalists from orchestras such as the London Symphony, which might account for the somewhat introvert, workmanlike attitude that was found. Rather different patterns of personality and stress were observed in pop and jazz musicians by Wills and Cooper (1988). The sources of stress declared by more than 20 per cent of a sample of pop musicians are shown in Table 10.4. Problems concerned with travel, equipment, night work, fatigue, lack of adequate rehearsal, work overload or absence, and artistic and economic disputes with other people in the business are featured in this list. Given all these stressors it is not surprising that pop and jazz musicians showed elevated neuroticism and psychoticism scores and perceived themselves as highly stressed. Above average levels of 'Type A' (coronary prone) personality were found (especially among guitarists, pianists, keyboard players, vocalists and drummers).

Table 10.4 The major sources of stress reported by pop musicians

Stressor	% reporting as highly stressful
Feeling that you must reach or maintain the standards of musicianship that you set for yourself	51.3
Instruments or equipment not working properly	44.8
Having to read and play a difficult part at a recording session or gig	41.8
Worrying because of lack of gigs	38.6
Playing when there is inadequate rehearsal or preparation	38.2
Effects of noise when the music is heavily amplified	37.4
Endangering your life by having to drive a long distance after a gig when you are tired	33.3
Finding it difficult to get a good recording or management deal for your band or musical project	32.1
Having to sack a musician if you are a bandleader	30.5
Stress put upon personal relationships, e.g. marriage	30.5
Having to play after travelling a long distance	30.1
Feeling that you need to become better known and/or better paid	28.9
As an artist, coming into conflict with recording, management or agency executives who are involved in your career and who do not share your musical ideals	28.5
Doing recording sessions or rehearsals during the day, then having to do a gig at night	28.5
Waiting around for long periods at the gig before it's time to play	27.6
Waiting for payment to come through from a gig or session	27.2

Table 10.4 The major sources of stress reported by pop musicians (continued)

Stressor	% reporting as highly stressful
Getting musicians to deputize at short notice	27.2
Having to play music you don't like, in order to earn a living	26.4
Doing an audition	24.4
Playing at a venue with bad conditions	23.5
Feeling lonely or bored in strange towns or hotels when on tour	23.2
Doing a long tour	23.1
Feeling tense or nervous when playing in the recording studio as a session musician	22.8
Having to work when work is available, making it difficult to take holidays	22.7
Worrying about all the musicians getting to the gig on time	22.0
Worrying about the lack of pensions and benefits in the music profession	22.0
Coping with an instrument that is physically difficult to play	21.5
Feeling tense or nervous when playing a live gig as a session musician	21.5
Worrying that your ability to play will leave you	20.4
Feeling that your musical ability is not appreciated because of the public's ignorance about music	20.3

Source: Wills and Cooper 1988

Despite the reputation of rock musicians for living on drugs and many famous deaths in the industry attributed to that cause (Janis Joplin, Brian Jones, Jimi Hendrix, Sid Vicious, etc.), Wills and Cooper (1988) did not find that alcohol and drug-abuse were especially rife in their sample. Cannabis was used 'sometimes' or more by 30 per cent of the sample, cocaine by 11 per cent and amphetamines by 4 per cent. Few admitted to even trying heroin or LSD and alcohol consumption was roughly similar to that of the general population.

The main predictors of ill-health among pop musicians were performance anxiety and poor work conditions (interestingly, not Type A personality). Jazz musicians suffered particularly from performance-related anxiety as well as the feeling that the public did not understand their music. On the other hand, they also enjoyed their work more than other musicians and used coping methods such as yoga and relaxation more often. Rock musicians were more concerned about commercial success and conflict with others in the industry such as agents and recording executives. They were also more likely to abuse drink and drugs. Commercial session musicians were the best-paid and most secure group, while freelancers were more stressed and suffered poorer health. The authors concluded that music colleges should run more popular music courses including training in stress management and how to deal with the problems that arise in the pop music business.

THE COST OF SUCCESS

While it might seem that failure to pass auditions and get work as a performer would be most distressing, fame also has a price. One problem is lack of privacy. Famous people feel watched by the public all the time and the likelihood that any affairs they have will be reported in the media increases the probability of marital breakdown. Marriage difficulties are also likely to occur because there are always plenty of 'groupies' willing to have sex with stars for various motives, including the sale of 'kiss and tell' stories.

In Chapter 3 we discussed the obsessed fans who follow and sometimes attack famous actors and singers so they cannot be ignored by them any longer – some even wish to go down in history with them as their assassins. In 1982, the actress Theresa Saldana suffered a near-fatal stabbing by a man who later claimed that God wanted them united in heaven. And in 1988, a youth charged with the murder of his step-brother was found to have been stalking Olivia Newton-John, Sheena Easton and Cher. Though confined to a psychiatric institution he continued to write to them. Most fans are harmless but there are usually one or two who threaten a famous performer.

Wills and Cooper (1988) describe the punishing schedules that are often required of successful rock bands on tour. For example, in 1964 the Beatles toured Scandinavia, Holland, the Far East, Australasia and America. In America, they played in 23 cities (always large venues like sports stadiums) and travelled over 600 miles per day. Everywhere they were assailed by hordes of fans. At San Francisco they were driven straight from the plane into an iron cage for protection, which was crushed by the crowd shortly after they left it at their destination. This is just one incident that typifies the pressured life style of the high-profile performer. Riotous behaviour among audiences and media vilification campaigns are also common. Ill-health, drug abuse or even suicide may result. A study of 164 stars in the US who died between 1964 and 1983 found that suicide was four times more common in famous performers than among the general population (Hurley 1988).

Of course, sometimes the sudden loss of fame is responsible for mental problems rather than fame itself. Performers are often rocketed to stardom from a poor background but abandoned equally quickly by the fickle pop industry after they have become attuned to an expensive lifestyle. Singer Tiny Tim, who achieved brief stardom with a rendition of 'Tiptoe through the Tulips' said that when his fame declined everything fell apart, including his marriage, and people would taunt him in the street. 'If you lose your work,' he said, 'the only people who know are your friends and family. If I lose my work, the whole world knows' (Hurley 1988).

Field (1991) has characterized performers as frequently suffering from 'love addiction'. Although she is talking mainly about approval-seeking and insecure self-esteem, the sudden withdrawal of fame, with its painful and sometimes fatal consequences, might well be understood in such terms.

CHAPTER 11

STAGE FRIGHT AND OPTIMAL PERFORMANCE

Why dost thou not speak? queried one.
'Tis that people stare so, I replied.
It maketh my heart to flutter,
my breath to pant, and
my tongue to stutter.
'Twould be death to continue, I cried.

Nay, they said, thou be a fool.
Assuredly thou dramatize thy plight
Speak, and thou wilt find favour
In other's sight.
They lied... I died!

Lucinda Scott-Smith (1991)

This poem was written by one of my students in Reno to express her own experience of stage fright which in her case, took the form of an anxiety concerning speech-making that she felt impeded her career development. Most amateur performers feel some degree of anxiety, if not total panic, when called upon to appear in public, but professionals are far from immune. At the height of his fame, Laurence Olivier apparently suffered from almost incapacitating stage fright – during a run of Othello he was so terrified of his soliloquies that he asked another actor to stand just offstage so he would not 'feel so alone' – and Richard Burton shook and sweated before going on stage for *Equus*, fearing that he had 'lost the ability to command' (Aaron 1986). Stage fright is experienced to a greater or lesser extent by nearly half of all performers, and sometimes to a degree that threatens their career. The key elements of the condition are described in Lucinda Scott-Smith's poem. There is, typically, a feeling of being subject to scrutiny and likely to fail and an awareness of the adrenaline effects that accompany fear, including palpitation, rapid respiration, sweaty palms, dry mouth, stammering and inability to think clearly. Under what circumstances does performance anxiety arise and what can be done to cope with it?

OPTIMAL AROUSAL

The first thing to note is that anxiety is not always detrimental to performance. A certain degree of emotional arousal is usually beneficial to performance, and this even applies to levels of anxiety that seem uncomfortable and unwelcome to the performer himself. Studies in which professional musicians have performed under conditions calculated to evoke high emotional arousal show that their performance (as judged 'blind' from recordings by other expert musicians) is generally superior to an equivalent rendition under relaxed conditions (Hamann 1982). Apparently, it is a good thing, for professional musicians at least, to be a little 'keyed up' for performance – this is one of the reasons commercial recordings are often made in the presence of a live audience. Radio and TV presenters likewise know that live broadcasts carry a certain 'charge' that is not easily obtained with pre-recordings.

An empirical demonstration of the beneficial effect of anxiety on performance has been provided by Konijn (1991). She studied four Dutch amateur actors (two male and two female) as they rehearsed and performed a one hour play called *Bende*. Their heart rate was continuously monitored as they performed two rehearsals and three actual performances. Self-reports were obtained of the quality of each performance and the levels of stress experienced, and four expert judges (members of the theatre company hierarchy) rated them independently using the same questionnaires. Heart rate data showed that the presence of an audience greatly increased arousal in comparison to rehearsals (the averages for the first five minutes of the play being 141 bpm and 96 bpm respectively for the first performance and first dress rehearsal). Despite the striking differences in overall level, performance and rehearsal showed the same pattern of peaks and troughs. Heart rate began increasing in the wings before entry, rose rapidly when the actor came on stage and decreased almost as quickly after the exit. The high point was reached during actual performance of a lengthy monologue, rising to 180 bpm, which is more than twice the baseline. This high level of stress was confirmed by the self-ratings and expert ratings (Figure 11.1). Both agreed that signs of nervousness were much greater for performances than rehearsals. However, the *quality* of performance was also judged higher, both by the actors themselves and the external judges, when an audience was present. In fact, stress and quality seemed to be positively related; both were highest for the first actual performance and lowest during the second rehearsal (which took place between performances as a refresher). Self-reports supported the popular theatrical belief in a 'second night dip' (an anti-climax after the excitement of opening night). However, the experts rated the quality of the third performance, which occurred a month later, as almost as low as the second rehearsal.

Konijn's study provides an excellent demonstration of the fact that emotional arousal sometimes has positive effects upon performance. There is a long-established principle in psychology called the 'Yerkes-Dodson Law' (Duffy 1962), which states that motivation increases performance up to a point beyond which

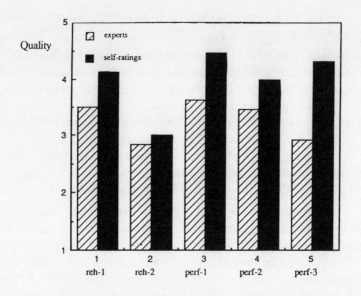

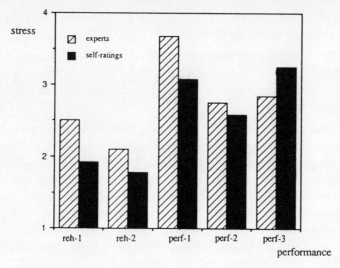

Source: Konijn 1991

Figure 11.1: Performance quality and degree of stress as rated by experts and actors themselves over two rehearsals and three performances of the same play

over-arousal leads to deterioration. The law further states that deterioration occurs more quickly when the task to be performed is complex or underlearned. Clearly, the more important a clear head is for performing a task effectively, the more anxiety is likely to interfere with it. In fact, there are probably three major groups of variables that need to be considered in understanding the circumstances in which arousal can go over the top:

1. The *trait anxiety* of the performer, i.e., his or her constitutional and learned tendency to become anxious in response to situations of social stress. This may reflect an overly reactive sympathetic nervous system, or low self-esteem, or some combination of the two. For whatever reason, some individuals are characteristically more sensitive than others to negative evaluation and fear of failure. Steptoe and Fidler (1987) have shown that performance anxiety relates to general neuroticism, but most particularly social phobias. Hence proneness to performance anxiety has a lot to do with fear of public humiliation.

2. The degree of *task mastery* that has been attained. A performance that is intrinsically simple, or one that has been so well prepared that it no longer presents any difficulties, is less susceptible to disruption due to over-anxiety than one that is complex or under-rehearsed. It has been demonstrated in many contexts that performance on simple, well-practised tasks is enhanced by stressful and arousing conditions, whereas complex, ill-prepared tasks are performed less efficiently under conditions of emotional stress.

3. The degree of *situational stress* that prevails. The point of over-optimal arousal is arrived at more quickly when social or environmental pressures are high (as in auditions, competitions or important public performances).

Whether or not anxiety will be detrimental to performance depends upon the interaction of these three groups of factors, in the manner depicted in Figure 11.2. Among the many inferences that can be made from this model are the following: highly anxious individuals will perform best when the work is easy and the situation relaxed, while performers low in anxiety will perform better when they are more challenged by the work and have a more exacting audience. By way of general advice, it follows that performers who are particularly prone to anxiety should choose easy pieces or works with which they are very familiar, at least for audition purposes or important public occasions. If the choice of work is outside the control of the performer, as very often is the case, then hard rehearsal can turn a difficult work into a relatively straightforward one.

The first thing the anxious performer should consider is whether their stage fright has a rational basis and is telling them something useful. Perhaps they have not prepared the work sufficiently and are justifiably afraid of mistakes and memory lapses. Perhaps they are out of their depth in having insufficient experience, skill or talent to attempt the work in question. Stage fright may occur as a result of the recognition by the performer, at some level of consciousness, that he has bitten off more than he can chew and is not really up to the mark. But that said, there are many cases in which talent and ability are not in doubt, but

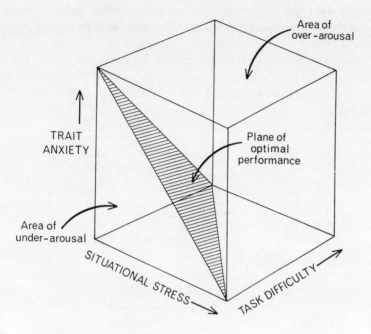

Source: Adapted from Wilson 1973

Figure 11.2: A three-dimensional extension of the Yerkes-Dodson Law, in which optimal performance is seen as a function of the interplay among three variables — trait anxiety, task difficulty and situational stress

still the performer is crippled by anxiety. When it matters most to perform well, these individuals are seriously hampered by visceral symptoms such as tremor, sweating, palpitation, 'butterflies' in the stomach, dry throat, even vomiting or incontinence. In cases of exceptionally high and unwarranted anxiety like this some kind of therapy will be necessary.

CATASTROPHE THEORY

Hardy and Parfitt (1991) have challenged the inverted-U hypothesis implied by the Yerkes-Dodson Law, suggesting that a 'catastrophe' model is more appropriate. Although they worked with athletic performance, the same arguments seem to apply to stage fright. According to catastrophe theory, once performers do go over the top in arousal the deterioration in performance is very large and dramatic rather than just a gradual tailing off. Once disaster is sensed in a high-stress competitive situation it is almost impossible to restore performance to even a mediocre level. Small reductions in stress will not push the performer back up to the top of the rainbow curve.

Hardy and Parfitt propose that the 'catastrophic' effect applies particularly to circumstances in which cognitive (mental) anxiety is high as well as somatic (bodily) agitation. If cognitive anxiety is low, they say, then the curve relating performance to physiological arousal follows the traditional Yerkes-Dodson inverted-U pattern. This theory is illustrated in Figure 11.3. Certain deductions from it were tested in the context of basketball goal-shooting performance and found to hold true.

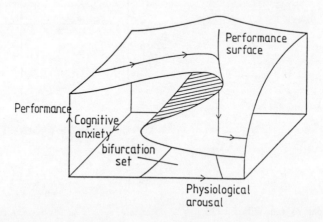

Source: Hardy and Parfitt 1991

Figure 11.3: A 'cusp catastrophe' model of the relationship between anxiety and performance. Performance is likely to fall apart completely when both mental and somatic anxiety are high

Somatic anxiety refers to bodily arousal that typically occurs in preparation for energy expenditure (e.g., increased heart rate) whereas mental anxiety refers to worries about whether the performance will be successful and fears of the social consequences of failure. It is clear why the latter is more likely to lead to the collapse of concentration and memory. Mental anxiety is likely to produce a vicious spiral whereby fear of failure becomes a self-fulfilling prophecy and early mistakes lead to an escalating pattern of distraction and worry. Relating this back to the three-dimensional model, mental anxiety could derive equally from individual proneness (trait anxiety), awareness that a work is complex or underprepared (task difficulty) and concerns about the consequences of failure (situational stress). Hence, Hardy and Parfitt's catastrophe model is not incompatible with an analysis based on the interaction of three stressor variables; rather it is an elaboration of it that makes much intuitive sense and certainly merits further research. The main point to note is that there are various types of anxiety and arousal and those that involve rumination concerning failure and embarrassment are more likely to be destructive to stage performance than agents such as coffee or exercise which stimulate bodily arousal.

THE TIMING OF ANXIETY PEAKS

Salmon *et al.* (1989) have drawn attention to the importance of when the peak of anxiety occurs in relation to the performance. They suggest that experienced performers learn to let their arousal peak sharply just *before* the performance whereas less experienced performers suffer anticipatory anxiety which builds over a long period of time and reaches its peak *during* the performance itself. This expectation was supported in a research study in which music students who were required to play before a 'jury' at the end of the semester rated their anxiety at various times leading up to the performance. As expected, there was a progressive build-up of anxiety as the time of the performance approached, but some students reached peak anxiety an hour before the performance while others were more anxious during the performance. Comparison of these two groups revealed that those who peaked during performance were less experienced and showed higher levels of anxiety at all phases (Figure 11.4).

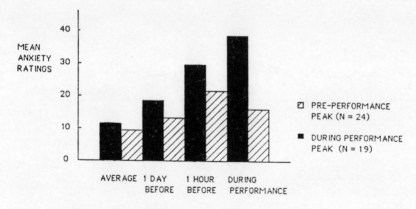

Source: Salmon *et al.* 1989

Figure 11.4: Levels of performance anxiety related to peak phase. Musicians whose peak anxiety occurred before the performance were more experienced and generally less anxious than those whose anxiety peaked during performance

The study by Salmon *et al.* replicates work with parachutists which found that seasoned jumpers also experience a peak of anxiety before the jump, whereas the novice is most frightened during it. Anxiety is not dispensed with entirely by the old campaigner, but displaced to a point in time where it may be useful for preparation rather than interfering with actual performance.

Apart from the timing of the anxiety peaks, there is probably also a change in their nature, with fearfulness giving way to a more adaptive focusing of attention and preparation for action. Figure 11.5 shows an EEG (brain wave) record obtained by telemetry from an orchestral horn player in the moments just before and during his solo. The graph moves upward (becomes electrically more negative) to reach a peak just before the solo begins, a pattern that is known to indicate a preparation in the brain for some kind of task performance – a kind of gathering of resources in expectation of a demand for response. If some kind of activity is anticipated the pattern is most obvious when recorded from the area of scalp above the 'motor' part of the cerebral cortex. Experiments show that performance is superior when preceded by these negative shifts in potential (Suter 1986) so it is clearly reflecting a useful kind of preparation. The changes observed by Salmon *et al.*, therefore, probably represent not just a shift in the timing of arousal with experience, but a change from anxiety toward focused attention.

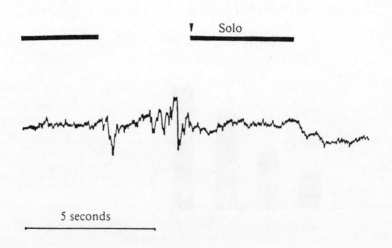

Source: Haider and Groll-Knapp 1981

Figure 11.5 The negative shift in brain potential immediately preceding a hornist's solo during an orchestral performance. This indicates mental preparation for accomplishing the task ahead

DRUG TREATMENT

What should be done when anxiety is clearly debilitating? Some performers attempt self-medication with 'anxiolytic' drugs such as alcohol, valium or marijuana. These drugs may get them through a performance, but they have side effects that are detrimental in the long run. Because they are general cerebral depressants, impeding all brain processes simultaneously, the 'fine edge' of a performance is lost and it may in fact become quite shabby. However, because these drugs also diminish judgement and induce a degree of mild euphoria, the performer himself is apt to believe that he did very well. Hence he acquires the superstitious habit of doping himself up with drink (or whatever) before every performance. The more he drinks the better he feels about his performance, although it is almost certainly getting worse as far as the audience is concerned. When he does try performing sober, he feels a great deal more exposed and anxious than usual, may suffer from state-dependent memory loss (Chapter 4), and whatever the quality of his performance, his discomfort reinforces the belief that he is better off on drink. Thus, a kind of dependence on the drug is established. As time goes by, the amount of drink needed to maintain the feeling of well-being increases, the quality of the performance is further reduced and memory lapses become a progressive problem. The spiral is insidious and, unless the performer can manage to break out of it in time, disastrous to a theatrical or musical career. Some of the same criticisms apply to the use of stimulants such as amphetamine and cocaine. While they may seem to give energy, euphoria and inspiration in the short term, they are habit-forming and ultimately destructive to general health (apart from usually being illegal). A cup of coffee may increase alertness, but even excessive amounts of caffeine cause a performer to become jittery, nervous and suffer from insomnia.

Although cerebral depressants and stimulants are not generally beneficial to performance, there are other drugs that may be helpful. A group of drugs known as *beta-blockers*, which selectively inhibit that part of the autonomic nervous system responsible for the visceral symptoms of anxiety (the adrenaline-based effects) without impairing the functioning of the central nervous system has quite frequently been prescribed to performers suffering from stage fright. A performer who is troubled by the bodily symptoms of anxiety, such as tremor, butterflies in the stomach or dry throat, may thus have this source of worry removed without any loss of mental alertness or memory. Controlled trials of beta-blockers such as *Propranalol* have shown them to be quite promising as a treatment for performance anxiety. Not only do musicians report feeling calmer before stressful public performances, and happier with their own playing, but external judges rate their performance as superior (James *et al.* 1977; James and Savage 1984). Around 20 per cent of orchestral musicians take beta-blockers as a matter of course before a performance, and an even higher proportion use them for special occasions such as auditions.

Against these indications of success for beta-blocking drugs in combatting stage fright must be put a long list of potentially harmful side-effects that require them to be controlled by prescription (e.g. nausea, tiredness, depression and sleep disturbance), certain ethical questions parallel to the doping of athletes and the general inconvenience of being dependent upon a chemical substance for emotional control. (The U.S. Food and Drug Administration has not approved the use of beta-blockers for performance anxiety.) It is therefore preferable in most respects to look to the psychological methods for coping with phobic anxiety.

DECONDITIONING OF ANXIETY

A method for treating phobias that has been used fairly successfully by clinical psychologists is called *implosion* or *flooding*. The idea is that unreasonable fears are maintained because the relief from anxiety that attends escape from the object of dread reinforces the irrational connection between fear and that object. Therefore, what is needed is continued exposure to the source of fear for long enough that reality is tested and the fear extinguishes. In the case of stage fright, this treatment might mean performing in front of an audience two or three times a day for several weeks. At the end of that time it is unlikely that any debilitating anxiety would remain.

If this is not practical, either because the opportunity is not available or because the client cannot be persuaded to 'take the bull by the horns', the technique of *systematic desensitization* may be tried. This begins with training in muscular relaxation by a semi-hypnotic procedure, though without suggestions of deep trance. Once the patient has learned how to relax, the phobic stimulus is introduced in gradual doses, usually by imagining approximations to the ultimate source of fear. The singer with performance anxiety may begin by imagining himself rendering 'Happy Birthday', along with several others at a warm and friendly family gathering. The stage-frightened actor may begin by imagining himself walking across the stage with only a couple of cleaners watching from the auditorium. Once it is established that the state of muscular relaxation can be maintained through these images, the next step up the 'fear hierarchy' is attempted, and so on until the ultimate horror (perhaps a booing and jeering audience at the Albert Hall) is confronted. Corny as this technique may sound in such brief outline, it has proved highly successful in practice (Allen *et al.* 1989).

PROGRESSIVE MUSCULAR RELAXATION

The relaxation technique most commonly used in connection with systematic desensitization was first described in 1929 by a physician called Jacobson. It consists of going through various parts of the body, one muscle group at a time, alternately tensing and then relaxing them. Usually, the procedure starts at the periphery (toes or fingers) and moves inwards towards larger muscles such as buttocks and shoulders. The idea is that through these exercises the individual becomes aware of muscle tensions and hence is better able to control them. Breathing exercises are also used, in which the client is asked to take deep breaths, hold them for a while and say 'relax' to themselves as they breath out. The idea is to train them to breath in a deep, slow, regular way and to associate this with the idea of mental relaxation. Once this technique has been acquired in ideal, quiet surrounds, the idea is then to work on transferring it to other more stressful situations such as driving a car or anticipating a public performance. That is where imagining scenarios that might induce stage fright comes in. Systematic desensitization amounts to rehearsing a relaxed response to situations that have evoked anxiety or panic in the past.

BIOFEEDBACK

A useful adjunct to either flooding or desensitization is the technology of *biofeedback* (mentioned already in Chapter 9). People learn to gain control of their autonomic processes much more quickly if they are supplied with immediate, graphic information concerning their progress. Mental relaxation, for example, is associated with a particular pattern of regular oscillations in the brain waves, called *alpha rhythm,* and this state can be achieved more efficiently if the subject is able to monitor the continuous electrical activity of his own brain on a video display. In learning how to produce alpha waves on the screen, it is hoped that the subject is simultaneously learning how to induce relaxation in himself, and there is some evidence that this skill can be carried over to other situations (such as waiting in the 'green room' for the show to commence).

Relaxation training programmes based on the biofeedback principle are now available for home computers. One very attractive package called *RelaxPlus* (Geake 1992) has a stress sensor in the form of finger electrodes monitoring electrical skin conductance and an infrared transmitter which alters the display on the computer screen. It begins with fish swimming forward when the subject relaxes or backwards when he gets tenser. As he relaxes, the fish turns into a mermaid, which then gets out of the water as a girl walking along a tropical beach. The girl then turns into an angel who flies into space. Ultimately, all that is left on the screen is a star and a congratulatory message. Alternatively, the biofeedback may be displayed as a straightforward graph. The programme also provides breathing and emotional exercises intended to help people learn to relax.

MEDITATION

Well before Western medicine became interested in stress self-control methods, the Eastern mystics had been using relaxation techniques that we call meditation. Typically, this involved adopting a passive yoga-like position and concentrating on a set word or saying (known as a *mantra*) designed to be uncomplicated and non-threatening. The belief is that this can slow down the body's functioning, reducing heart rate, blood pressure and respiration rate and metabolism. A Western adaptation of meditation is to sit quietly for 10–20 minutes each day repeating the word 'one' or its Eastern equivalent 'om' (Benson 1975). A set of instructions for a combined meditation/muscle relaxation programme is shown in Table 11.1. Quite a number of performing artists are known to favour such an approach to relaxation, especially just before an important appearance or concert.

Table 11.1 Six steps to relaxation as recommended by Benson (1975)

1. Get into your relaxed position and close your eyes.

2. Begin to concentrate on your breathing, and slow it down. Breathe through your nose, making your exhale longer than your inhale. You will notice a little tension associated with inhaling, and relaxation brought about by your exhaling. Concentrate on making exhaling feel as pleasurable as possible.

3. Pay attention to the position you are in, and feel each part of you being supported by the couch or bed so that you can relax your muscles further.

4. Begin searching your body for any signs of tension. Start at your feet and work your way up your body. As you find any tension, focus your attention on it, and as you exhale, try to relax it away.

5. Keep breathing slowly through your nose, and begin to think or say the word 'one' to yourself. Keep doing this for five to ten minutes. If you get distracted, go back and continue repeating it. After a few sessions you may want to substitute a word that is more conducive to relaxing such as 'calm'.

6. When you are ready to end your relaxation training session, open your eyes and sit up slowly. Take one or two more deep, slow breaths.

AUTOGENIC TRAINING

Another self-suggestion approach to relaxation that has gained some popularity in Europe and the US is called *autogenic training*. This was first described by a German neurologist called Johannes Schulz in 1932. Again it consists of a set of daily exercises intended to slow down the heart and switch off the body's alarm system. These range from focusing on feelings of heaviness in the limbs and breathing easily to imagining feelings of warmth in the limbs and upper abdomen and feelings of coolness in the forehead. As with meditation, standard phrases are repeated to oneself, but these are aimed at a more specific body reaction, for example, 'my hands are becoming warm' or 'my muscles are becoming heavier'. The therapeutic attitude is supposed to be permissive rather than intense and compulsive, and the mental state that is sought is described as one of 'passive concentration' (Suter 1986). As with other types of relaxation training, this method has found application in a variety of different settings. Business managers, athletes, astronauts and psychiatric patients have claimed benefit as well as performing artists (Groisman *et al.* 1990).

HYPNOTIC SUGGESTION

The most direct form of suggestion therapy is that which makes use of a deep hypnotic trance. This is induced through suggestions of heaviness of the limbs and eyelids, deep slow breathing, feelings of sleepiness and focusing attention on the voice of the hypnotist. In this state of heightened suggestibility instructions to relax may be particularly effective in reducing anxiety. However, other more positive and direct suggestions may also be useful to a performer such as telling them they are 'great performers'; that they 'can perform certain feats with ease' and that 'the audience love them'. Hypnosis then becomes an aid to implanting a form of positive self-talk or success imagery into the subconscious (Groisman *et al.* 1990).

Initially a hypnotist is needed for this procedure, but people can learn to develop auto-suggestion and tape-recorded sessions can be conducted in the home. Various tapes for relaxation training and self-hypnosis are commercially available, or they can be tailor-made for the particular goals of the client. The main limitation of hypnotism is that not everybody is a good hypnotic subject. Some people do not achieve the trance state easily and are inclined to be resistant to suggestion, so for them other, less mystical, methods are preferable.

AEROBIC EXERCISE

Recently there has been much interest in the psychological benefits of regular aerobic exercise. This is exercise sustained for at least half an hour in which the heart is made to race moderately. The ideal heart rate during exercise is said to be calculated as 60–75 per cent of the difference between your age and 220. Exercise of this kind (whether it is jogging, swimming or dancing) seems to be an antidote to anxiety and depression. Various explanations have been put forward to account for this, including the idea that exercise releases endorphins – naturally occuring opiates in the brain that reduce pain and give a feeling of well-being. It also appears that people who are fit are more resistant to psychological stress (Holmes and McGilley 1987). Add these benefits to the advantages of looking trim and attractive and it is clear why so many performers swear by physical fitness routines.

Sleep is equally important to fitness, health and ability to cope with stress. Late nights, especially with excessive drinking, make it a great deal more difficult to concentrate and remember lines and it is therefore important to have an early night before an important audition or performance. Sometimes going to bed for a few hours in the afternoon before an evening performance is beneficial, whether the time is spent in mental preparation or just snoozing.

ALEXANDER TECHNIQUE

A type of therapy that is particularly favoured by performers in Britain (though it is little known in the US or other countries) is called the *Alexander Technique*. This was named after an Australian actor called Fred Alexander who died in London in 1955, after seeking (and apparently finding) a solution to his own problem of voice loss under stress. Alexander believed that tensions were due to (or manifested as) unsatisfactory posture, especially the position of the head relative to the neck and back. He reckoned that, perhaps due to the failure of the instinctive control of body posture following the recent evolution of upright stance, many people develop patterns of habitual misuse. A common fault, which included Alexander's own, is said to be pulling the head back and down, as in a startle reaction, whilst performing simple acts like sitting down. However, faults are also idiosyncratic, so the programme of 'postural re-education' needs to be tailored to individual needs by one-to-one work with a specialist teacher.

The general aim of Alexander Technique is to retrain posture and movement in everyday activities such that 'uptight' feelings are removed and greater relaxation possible. This is achieved in therapy sessions by the teacher giving physical guidance as to ideal movements (e.g. holding the head in an appropriate position as the person stands up). The teacher also imparts suitable verbal cues which can be used by the client as helpful self-talk (e.g. 'direct the head forward and up', 'lengthen the back').

The importance of postural ease to actors, dancers, singers and musicians is clear (recall the various overuse syndromes described in Table 10.3). Around 20 per cent of British performers have Alexander lessons at some time in their career, making it the most widely used system of professional help. Empirical validation of the usefulness of the approach is so far limited (Valentine 1991). There is some physiological evidence that guided movements in which habitual posture adjustments of the head and neck are inhibited require less muscle activity and force and are quicker and smoother than before. There is also a Danish study which shows a 50 per cent reduction in pre-concert blood pressure in musicians using the Alexander Technique, supporting its claim as a stress reducer. Unfortunately, most of the studies have been done by committed Alexander teachers rather than independent scientists and they lack proper controls.

A recent exception is that reported by Valentine (1993) in which groups of music students with and without Alexander training were compared in various performance situations before and after Alexander lessons. Two of these were high-stress situations (audition and major recital) and two were low-stress (ordinary class performance). Physiological and self-assessment measures were taken, as well as video recordings which were subsequently rated for quality of performance by musicians and for postural quality ('use') by the Alexander teachers. The Alexander group showed an advantage on various measures, including overall musical and technical quality as rated by judges who were blind to treatment assignment, heart rate variability, anxiety, concentration and positive attitude to performance. However, these benefits were largely confined to the low-stress performance situation and did not transfer to the high-stress (recital) situation. Furthermore, these improvements were not related to postural use criteria as judged by Alexander teachers. Thus it appears that Alexander training produces some benefit to performers, though it is likely to be lost at the most critical junctures, and insofar as it is effective, it probably works through some mechanism other than postural improvement. One possibility is distraction from anxiety-evoking thoughts and destructive self-talk, similar to the basis of the meditation procedure.

COGNITIVE ORIENTATION

Wolverton and Salmon (1991) point out that we have a limited amount of attention to allocate in any situation and where it goes may be critical to the quality of a performance. In music there are three main possibilities:

1. The *self*. How am I looking? Am I playing to the level of my own expectations?

2. The *audience*. How are they reacting? Are they impressed or are they showing signs of boredom or dislike?

3. The *music*. Absorption in its technical intricacies, overall shape, or the emotions that it evokes.

A similar kind of breakdown would apply to acting and other forms of performance.

Not surprisingly, Wolverton and Salmon found that absorption in the artistic work itself was associated with the lowest levels of anxiety. Almost certainly this would also go with optimal performance. Hence cognitive therapy aimed at persuading performers to focus attention on the artistic effect itself rather than the self or the audience reactions is likely to be helpful in cases where this is found to be a problem.

Steptoe and Fidler (1987) asked orchestral musicians what was going on in their head just prior to performance. Two groups of self-statements emerged as most interesting. One was called *catastrophizing* (e.g. 'I think I am going to faint', 'I don't think I will be able to get through to the end without cracking up', 'I'm almost sure to make a dreadful mistake, and that will ruin everything'.) The other was called *realistic appraisal* ('I'm bound to make a few mistakes, but so does everyone', 'The audience wants me to play well and will make allowances for any slips', 'I'll concentrate on technical aspects of the music and the interpretation I've prepared'). Catastrophizing was most clearly related to performance anxiety; individuals with stage fright being inclined to exaggerate the imagined consequences of minor mishaps and to fear complete loss of control. Realistic appraisal was interesting because it showed a curvilinear relationship with performance anxiety, being used most by those with moderate (optimal?) levels of anxiety. Statements in this category, which includes recognition of the likelihood of some mistakes being made together with a positive attitude toward the audience, may be the most adaptive.

STRESS INOCULATION

Developing realistic expectations about performance is the basis of stress inoculation training as an approach to dealing with anxiety (Meichenbaum 1985). The idea is that performers can be taught to expect and make constructive use of the symptoms of anxiety that are bound to occur before an appearance. In this way, anxiety cues are 'reframed' as less threatening, even desirable, reactions.

One danger of catastrophizing is that the performer may react with repression and denial, avoiding anything associated with the performance, including practice. Stress inoculation training is aimed at helping the performer recognize anxiety as a signal that something has to be attended to in a positive kind of way, by making appropriate preparations (Salmon 1991). At the same time, the performer is taught to re-appraise the adrenaline effects (pounding heart, sweating, shallow breathing, etc.) as perfectly normal reactions that are not conspicuous to the audience and which can contribute to a more lively, exciting interpretation. The procedure of desensitization mentioned above (gradual exposure combined with relaxation) can also be used to habituate the performer to their own body symptoms so they are experienced as less distressing.

SELF-TALK

Many of the methods described above share the component of delivering verbal cues to oneself that prepare the mind and emotions for optimum performance. Indeed, self-talk is used by many performers to 'psyche themselves up' while others seem to specialize in 'talking themselves down'. The crippling effect of negative self-talk is well recognized. Lloyd-Elliot (1991) discusses internal voices as 'demons' prompting us to destruction on important occasions such as auditions. These demons often date from childhood when somebody made a particularly ego-insulting comment. For example, a mother turns to her five-year-old whose father is bedridden and says, 'Don't sing dear, it makes your father sick'. A drama teacher is overheard talking to her colleagues: 'The poor girl is hopeless, can't project to save her life; and her interpretation is terrible'. A music teacher says quite viciously, 'Mark, have you ever thought that chemistry might suit you better than the clarinet?'. Hurtful comments like these may be imprinted for life and return to haunt the insecure performer whenever they feel under scrutiny.

In the terminology of transactional analysis, we sometimes generate our own 'critical parent' scripts. On making one mistake in a Shakespeare recital, a young student instantly switched on an internal tape saying 'If you can't remember that, you might as well give up'. A member of an audition panel frowns and the actress says to herself, 'They hate my face. I might as well walk out'. Lloyd-Elliot goes further and suggests that some performers answer their 'critical parent' with a 'rebellious child' and deliberately sabotage their own performance just to 'get back'. There can be little doubt that 'inner games' of this kind do go on, and they can interfere greatly with performance (Green 1986).

However, if self-talk can be so destructive, it should be possible to harness it for positive purposes. This means using affirmations like 'I am a talented singer' or more detailed directives like 'I love the audience and they will love me', 'Relax and concentrate on enjoying the music as you play it'. It may be necessary to watch out for negative self-talk during performance and be ready to replace it with pre-rehearsed positive phrases (Kubistant 1986). Many performers find it useful to deliver motivational scripts to themselves before and during performance, but clearly the method does not work for everybody. Beach (1977) describes the case of the cellist Piatigovsky who suffered from pre-performance nerves and told a friend 'Before a concert, I say to myself, 'Grischa, don't be nervous, You are the great Piatigovsky!' The friend asked, 'And does it help?'. 'No. I don't believe myself'.

GOAL IMAGING

Rather than use self-talk some performers adopt visual imagery depicting perfect accomplishment. This may involve imagining that they are Olivier playing the part, Ashkenazy seated at the piano or Pavarotti singing the role rather than themselves. Grandiose fantasies of this kind may be employed more often than some performers are prepared to admit, and there is reason to think they might sometimes be successful. Some people who have demonstrated little talent as performers in the past have turned in quite impressive performances when told under hypnosis that they are highly accomplished, famous artists.

A method of training that has proved successful in athletics is that of *mental rehearsal* (Suter 1986). Usually, progressive muscle relaxation is first induced and then the athlete is asked to conjure vivid, detailed pictures of correctly executed movements (e.g. putting darts in a bulls-eye, scoring basketball goals or performing figure-skating routines). Subsequent testing of skills reveals improvement due to the imagery alone, without actual physical practice. This technique is most effective for skills that involve an important mental component and long, complex sequences of movements (Feltz and Landers 1983). Playing the piano or another musical instrument, or performing a play would seem to fit this description very well.

Positive self-talk and goal imaging have something in common that is probably essential to their efficacy. They direct attention to the outcome one is seeking, as opposed to distracting thoughts regarding the things that might go wrong and the unpleasant consequences that would ensue. Probably the most important thing about mental rehearsal, whether it be verbal or visual, is that it be *optimistic* (Seligman 1989). Those who envisage success, whether it be in sport, business, or on stage are more likely to perform at their best. The trick is to 'picture it perfect'.

SELF-HANDICAPPING

A potentially harmful strategy that 'hedges bets' concerning the outcome has been identified by Jones and Berglas (1978). In many competitive contexts some people seem so afraid of losing self-esteem that they set up excuses for failure in advance. For example, they deliberately have a late night before an exam, or drink alcohol before a musical performance so that they can say to others and themselves in the event of failure, 'I would have done better if it wasn't for this, that or the other'. The danger, of course, is that they increase the chances of needing an excuse.

Many performers enjoy taking over a part or gig at short notice (e.g. due to the illness of another performer) because this absolves them of responsibility. If they succeed they are the hero that stepped in and saved the day; if they fail it is because they had insufficient time to prepare. Some have a reputation for always giving themselves excuses in advance, 'I have a sore throat at the moment', 'I've never seen this music before', 'The director is forcing me into a characterization that doesn't suit me'. It is easy to see how such excuses can approximate to negative self-talk and become self-fulfilling prophecies of failure. The next step in this process is to sabotage one's own performance by actual self-handicapping, such as failing to attend rehearsals, damaging one's instrument or getting drunk beforehand. Susceptible individuals should watch for signs of this in themselves and try to replace them with some of the positive strategies above.

A CHECKLIST FOR PERFORMERS SUFFERING STAGE FRIGHT

Much of what has been said above can be summarized in the series of steps offered below for performers who are concerned about their own level of performance anxiety.

1. Ask yourself if the tension you are feeling is definitely detrimental to your forthcoming performance? Remember that a certain degree of arousal helps give 'spark' to a performance even though it might seem uncomfortable to the performer. Remind yourself that the symptoms of bodily arousal are perfectly normal and not noticeable to an audience.

2. If your anxiety is definitely 'over the top', ask yourself if it is telling you something about your readiness for the assignment in hand. Should you find some way of reducing the pressure, for example choosing an easier work, sharing the concert platform with other performers, or doing more rehearsal. Don't let the anxiety lead you to avoid thinking about what needs to be done to improve it – thorough preparation may largely solve the problem.

3. If after that you still think the anxiety is unreasonable then consider how best to manage it. Drugs are very much a desperation measure and should be used only as a 'stop-gap' until psychological coping methods

can be learned. Remember that the use of drugs often sets back the development of self-mastery.

4. Which psychological approach is best depends upon the individual performer and the nature of their problem. If you are generally over-reactive to stress, then some of the all-purpose relaxation techniques such as biofeedback, meditation, autogenic training, hypnosis, aerobics and progressive muscular relaxation may be useful. Ultimately, however, it will probably be necessary to confront the performance situation itself with methods such as desensitization, flooding, stress inoculation, positive self-talk, and goal imaging. Any of these can be undertaken either through self-study or with the help of a professional counsellor.

5. The most effective cognitive strategies seem to be those that: (a) prepare the performer to accept a degree of tension and minor mishaps as par for the course; (b) focus on the process and personal enjoyment of the performance rather than audience evaluation of it; and (c) use positive, optimistic self-talk and visual imagery rather than self-doubt or catastrophizing.

CHAPTER 12

THERAPEUTIC USE OF PERFORMING ARTS

There is a sense in which all theatrical experience may be therapeutic. It provides 'catharsis', the opportunity to feel and express profound passions like fear, grief, love and triumph in a safe setting, which is precisely what is claimed of psychotherapy. The cathartic value of drama has been extolled since the days of ancient Greece (Chapter 1). Dance, as we have seen (Chapter 6), is an artistic form of body expression and the power of music to move us emotionally is undoubted (Chapter 8). It is no surprise, therefore, that various attempts have been made to harness the psychological value of drama, dance and music within clinical settings. This chapter outlines the theory and practice of some of these approaches.

Unfortunately, little in the way of objective evaluation is available. As with most schools of psychotherapy, advocates of these techniques usually take their value as granted and do not seek to scrutinize them scientifically. In fact, their objectives are often so esoteric (abreaction, personal growth, insight, etc.) that it is difficult to imagine what sort of evidence could be used to support or refute them. Nevertheless, these therapies are popular and interesting and hence worthy of discussion.

WAGNER AND PSYCHOANALYSIS

Wagner, above all composers of his time, was deliberately trying to evoke Greek-style catharsis in his audiences. All the innovations that he introduced at Bayreuth were to this end, including the return to an amphitheatre seating arrangement, shutting the doors and darkening the auditorium during performance, hiding the orchestra in a pit below the stage, the parting (as opposed to descending) curtain and the use of magic lanterns to create visual effects. Everything was geared to 'hypnotising' the audience – transporting them to a fantastic, fairy-tale world that derives from the unconscious. The settings, the characters, their conflicts and their ecstacies are typically infantile and ancestral, like the dreams, myths and symbols that Freud and Jung later claimed were fundamental to human psychology and neurosis.

In fact, through his prose writings as well as his operas, Wagner was probably a major influence on both Freud and Jung. Two of Wagner's most interesting works, *Opera and Drama* and *A Communication to my Friends*, coming half a century before the prime of psychoanalysis, precede many of the central 'discoveries' of the analysts (Wilson 1982). That is not to say they were necessarily original to Wagner, for he in turn borrowed much from German philosophers such as Schopenhauer, but the fact remains that much of what we think of as twentieth century psychoanalytic thought was understood and discussed by Wagner. His personal death wish, and belief in its universal existence, embodied in several of his operas (notably *The Flying Dutchman* and *Tristan and Isolde*) was mentioned in Chapter 1; Here I shall concentrate on two prime examples of Wagner's 'psychoanalytic thinking' – the Oedipus complex and the collective unconscious. (References are to the W.A. Ellis 1893 translation of Wagner's prose works.)

THE OEDIPUS COMPLEX

The notion of the Oedipus complex is one of the most celebrated of Freud's contributions and there have been many speculations about the source of his inspiration. Oliver Gillie (*Sunday Times*, 3rd January 1982) makes a case that Freud had a long-term affair with his sister-in-law Minna. Since this would be deemed incest under Judaic law, it may have helped to persuade Freud that humans were naturally incestuous.

In fact, Freud was wrong about incest being a universal human tendency. The truth is nearer the reverse; all higher animals display incest *avoidance*, the evolutionary function being that this reduces the likelihood of harmful inbreeding (Bixler 1981). However, the mechanism of incest avoidance appears to be simple *exposure* to the family with the result that 'familiarity breeds contempt' (Pusey 1990), so it does not apply to family members who have not grown up together (as was the case with Oedipus and Jocasta). Since there is evidence that physical characteristics of the opposite-sex parent partly determine sexual preferences in adulthood (presumably as a result of sensory imprinting in early childhood) powerful attraction to close relatives is quite likely provided that upbringing has been separate. Testimony to this is seen in the many instances of sexual attraction in reunited family members, for example the case in Tennessee in which a 43-year-old woman discovered that she had married her own son whom she had given up for adoption as a baby (*The Times*, 12th September 1984).

Several decades earlier than Freud, Wagner seems to have had a clearer grasp of these dynamics. He was intrigued by the Oedipus legend, believing it to hold the key to much of human psychology: 'Today we need only expound faithfully on the myth of Oedipus according to its inmost essence, and we in it win an intelligible picture of the whole history of mankind...' (p.91). His most thoroughly developed operatic treatment of the incest theme is found in the meeting of Siegmund and Sieglinde in Act I of *The Valkyrie* in which brother and sister are instinctively drawn to one another and fall passionately in love before realizing that they are twins separated in infancy. The idea that their love at first sight stems from childhood imprinting is strongly implied by the musical and poetic treatment of their fast-developing interest in each other. Sieglinde even associates Siegfried with her memory of their father Wotan, who had recently visited her in the guise of 'The Wanderer'.

> SIEGLINDE: A marvel stirs in my memory;
> although you came but today,
> I've seen your face before!

> SIEGMUND: I know your dream,
> and feel it too:
> in ardent yearning
> you were my dream.

> SIEGLINDE: The stream has shown my reflected face –
> and now I find it before me;
> in you I see it again,
> just as it shone from the stream!

> SIEGMUND: You are the dream
> that I felt in my heart

> SIEGLINDE: Be still! Again
> that voice is sounding,
> the voice which I heard
> once as a child –
> But no! I know where I heard it:
> when through the woods I called
> and echo called in reply

> SIEGMUND: Oh loveliest music
> voice that I longed for!

> SIEGLINDE: And your gleaming glance
> I've seen it before.
> The stranger in grey
> gazed on me thus
> when he came to console my grief
> By his glance
> his child knew him well –
> I knew by what name I should call him.

> (*The Valkyrie*, Act I Scene 2, Andrew Porter trans.)

On the discovery of their social transgression, Siegmund and Sieglinde are not racked with guilt and remorse as was Oedipus. Rather they seem further convinced that their love is natural and not to be denied. Such is the power of Wagner's music and poetry that the audience is equally persuaded that the sexual consummation of their passion is wholly justified. Objectively viewed, a stranger has stumbled upon Hunding's stable domestic scene seeking shelter from a storm, enjoyed his hospitality and stolen his wife, committing incest with his sister into the bargain. And yet all this, in context, is made to seem right and proper because it is spontaneous and powered by instinctual forces that transcend the rules of men. This is the reason so many people fear an antisocial component to Wagner; like psychoanalysis, he appears to preach the priority of passion over convention.

'Oedipal' references are found in two other Wagner operas, *Siegfried* and *Parsifal*. In each case an innocent hero encounters a woman for the first time, awakens her with a kiss, confuses the emotions of sex and fear and is reminded of his mother for whom he passionately longs. Apparently, Wagner regarded this transfer of infantile attachment to the mother to adult heterosexuality as an important element of human psychology and was insightful enough to see that it would be particularly manifest if mother and child were separated early in life. The difficulty that his heroes have in distinguishing the passions of love and fear when confronted with female sexuality could be interpreted either as Oedipal guilt or the foreshadowing of an important principle in 'attribution theory' (Chapter 3). Emotional arousal is so non-specific as regards its physiological basis that it can readily be misidentified in a manner consistent with our expectations.

THE COLLECTIVE UNCONSCIOUS AND ARCHETYPES

The idea that man's most powerful instincts and emotions predate his own evolution is explicit in much of Wagner's writing and the notion of a collective unconscious is also well developed both in his operas and his explanation of them. 'This *Lohengrin* is no mere outcome of Christian meditation... Not one of the most affecting, most distinctive Christian myths belongs by right of generation to the Christian spirit such as we commonly understand it; it has inherited them all from the purely human intuitions of earlier times, and merely moulded them to fit its own particular tenets. [These yearnings come] from the truest depths of universal human nature' (p.261).

Most of Wagner's characters are archetypes in the Jungian sense of the term; he is quite explicit about this, and the actual word 'archetype' is used (p.165): 'The figure of the Flying Dutchman is a mythical creation of the folk: a primal trait of human nature speaks out from it with heart-enthralling force. This trait in its most universal meaning is the longing after rest from amid the storms of life.' The Devil who lays the curse upon the Dutchman is 'obviously the element of flood and storm' and Senta is the 'quintessence of womankind, as yet still unmanifest, the longed for, the dreamed of, the infinitely womanly woman' (p.307). Wagner was clear that the Dutchman's yearnings emanated from deep within his own subconscious. 'It was bidden me by my inner mood, and forced upon me by the pressing need to impart this mood to others... That which drives a man hereto is necessity, deeply felt, unrecognizable by the practical reason...' (p.307).

About Siegfried he wrote: 'What here I saw, was no longer the figure of conventional history, whose garment claims our interest more than does the actual shape inside; but the real naked man, in whom I might spy each throbbing of his pulses, each stir within his mighty muscles, in uncramped, freest motion; the type of true *human being* (p.264, italics Wagner's). It takes little imagination to interpret the symbolic significance of Siegfried's first encounter with Brunhilde in which he breaks open her armour with his sword, which is called 'Nothung' (needful).

Although the contribution of Jung in assembling and discussing a great variety of different archetypal themes cannot be denied, the importance of myths and dreams as revelations of the collective unconscious and the notion of archetypal characters and symbols were well understood by Wagner much earlier.

Other similarities between the thinking of Wagner and that of Freud and Jung could be noted, but enough has been said to suggest that the two major figures in the psychoanalytic movement may well have derived some of their most celebrated ideas from the composer. Freud and Jung scarcely mention Wagner in their writings, and when they do it is usually in some peripheral context. Freud, in particular, avoids reference to Wagner's prose works to an extent that might be thought deliberate (if indeed he had read them, which seems probable considering that most European intellectuals of the day did so). In a letter to Wilhelm Fliess he notes in passing having attended a performance of *The Mastersingers of Nuremberg* and being impressed by the way feelings and ideas were integrated, but nowhere does he acknowledge Wagner as a source of psychoanalytic inspiration.

Jung shows himself to be aware of the *Ring Cycle*, but proceeds to analyse it as though Wagner was unaware of his own intentions in constructing it. Wotan is interpreted as the embodiment of the spirit rife within the German people which predisposed them to Nazism. But Jung, too, chooses to ignore the fact that Wagner's operas were explicitly derived from theoretical formulations about the human mind remarkably prescient of his own. Perhaps one of the reasons why Wagner is not recognized as the father of psychoanalysis is that the twentieth century leaders of the movement neglected to register their considerable debt.

Like Freud, Wagner identified life's central problem as the conflict between individual, instinctual needs and the internalized representations of society that we call conscience. What Wagner called 'nature-necessity', Freud called the id and Wagner's 'physical life bent' is much like *libido*. There are frequent references to repression as the basis of neurosis in Wagner's writing (e.g. p.179) and the explicit aim of his operas was 'to bring the unconscious part of human nature to consciousness within society' (p.193). In line with modern psychoanalysts and 'ego theorists', Wagner maintained that consciousness only arises out of social interaction (p.195–196). The idea that dreams reveal the unconscious mind also appears in several places (e.g. p.181).

Magee (1969) notes that Wagner uses the orchestra to express primitive unconscious feelings, while the singer's voice plays a kind of ego role, attempting to reconcile these urges with situational demands. Wagner himself stated this explicitly:

> 'In the instruments the primal organs of creation and nature are represented. What they articulate can never clearly be determined or stipulated because they render primal feeling itself, emergent from the chaos of the first creation, when there may even have been no human beings to take it into their hearts. The particular genius of the human voice is quite different from this. It represents the human heart and all its delimitable, individual emotion... The thing to do now is bring the two elements together – make them one. Set the clear, specific emotion of the human heart represented by the voice, against the wild primal feelings, with their ungovernable urge towards infinitude, represented by the instruments; it will appease and smooth the violence of these feelings and channel their cross-currents into a single, definite course. Meanwhile the human heart itself, insofar as it absorbs the primal feelings, will be infinitely enlarged and strengthened, and become capable of experiencing with godlike awareness what previously had been a mere inkling of higher things.' (Wagner, 1851, quoted in Magee, p.67)

It seems, then, that Wagner was claiming for his operas much the same benefits as Freud claimed for psychoanalysis, the power to expand people's consciousness to include an appreciation of the primitive, instinctual urges that previously were suppressed in lower recesses of the mind. Wagner could therefore be regarded as something of a group therapist, in that he attempted to treat the whole of society, or at least an entire audience simultaneously by a Greek-style emotional catharsis. What Freud and Jung seem to have done is transfer the ideas of Wagner from the theatrical context to the psychiatric clinic.

PSYCHODRAMA

A similar kind of evolution can be seen in the psychodrama of J.L. Moreno (1959, 1964, 1969) – a method of psychotherapy, conducted in group form, that uses theatrical role-playing as a means of exploring patients' problems, conflicts, motives and fantasies.

Psychodrama began in Vienna in the early 1920s with Moreno's experiments in improvisation which he called the 'theatre of spontaneity'. At this stage he was concerned not with the actor's private problems but with introducing greater realism and 'relevance' into the theatre through warm-up techniques and im-promptu reactions. One such technique was called the 'living newspaper'. A topical event, such as a student uprising, would be described to the players who would then act out the roles and situation before an audience. However, Moreno discovered that those who were best at improvisation gravitated towards traditional theatre and movies leaving him with lesser talent. At the same time he realized that audiences were generally suspicious and resistant to this kind of theatre, so he decided to adapt his methods for therapeutic purposes with non-specialist actors.

The idea for this method of psychotherapy stems from a convergence of several concepts with which Moreno would have been familiar: (1) the classical Greek goal of 'catharsis'; (2) Wagner's exploration of the unconscious through opera; (3) the Freudian pursuit of abreaction through 'free association'; and (4) Stanislavski's stress on 'emotional memory'. Moreno pointed out that psychodrama goes beyond 'couch therapy' by plunging the individual directly into the emotional reality of his problem rather than have him simply talk about it in a dispassionate way. Ambivalence towards one's father, for example, would not just be discussed, it would be acted out with the help of others. This method of reliving experience he believed to be more vivid and intense, so there ought to be a better chance of releasing tension or learning to cope with it.

Because of its theatrical origins, psychodrama has a jargon drawn from the stage. The patient is called the 'protagonist', other members of the group who play the role of significant others in the life of the patient (or other aspects of the patient himself) are called 'auxiliary egos', and the therapist is called the 'director'. Each member of the group chooses a time when he feels ready to have his personal drama played out on stage with the assistance of the director and other group members who function as supporting cast (auxiliaries) and audience. The protagonist is encouraged to move about the stage, improvise lines, and act out episodes relating to his childhood experience or current situation that are regarded by himself or the director as central to his difficulty. As in psychoanalysis, the hope is that, through emotional catharsis and gains in insight, the patient will become better adapted to cope with his emotions and day-to-day problems. Group members are supposed to gain understanding not just by airing their own problems, but by helping other people come to grips with theirs. Although one patient (the protagonist) is the focus of attention at any one time, all group members are involved either as auxiliary egos in the drama or as audience, and are supposed to benefit indirectly from the protagonist's 'agonizing'.

Psychodrama is said to proceed through three main phases (Greenberg 1974):

1. The *warm-up*, consisting of a gradual increase in physical movement, spontaneity and group rapport and the focusing of attention toward a specific idea or goal. The director may achieve this through a variety of methods ranging from general discussion and intimate revelations to physical games and activities.

2. The *action*, which comes out of a discussion of a particular person's situation. This protagonist, with the co-ordination of the director, sets the scene on stage and selects auxiliary egos for the performance. The director then supervises the enactment, manipulating the degree of

emotional involvement so that the protagonist is challenged without being overwhelmed, and changing the scenes as new insights emerge. At the same time, he tries to remain aware of the audience mood so that all group members participate in some way, however indirectly.

3. *Closure* or *sharing* follows the action, the director leading a group discussion in which he seeks to ensure that maximum insight is gained by all. This is supposed not to be an intellectual exercise, but one in which other group members 'share with the protagonist their emotional reactions to the drama'. Some cathartic release is expected to occur at this time as well as during the action.

PSYCHODRAMATIC TECHNIQUES

There are a number of specific methods that may be adopted within the course of psychodramatic therapy. Those described below are culled from Moreno's own writing as well as reviews by Blatner (1973), Starr (1977 1979) and Gold (1991).

The double

This technique involves using an auxiliary ego to play the specialized role of the patient's 'alter ego' or inner self – a kind of Jiminy Cricket who speaks in the first person singular to express the protagonist's deeper thoughts and feelings. If the protagonist is caught in cross-fire between two or more 'inner voices' (aspects of his personality), then more than one alter ego may be called upon. The various doubles can verbalize different sides of the conflict, in order to help the protagonist to see the issues more clearly. It is like deliberately splitting the patient's personality along the lines of id, ego and superego (or some other appropriate division), so that conflicting pressures can be brought more quickly to the surface and effective decisions for future behaviour arrived at.

Sometimes a double may be assigned to other participants in the drama, such as an auxiliary father figure, or the director. Even the audience may be given a double. For example, if the psychodrama has become 'bogged down' in over-intellectualized verbosity, the audience double may stand behind some group member and announce: 'I am getting bored... I want Mary to reach out', the hope being that this would catalyze a reaction which would further the action of the drama.

Mirroring

One special use of the double is to provide a kind of feedback to the protagonist by reflecting his postures, gestures and expressions, or mimicking his spoken comments or voice tones. According to Moreno and his followers, this can be a useful means of provoking constructive aggression and change, though it is also potentially cruel and needs to be handled judiciously.

The soliloquy

In the technique of soliloquy, the action of the drama is held static for a period while the protagonist discloses his normally private thoughts and feelings to the audience and other players. He turns his head out in the manner of an aside, and in a different, more whispered, tone of voice, expresses his inner feelings with respect to the ongoing action. This is said to be helpful in communicating feelings that are aroused by certain events which would not otherwise be observable. A variation on this technique is called 'walk and talk' in which the director leads the protagonist away from the action, which remains 'frozen', in order to explore his feelings more deeply.

The monologue

The monologue is an extended soliloquy in which the protagonist assumes the roles of all the other players, shifting his position around the stage accordingly. This amounts to a self-directed one-man show, and may be preferable for patients who find the spontaneity of auxiliary egos too disturbing, or who insist on having their scenario ritualistically replayed exactly as they remember it from the original experience.

Role reversal

Another technique sometimes used in psychodrama is that of exchanging the roles of people at crucial interludes. For example, a husband may be required to take over the role of his wife, while the auxiliary previously playing his wife assumes his position, or a son may suddenly have to 'step into the shoes' of his mother. The presumed benefit of this procedure is that the protagonist is brought to see the point of view of significant others in his life, the hope being that this insight might lead to productive changes of attitude and behaviour. In effect, it is an empathy training procedure, providing patients with a better appreciation of other people's position.

Another reason for employing role-reversal may be to by-pass a 'block' in the psychodrama that is due to an auxiliary ego misrepresenting a significant other. By temporarily taking over that role himself, the protagonist can make an appropriate correction with minimal disruption to the psychodrama. Role reversal can also be used by a protagonist to demonstrate how he *wants* to be treated by the other person, thus pointing to a possible resolution of the conflict.

The behind-the-back technique

Related to role-reversal is the procedure of having the protagonist turn his back and 'overhear' what the others are saying about him when he is not present. If he is not overwhelmed with anger or ego-threat this may also give insight into the perspective of other people. It may be a powerful way of discovering one's good and bad points as seen by others, a way of rousing an inhibited patient toward a cathartic expression of retaliatory emotion, or a means of learning to cope with 'paranoid' fears about what other people might be saying.

Other techniques

Among other role-playing methods that are sometimes used for special purposes in psychodrama are: *dream and hallucination presentation* (acting out central fantasies so they are more graphically communicated to others than by simply describing them); *future projection* (in which the patient portrays in dramatic form what he thinks the future holds for him); *hypnodrama* (similar to the nightclub entertainment routines); and *psychodramatic shock* (the deliberate recall of painful memories in the hope of exorcising their disruptive effect upon the personality).

The diffuse aims of psychodrama make it difficult to assess its effectiveness by empirical means. It is therefore no surprise that controlled evaluations have not been reported. Extrapolating from research findings concerning related group-dynamic and insight-oriented therapies (Rachman and Wilson 1980), psychodrama would probably not turn out to be an efficient way of ridding patients of highly specific symptoms such as compulsions, delusions or depression. Nevertheless, its continued popularity proves that it is an entertaining diversion, at least, for people who feel they have relationship problems and it is probable that some people gain genuine lifestyle benefits, however difficult these may be to define and measure. Gold (1991) describes the benefits as follows:

> 'It allows us to understand more about what is frequently left unsaid or censored. It permits us to act out our fears, desires or conflicts within a safe and comfortable milieu. It allows us the opportunity to try on new behaviours that might otherwise have been difficult. Finally, it lets us see how others confront, avoid and dance around the quintessential dramas of life'. (p.274)

It is notable that role-playing techniques have been widely adopted as components of other types of therapy, including those that are generally classified as 'behavioural', such as assertiveness training, social skills learning and the desensitization of speech anxiety. Group therapy has also become widely used, particularly in institutional settings. Even if some of Moreno's philosophy and jargon is considered unnecessary by mainstream psychologists, his contribution in terms of inventive therapeutic methods merits recognition.

DRAMATHERAPY

Therapeutic applications of drama that are more eclectic (i.e. not based on the Moreno tradition) are usually called *dramatherapy* (Jennings 1990). Like psychodrama, dramatherapy involves 'acting out' rather than just talking out, but the plays used are more general and not just based on personal material. There is more emphasis on the art form of drama itself and its universal application to life's problems. For example, a scene between Antigone and Creon from the classic Sophocles tragedy may be chosen as relevant to the archetypal conflict between father and daughter. A scene from *A Doll's House* by Ibsen may be used to explore a woman's feeling of being suffocated by her marriage, or a man's unreasonable jealousy may be better understood by playing part of *Othello*. Because time and space are condensed in the theatre, whole life experiences can be contained and understood that would otherwise be too enormous to grasp.

Dramatherapy shares with psychoanalysis the concept of 'transference'. It is presumed that we are able to (or inevitably do) transfer feelings and attitudes relating to people from our past experience to present people who are reminiscent in some way, including the characters in a play. It is further presumed that by playing fictional characters we understand ourselves better and communicate things we otherwise could not. Because we are able to distance ourselves from the role we are playing, less threat is aroused and greater depth can be explored. The symbolic scenes and metaphors in the drama have meaning at several different levels of the patient's life. Jennings says it is best not to attempt interpretations or explanations of the connection between the drama and the patient's own life problems as this is likely to be oversimplified and could interfere with multi-layered understanding. (This preference for non-interpretation is one way in which dramatherapy departs from psychoanalysis.)

The concept of *appropriate distance* between drama and real-life was discussed in connection with Scheff's (1976 1979) theory of catharsis (Chapter 1). Therapeutic change is most likely to occur when the evocation of emotion is moderate rather than overwhelming. The patient should be brought into mild contact with hurtful past experiences, not retraumatized or threatened to the point that defences are mobilized.

There is a famous section in Shakespeare's *Hamlet* in which Hamlet envies the freedom of actors to express emotion 'in a fiction, in a dream of passion', when ordinary people 'can say nothing'. He goes on to plot the use of a play to diagnose his uncle's guilt.

> '... I have found
> That guilty creatures sitting at a play
> Have by the very cunning of the scene
> Been struck so to the soul that presently
> They have proclaimed their malefactions.
> For murder, though it hath no tongue, will speak
> With most miraculous organ. I'll have those players
> Play something like the murder of my father
> Before mine uncle. I'll observe his looks.
> I'll tent him to the quick. If 'a do blench

> I know my course.... The play's the thing
> wherein I'll catch the conscience of the King.'

> *(Hamlet*, Act II, Scene 2)

This mechanism, so astutely observed by Shakespeare, is according to Jennings, one of the main functions of dramatherapy. A play that bears the right relationship to the patient's life will 'catch his conscience' and reveal home truths. Devices such as costumes, masks and puppets may be used to adjust the distance between the role and reality to its optimal point. Sometimes it is necessary to start with patients 'on the outside looking in' and only venture inside (close the distance) as they become more relaxed and adventurous.

Jennings believes that another important part of the therapeutic process is the *re-working of experience* that drama allows. Assuming dramatic roles permit people to review the unhelpful and destructive stages of their lives and to transform them mentally in such a way that greater control and freedom is achieved. The facts may remain much the same but the manner in which the story is told (dramatized) can be altered, and hence the individual's own perception of it. In this way, people who have been stuck at some point in their lives can be helped to move on.

Dramatherapy encourages people to express suppressed thoughts and feelings, to behave in previously untried ways, and hence discover new aspects of themselves. Grainger (1985) says that dramatherapy is liberating because it helps people to learn that 'roles can be taken up, laid down, exchanged: that we can be, and in fact are, a great range of people'. Rather than being concerned with trying to make drama more life-like, people are brought to an awareness that life involves role-playing and hence contains a strong element of play. This is a useful insight to many patients.

Concern is sometimes expressed that drama is confusing for mental patients, particularly if they have identity problems in the first place. (After all, in Chapter 10 we considered the question of whether professional actors are destabilized in identity by the variety of roles they play.) This does not seem to be a problem with dramatherapy, however. Grainger (1990) has shown that people suffering from thought disorder actually become less confused following work in a dramatherapy group. Not only did dramatherapy lead to an enhanced capacity to relate to other people but there were gains as regards clarity of self-perception.

An interesting case history of a schizophrenic patient called Peter who was treated with dramatherapy is described by Snow (1991). Peter had actually written a play based on his own psychotic fantasies. In this play, the protagonist (with whom Peter identified), called Nelson Neuron, has the heroic task of proving the Devil's innocence in a trial located in hell, over which the Lord God Almighty presides. The Devil is depicted as a woman, Lana Love, who was based on the personality of a real-life newscaster with whom Peter was obsessed. In the play, the Devil is actually innocent of creating all the world's evil, and Nelson Neuron successfully defends her in a heated court battle with the prosecuting attorney. The therapist helped Peter to produce his play, casting him in the role of Nelson Neuron and assigning roles to other patients in the group. This apparently provided Peter with a kind of reality orientation. As the play was rehearsed over a period of months, the presence of a supporting cast who could be trusted not to be phased by his bizarre thoughts and behaviour, but to actually participate in the fantasy with him, seemed to have a stabilizing effect upon him. The rehearsal periods provided a 'safe haven' in which he felt free to explore variations on the characters and actions set down in the script: 'The self-centred nature of the script was Peter's anchor; in the rehearsal space he could float, sometimes playfully, sometimes chaotically, but with the assurance that his imagery and actions were safely contained'. Although it would be difficult to assess the role of dramatherapy in Peter's recovery, at last count he was being rehabilitated and was thinking of studying law.

The benefits attributed to dramatherapy depend upon the group to whom it is applied. For psychotics it may provide social support while the boundaries between reality and delusion are explored. For patients with neurotic conditions it is more concerned with the re-evaluation of life experiences and personal relationships. For people with learning disabilities dramatherapy is most valuable as a means of building self-esteem and communication skills. Psychopaths may be helped to focus on the interplay between human nature and social forces in determining evil behaviour – an interesting analysis of the experience of performing Shakespear-ean tragedies in a secure psychiatric hospital is provided by Cox (1992). Work in the community using theatre as an educational tool for examining social issues such as drugs, abortion, AIDS, and problems of the elderly is described by Bryan (1991). As with psychodrama, the benefits of dramatherapy are varied and esoteric and it is, therefore, hardly surprising that scientific evaluation has not been attempted.

DANCE MOVEMENT THERAPY

Dance movement therapy is one of the newest applications of performing arts for clinical purposes. 'It uses the relationship between motion and emotion as a vehicle through which an individual can engage in personal integration towards a clearer definition of self' (Payne 1992). The idea is that movement is a more direct and immediate form of self-expression than words and is shared by all people, including some that have no other means of communication (e.g. autistic or learning disabled children). Dance movement therapists therefore, observe the posture and movements of their clients as a form of assessment and use this as a point of departure for development and change of maladaptive life habits. As with other arts therapies, a contained and supportive environment is provided in which clients feel safe in expressing their feelings.

Dance movement therapists work in the same settings as art, music and drama therapists, including psychiatric hospitals, special schools, community homes, day centres, prisons and in industry. Dance was conceived by tribal peoples as a means of 'communing with the gods', or the vast unknown, and uses primitive means to communicate feelings, such as posture, gesture and imitation. It is this phylogenetic priority that is said to make dance such an important window to the subconscious aspects of human motivation.

Because of the nature of the medium, dance movement therapy makes use of spatial and somatic *metaphors* and visual *images*. It is easiest to illustrate this point with some examples.

> A high functioning woman suffering from depression, began a session saying she felt low and shaky. When she stood up, she feared that she would fall down. The image of falling down became the theme of the session. As the patient and therapist moved and played with what the movement metaphor of falling down meant for her, verbal associations followed. When she was a little girl, her mother fell down one day at the bus stop. When the mother fell, she cried, and the girl (patient) responded by laughing. Within the session, she realized that she feared that if she fell the group would laugh, leaving her feeling rejected. As her story unfolded, the next connection she made was to falling in love with her present husband 12 years ago and consequently being rejected by her family. At this point she wanted to leave her husband, on whom she was very dependent, but feared falling down emotionally and financially. (Webster 1991, p.290)

> A woman, Marge, felt very low and depressed after an exhausting day. Her body was sensed as stiff and rigid. The image that came up was a barren leafless tree in a bleak wintery landscape. The image was held in consciousness and explored through movement. A very slow and gradual process unfolded. Subtle changes in posture, which were barely visible to the observer outside, related to a conscious sensation of gravity and led to a sense of rootedness in the earth and the sensations of sap rising inside the trunk. Light movements of fingers and arms started and the neck relaxed. A swaying movement of the whole body followed, which suggested to the observer the image of a tree rocked gently by the wind, and this was confirmed later. Her arms started to move up and out and, while still standing on the same spot, her whole body looked open, relaxed and alive, and a smile appeared on her face. Marge finished by opening her eyes and announced 'Spring has come'. (Noack 1992, p.195)

These examples give the general flavour of dance movement therapy. From the observation of spontaneous movement, images and metaphors are derived that are believed to relate to intrapsychic struggles. With the help of the therapist these conflicts are 'worked through' until some satisfactory resolution is achieved both physically and mentally. This may even involve a long-term life change, such as a divorce or a change of occupation.

The same difficulties in assessing the benefits of dramatherapy apply also to dance movement therapy. Leste and Rust (1984) found that dance was more effective in reducing anxiety than either music therapy or physical education control groups and there is no doubt that dance is a pleasurable form of energy expenditure (witness the popularity of 'dancercise' aerobics). We have seen that long periods of rhythmic dancing can induce altered (trance-like) states of consciousness and intense physical activity leads to endorphin production which creates a feeling of well-being. Altogether, it is reasonable to conclude that dance is a good way of increasing fitness and reducing stress. However, the claimed benefits of dance movement therapy go well beyond this to specific psychological and lifestyle changes and these are more difficult to verify.

MUSIC THERAPY

The use of music as a therapeutic aid is better established than either drama or dance therapy (Heal and Wigram 1993). We have noted the power of music to lift the spirits or 'soothe the savage breast' (Chapter 8). Now we outline the ways in which it has been applied in clinical and community settings to reduce stress, ameliorate pain, revive memories, restore vitality and enhance life generally.

One of the arguments in support of music therapy, which is similar to one used for dance movement therapy, is that music offers a channel of expression that is non-verbal. It was noted in Chapter 9 that speech communication is primarily a function of the left (dominant) hemisphere of the cerebral cortex, while music making and appreciation is dealt with to a greater extent by the right (non-dominant) hemisphere. Since verbal skills are mostly used to assess a person's mental competence, for example in assigning children to special homes for the learning disabled, or old people to geriatric wards, it is not unusual for people with a perfectly well functioning capacity for musical processing to be submerged in what for them is an impoverished or alien environment. Such people have the unfortunate plight of being assumed to have no high level mental ability just because they are not effective with words (Lipe 1987).

We have seen that children with learning disabilities sometimes display absolute pitch. This is one illustration of the fact that although verbally, and perhaps physically disadvantaged, they may still possess normal, or even exceptional, musical comprehension. The assumption that people with learning disabilities can only respond to babyish action songs or banal pop music does gross injustice to certain individuals in this category at least. A trained music therapist can watch out for such individuals and see they are provided with forms of music that are more stimulating and rewarding to that part of their brain which is fully functioning. The same is true of patients who have suffered brain damage later in life, perhaps through stroke or head injury. If, for example, the focus of the brain malfunction is in the left frontal region, they are likely to be paralysed to some extent on the right side of the body and have difficulty in expressing themselves verbally, yet their appreciation of complex music may be unimpaired. Again, it would be offensive to such people, who are in effect trapped within a highly sensitive right cerebral hemisphere that cannot stick up for itself, to bombarb them perpetually with pop music from a ward radio.

A further example is that of the elderly person whose senility takes the form of a loss of memory for recent events – one of the most common symptoms of the aging brain. This, again, should not be taken as indicating all-round idiocy and insensitivity. Despite the difficulty with new learning, elderly patients usually retain memories of their early life perfectly well, and one of the best ways of reviving the feelings associated with their prime of life is to play them the music of that era. Such music may be the starting point for 'a trip down memory lane' that results in a reawakening of consciousness in an otherwise vegetative patient. They may smile and laugh or sob and weep, but either way their renewed interest in life is unmistakable (Hanser 1990). Hence music may be used as an important component of what has come to be called *reminiscence therapy*, the provision of a familiar environment from the past to restimulate memories and promote feelings of security.

In Britain there is a charitable organisation called *Music in Hospitals* which arranges live concerts in hospitals, hospices and homes for the elderly and infirm (Lindsay 1991). The performers are professional singers and instrumentalists, chosen not just for their musical training and talent, but also for their ability to communicate with patients, many of whom have been underestimated and misunderstood in the ways described above. Both the artists themselves and the medical staff have been amazed at the improvement seen in some of the patients following these concerts. Some who appear to have abandoned all hope, or are even comatose, are restored to new interest in life. As one of the performers was leaving after a concert, an elderly lady reached out, grasped her by the arm and said, 'Thank you dear, that was nice'. According to the nurses, this was the first time this patient had spoken in twenty years. Stories like this are consistent with clinical evidence that familiar sound is one of the best ways of waking a person from deep coma.

Artists who are experienced in performing to people with learning disabilities note how easy it is to be deceived as regards their musical sophistication. Because they have the mental age of children (and may look like children well into middle age, especially in the case of individuals with Down's Syndrome), there is a temptation to patronize them by performing only nursery rhymes and suchlike. While they will clap along good-naturedly with simple tunes such as this, they are often more delighted with nostalgic songs and ballads (every word of which they frequently know) and even classical opera such as Mozart and Rossini. Because so few people recognize their true chronological age or give them credit for such a high level of musical appreciation, a classical concert delivered live to such people may be a great and memorable occasion which has them buzzing with enthusiasm for many days afterwards.

Different kinds of benefit are seen in psychiatric patients. Sometimes the music enables them to express emotions that have lain dormant or been suppressed for long periods of time, providing the breakthrough that allows verbal therapy to commence. In cancer hospitals patients are helped to forget their pain and feel released from fear and discomfort for a short time at least. Lindsay (1991) quotes an elderly gentleman who said of a concert, 'Ah, that beats diamorphine any day!'. And for all patients there is the general tonic that somebody has taken the trouble to dress up for them and try to make them happy – the feeling that somebody cares.

Scientific research has generally supported the efficacy of music as an agent of pain control (Brown, Chen and Dworkin 1989) and as a sedative (Schuster 1991, Curtis 1986, Thaut 1989, Davis and Thaut 1989). Appropriately chosen music can calm or activate schizophrenics and depressives in much the same way as it does normal people (Weidenfeller and Zimny 1962), even though these effects are often short-lived (Skelly and Haselrud 1952). Self-chosen musical tempo also has diagnostic significance: depressed patients play instrumental music more slowly than non-depressed people (Steinberg and Raith 1985).

Recently, there has been developed a 'music bath' for the delivery of what is called *vibroacoustic therapy*. Sufferers of conditions such as arthritis, cerebral palsy, asthma, back pain or circulatory problems lie in a bed of speakers enveloped by soothing sound and vibrations. This apparently produces deep relaxation and is already finding wider applications such as post-sport relaxation for skiers and runners and stress reduction for business executives (*Sunday Correspondent*, 14th October 1990).

Music therapy is fast developing as a specialist profession. Those trained in the tradition of Nordoff and Robbins (1977) favour a one-on-one approach. In fact, there are sometimes two therapists to one patient (who is most often a profoundly disabled or disturbed child) – in this case one therapist might sit at a piano improvising an accompaniment to any activity the child chooses, while the other would help the child to move impaired limbs, articulate a sound, join in a song, or respond in some other appropriate way. Treatment is always geared to the needs of the individual patient, but usually takes the form of some kind of dialogue based on instrumental or vocal sound rather than words (recall the *Dualling Banjos* scene in the film *Deliverance*). Again, the theory is that the musical channel of communication is often available even though speech is perfunctory or absent. The flavour of Nordoff-Robbins therapy is gained from this description of a typical session with an adolescent with multiple disabilities.

> A fourteen-year-old girl with a mental age of five, an uncontrollable temper and poor speech patterns, meets her therapist for the first time. The therapist begins the session by playing crashing dissonant chords on the piano to match the girl's own angry mood and constant swearing. Surprised to silence by what she hears, the girl takes the drumstick given to her by her therapist and begins to make her own 'music' on a drum

and cymbal. The therapist's job is now to play along with the girl, turning her chaotic music into gentler, more controlled musical phrases. The girl follows suit, her violence subsides and she dissolves into tears. The therapist changes the mood in her improvisation to sad, gentle music. After the session, the girl leaves the room quietly and calmly. Over the next few months, the relationship between the two develops. Gradually, the girl begins to display better behaviour and improved speech, and the children's home where she lives reports less frequent violent outbursts from her.

(Julienne Cartwright in *Cosmopolitan* 1984).

This kind of therapy is clearly very labour-intensive and requires the ability to improvise a wide variety of musical styles on a piano or other instrument as well as some clinical intuition. Some remarkable gains are reported by parents, teachers and doctors, as well as the practitioners themselves, although the evidence consists mostly of uncontrolled clinical case studies (e.g. Heal and O'Hara 1993).

When music therapy is performed in a group setting various other benefits are claimed in addition to opening a new channel of communication. The experience of participating in a group provides valuable training in social co-operation. It is an opportunity to get 'in tune' with others. For example, a group of patients may be assigned instruments and vocal parts in accordance with their preferences and special talents and some kind of symphonic arrangement is built up over a period of time. All this takes place under the guidance of the music therapist, who perhaps directs and conducts from the piano. Some patients may learn (or be able) to play an instrument quite respectably, especially a pentatonic instrument that is less likely to produce discordant sound. For others, the extent of their contribution may be to hum along roughly with the tune or bash a drum in time with the beat. But even this may amount to the most socially communicative gesture of which they are capable and as such constitute a rewarding experience to them.

Music therapists question the assumption that only a minority of people are musically talented and the rest not. They note that talent is subjectively defined in music and that most people, including those who are severely disabled, can be helped to participate in some way. In so doing, they will gain great pleasure from the achievement and their self-esteem will be enhanced (Henderson 1983, Brodsky and Niedorf 1986). Like drama and dance, music opens a channel of communication that by-passes words to engage the emotions directly, promoting activity, social cooperation and feelings of well-being.

REFERENCES

Aaron, S. (1986) *Stage Fright: its role in acting.* Chicago: University of Chicago Press.

Alexander, A. (1971) *Operanatomy.* London: Orion.

Allen, M., Hunter, J.E. and Donahue, W.A. (1989) Meta-analysis of self-report data on the effectiveness of public speaking anxiety treatment techniques. *Communication Education,* 38, 54–76.

Ardrey, R. (1966) *The Territorial Imperative.* New York: Athenium.

Argyle, M. (1975) *Bodily Communication.* New York: International Universities Press.

Argyle, M. and Cook, M. (1976) *Gaze and Mutual Gaze.* Cambridge: Cambridge University Press.

Arnold, N. (1990) The manipulation of the audience by director and actor. In G.D. Wilson (ed) *Psychology and Performing Arts.* Amsterdam: Swets and Zeitlinger.

Asch, S.E. (1956) Studies of independence and conformity: a minority of one against a unanimous majority. *Psychological Monographs,* 70, (9, Whole No. 416).

Atkinson, M. (1984) *Our Master's Voice.* London: Methuen.

Austin, B.A. (ed) (1985) *Current Research in Film: audiences, economics and law.* Norwood, NJ: Ablex Publishing Corp.

Bakker, F.C. (1988) Personality differences between young dancers and non-dancers. *Personality and Individual Differences,* 9, 121–131.

Bakker, F.C. (1991) Development of personality in dancers: a longitudinal study. *Personality and Individual Differences,* 12, 671–681.

Bamberger, J. (1982) Growing up prodigies: the midlife crisis. *New Directions in Child Development,* 17, 61–77.

Bandura, A. (1973) *Aggression: a social learning analysis.* New York: Prentice Hall.

Barr, H.L., Langs, R.J., Holt, R.R., Goldberger, L. and Klein, G.S. (1972) *LSD: personality and experience.* New York: John Wiley and Sons.

Barrick, A.L., Hutchinson, R.L. and Deckers, L.H. (1990) Humour aggression and aging. *Gerontologist,* 30, 675–678.

Bates, B.C. (1986) *The Way of the Actor.* London: Century Hutchinson.

Bates, B.C. (1991) Performance and possession: the actor and our inner demons. In G.D. Wilson (ed) *Psychology and Performing Arts.* Amsterdam: Swets and Zeitlinger.

Beach, S. (1977) *Musicdotes.* Berkeley: Ten Speed Press.

Benedetti, R.L. (1976) *The Actor at Work.* Englewood Cliffs, NJ: Prentice Hall.

Benson, H. (1975) *The Relaxation Response.* New York: Morrow.

Berlyne, D.E. (1971) *Aesthetics and Psychobiology.* New York: Appleton-Century-Crofts.

Bernstein, L. (1976) *The Unanswered Question.* Cambridge MA: Harvard University Press.

Bettelheim, B. (1943) Individual and mass behaviour in extreme situations. *Journal of Abnormal and Social Psychology*, 38, 417–452.

Bever, T.G. and Chiarello, R.J. (1974) Cerebral dominance in musicians and non-musicians. *Science*, 185, 537–539.

Bixler, R.H. (1981) The incest controversy. *Psychological Reports*, 49, 267–283.

Blackwell, H.R. and Schlosberg, H. (1943) Octave generalisation, pitch discrimination and loudness thresholds in the white rat. *Journal of Experimental Psychology*, 33, 407–419.

Blatner, H.A. (1973) *Acting In: practical applications of psychodramatic methods.* New York: Springer.

Bloch, S., Orthous, P. and Santibañez, H.G. (1987) Effector patterns of basic emotions: a psychophysiological method for training actors. *Journal of Social and Biological Structure*, 10, 1–19.

Bond, C.F. and Titus, L.J. (1983) Social facilitation: a meta-analysis of 241 studies. *Psychological Bulletin*, 94, 265–292.

Bond, D.B. (1952) *The Love and Fear of Flying.* New York: International Universities Press.

Boorman, J. (1985) *Money into Light.* London: Faber and Faber.

Bower, G.H. (1981) Mood and memory. *American Psychologist*, 36, 129–148.

Brady, P.T. (1970) Fixed-scale mechanism of absolute pitch. *Journal of the Acoustical Society of America*, 48, 883–887.

Brehm, J.W. and Cohen, A.R. (1962) *Explorations in Cognitive Dissonance.* New York: John Wiley and Sons.

Brehm, S.S. and Brehm J.W. (1981) *Psychological Reactance: a theory of freedom and control.* New York: Academic Press.

Brodsky, W. and Niedorf, H. (1986) 'Songs form the heart': new paths to greater maturity. *Arts in Psychotherapy*, 13, 333–341.

Brown, C., Chen, A.C. and Dworkin, S.F. (1989) Music in control of human pain. *Music Therapy*, 8, 47–60.

Brown, M., Amoroso, D.M. and Ware, E.E. (1976) Behavioural effects of viewing pornography. *Journal of Social Psychology*, 98, 235–245.

Bryan, V. (1991) Use of theatre as a therapeutic and educational tool within community structures and social service programmes. In G.D. Wilson (ed) *Psychology and Performing Arts.* Amsterdam: Swets and Zeitlinger.

Bücher, K. (1919) *Arbeit und Rhythmus.* Berlin: Springer Verlag.

Buchwald, A. (1967) Art Buchwald in conversation. *Psychology Today,* 14–23.

Bull, P.E. (1987) *Posture and Gesture.* Oxford: Pergamon.

Burton, A., Morton, N. and Abbess, S. (1989) Mode of processing and hemisphere differences in the judgement of musical stimuli. *British Journal of Psychology,* 80, 169–180.

Butland, M.J. and Ivy, D.K. (1990) The effects of biological sex and egalitarianism on humour appreciation. *Journal of Social Behaviour and Personality,* 5, 353–356.

Bynum, W.F. and Neve, M. (1986) Hamlet on the couch. *American Scientist,* 74, 390–396.

Cameron, P. and Fleming, P. (1975) Self-reported degree of pleasure associated with sexual activity across the adult life-span. Mimeographed report. Division of Human Development, St Mary's College of Maryland.

Campbell, J. (1949) *The Hero with a Thousand Faces.* New York: Meridian Books.

Cantor, M.G. (1991) The American on television: from Molly Goldberg to Bill Cosby. *Journal of Comparative Family Studies,* 22, 205–216.

Cantor, J.R. and Zillman, D. (1973) Resentment toward victimized protagonists and severity of misfortunes they suffer as factors in humour appreciation. *Journal of Experimental Research in Personality,* 6, 321–329.

Chaliapin, F. (1933) *Man and Mask.* New York: Knopf.

Chalmers, B. (1978) The development of a measure of attitude towards instrumental music style. *Journal of Research in Musical Education,* 26, 90–96.

Chapman, A.J. and Foot, H.C. (1976) *Humour and Laughter: theory, research and applications.* Chichester: John Wiley and Sons.

Clément, C (1989) *Opera, or the Undoing of Women* (trans B Wing) London: Virago.

Clore, G.L., Wiggins, N.H. and Itkin, S. (1975) Judging attraction from non-verbal behaviour: the gain phenomenon. *Journal of Consulting and Clinical Psychology,* 43, 491–497.

Clynes, M. (1986) Music beyond the score. *Communication and Cognition,* 19, 169–194.

Cole, D. (1975) *The Theatrical Event: a mythos, a vocabulary, a perspective.* Middleton, Conn: Wesleyan University Press.

Conrad, P. (1987) *A Song of Love and Death: the meaning of opera.* London: Chatto and Windus.

Cook, R.F., Fosen, R.H. and Pacht, A. (1971) Pornography and the sex offender: patterns of previous exposure and arousal effects of pornographic stimuli. *Journal of Applied Psychology,* 55, 503–511.

Coon, H. and Carey, G. (1989) Genetic and environmental determinants of musical ability in twins. *Behaviour Genetics,* 19, 183–193.

Coslin, P.G. (1980) The adolescent through the works of the Research Group on Juvenile Adjustment of the University of Montreal. *Bulletin de Psychologie,* 33, 627–629.

Cousins, N. (1979) *Anatomy of an Illness as Perceived by the Patient.* New York: Bantam Books.

Cox, M. (ed) (1992) *Shakespeare Comes to Broadmoor: 'The actors are come hither'.* London: Jessica Kingsley Publishers.

Cox, J.A., Read, R.L. and Van Auken, P.M. (1990) Male–female differences in communicating job-related humour: an exploratory study. *Humour: International Journal of Humour Research,* 3, 287–295.

Crandall, R. (1974) Social facilitation: theories and research. In A. Harrison (ed) *Explorations in Psychology.* Monterey, CA: Brooks/Cole.

Crisp, A.H., Matthews, B.M., Oakey, M. and Crutchfield M. (1990) Sleepwalking, night terrors and consciousness. *British Medical Journal,* 300, 360–362.

Cuddy, L.L. (1971) Absolute judgement of musically-related pure tones. *Canadian Journal of Psychology,* 25, 42–55.

Curtis, S.L. (1986) The effects of music on pain relief and relaxation of the terminally ill. *Journal of Music Therapy,* 23, 10–24.

Dabbs, J.M., De la Rue, D. and Williams, P.M. (1990) Testosterone and occupational choice: actors, ministers and other men. *Journal of Personality and Social Psychology,* 59, 1261–1265.

Daly, M. and Wilson, M. (1979) Sex and Strategy. *New Scientist,* 4 January, 15–17.

Darwin, C.R. (1872) *The Expression of the Emotions in Man and Animals.* London: John Murray.

Darwin, C.R. (1883) *The Descent of Man and Selection in Relation to Sex.* London: Macmillan.

Davies, A. and Roberts, E. (1975) Poor pitch singing: a survey of its incidence in schoolchildren. *Psychology of Music,* 3, 24–36.

Davies, C. (1986) Jewish jokes, anti-Semitic jokes and Hebredonian jokes. In A. Ziv (ed) *Jewish Humour.* Tel Aviv: Papyrus Publishing House.

Davies, D.R., Lang, L. and Shackleton, V.J. (1973) The effects of music and task difficulty on performance at a visual vigilance test. *British Journal of Psychology,* 64, 383–389.

Davies, J.B. (1978) *The Psychology of Music.* London: Hutchinson.

Davis, W.B. and Thaut, M.H. (1989) The influence of preferred relaxing music on measures of state anxiety, relaxation and physiological responses. *Journal of Music Therapy,* 26, 168–187.

Davitz, J.R. and Davitz, L.J. (1989) The communication of feelings by content-free speech. *Journal of Communication,* 9, 6–13.

De la Cruz, B.J.A. (1981) Laughter in children as a function of social facilitation. *Philippines Journal of Psychology, 14, 55–63.*

Dench, J. (1990) Reflecting nature: a conversation with Dr Michael Parsons. *The Psychologist,* July 1990, 312–314.

De Paulo, B.M., Kirkendol, S.E., Tang, J. and O'Brien T.P. (1988) The motivational impairment effect in the communication of deceptions: replications and extensions. *Journal of Non-Verbal Behaviour,* 12, 177–202.

Desmione, R., Albright, T.D., Gross, C.G. and Bruce, C. (1984) Stimulus-selective properties of inferior temporal neurons in the macaque. *Journal of Neuroscience, 4,* 2051–2062.

De Turck, M.A. and Miller, G.R. (1990) Training observers to detect deception: effects of self-monitoring and rehearsal. *Human Communication Research,* 16, 603–620.

Deux, K. and Wrightsman, L.S. (1984) *Social Psychology in the 80s.* Monterey: Brooks/Cole.

De Vries, B. (1991) Assessment of the affective response to music with Clyne's sentograph. *Psychology of Music,* 19, 46–64.

Dorinson, J. (1986) The Jew as comic: Lenny Bruce, Mel Brooks, Woody Allen. In A. Ziv (ed) *Jewish Humour.* Tel Aviv: Papyrus Publishing House.

Dowling, W.J. and Harwood, D.L. (1986) *Music Cognition.* London: Academic Press.

Doxey, C. and Wright, C. (1990) An exploratory study of children's music ability. *Early Childhood Research Quarterly,* 5, 425–440.

Drummond, J.D. (1980) *Opera in Perspective.* Minneapolis: University of Minnesota Press.

Duffy, E. (1962) *Attention and Behaviour.* New York: John Wiley and Sons.

Duncan, S. and Fiske, D.W. (1977) *Face to Face Interaction.* Hillsdale, NJ: Erlbaum.

Durant, J. and Miller, J. (1988) *Laughing Matters: A serious look at humour.* Harlow: Longman.

Dutton, D.G. and Aron, A.P. (1974) Some evidence for heightened sexual attraction under conditions of high anxiety. *Journal of Personality and Social Psychology,* 30, 510–517.

Eden, D. (1986) *Gilbert and Sullivan: the creative conflict.* London: Associated University Presses.

Eggebrecht, R. (1983) Sprachmelodie und musikalische Forschungen im Kulturvergleich. University of Munich dissertation (quoted in Eibl-Eibesfeldt 1989).

Eibl-Eibesfeldt, I. (1989) *Human Ethology.* New York: Aldine de Gruyter.

Ekman, P. (Ed.)(1972) *Emotion in the Human Face (2nd edition).* New York: Cambridge University Press,

Ekman, P. and Friesen, W.V. (1974) Detecting deception from the body or face. *Journal of Personality and Social Psychology,* 29, 288–298.

Ekman, P., Levenson, R.W. and Friesen, W.V. (1983) Autonomic nervous system activity distinguishes among emotions. *Science,* 221, 1208.

Ellis, L. and Ames, M.A. (1987) Neurological functioning and sexual orientation: a theory of homosexuality and heterosexuality. *Psychological Bulletin,* 101, 233–258.

Epstein, D. (1985) Tempo relations: a cross-cultural study. *Music Theory Spectrum,* 7, 34–71.

Epstein, D. (1988) Tempo relations in music: A universal? In I., Rentschler, B. Herzberger and D. Epstein (eds) *Beauty and the Brain.* Boston: Birkhauser.

Esslin, M. (1976) *An Anatomy of Drama.* New York: Hill and Wang.

Evans, R.I. (1981) *Psychology and Arthur Miller.* New York: Praeger.

Eysenck, H.J. and Eysenck, M. (1985) *Personality and Individual Differences: a natural science approach.* London: Plenum.

Eysenck, H.J. and Eysenck, S.B.G. (1975) *Manual of the Eysenck Personality Questionnaire.* London: Hodder and Stoughton.

Eysenck, H.J. and Nias, D.K.B. (1978) *Sex, Violence and the Media.* London: Temple Smith.

Feggetter, G. (1980) Suicide in opera. *British Journal of Psychiatry*, 136, 552–557.

Fein, I.A. (1976) *Jack Benny: an intimate biography.* New York: G.P. Putnam & Sons.

Feltz, D.L. and Landers, D.M. (1983) The effects of mental practice on motor skill learning and performance: a meta-analysis. *Journal of Sport Psychology*, 5, 25–57.

Feshbach, S. (1961) The stimulating versus cathartic effects of a vicarious aggressive activity. *Journal of Abnormal and Social Psychology*, 63, 381–385.

Feshbach, S. and Singer, R.D. (1971) *Television and Aggression.* San Francisco: Jossey-Bass.

Field, C.H. (1991) Love addiction in performers. In G.D. Wilson (ed) *Psychology and Performing Arts.* Amsterdam: Swets and Zeitlinger.

Fisher S. and Fisher R.L. (1981) *Pretend the World is Funny and Forever: a psychological analysis of clowns and actors.* Hillsdale, NJ: Erlbaum.

Freud, S. (1905) *Jokes and their Relation to the Unconscious.* London: Routledge and Kegan Paul (reprinted 1960).

Friedman, H.S., Prince, L.M., Riggio, R.E. and Di Matteo, M.R. (1980) Understanding and assessing non-verbal expressiveness: the Affective Communication Test. *Journal of Personality and Social Psychology*, 39, 333–351.

Frosch, W.A. (1987) Moods, music and madness: I. Major affective disease and musical creativity. *Comprehensive Psychiatry*, 24, 315–322.

Fry, H.J.H. (1986) Overuse syndrome in musicians: prevention and management. *Lancet*, 2, 728–731.

Furnald, A. (1992) Human maternal vocalizations to infants as biologically relevant signals: an evolutionary perspective. In: J.H. Barkow, L. Cosmides and J. Tooby (eds) *Evolutionary Psychology and the Generation of Culture.* Oxford: Oxford University Press.

Gardano, A.C. (1986) Cultural influences on emotional response to colour: a research study comparing Hispanics and non-Hispanics. *American Journal of Art Therapy*, 24, 119–124.

Gardner, H. (1981) How the split brain gets a joke. *Psychology Today*, February, 74–77.

Gaver, W.W. and Mandler, G. (1987) Play it again Sam: on liking music. *Cognition and Emotion*, 1, 259–282.

Geake, E. (1992) *New Scientist*, 19, 27th July.

Girodo, M. (1984) Entry and re-entry strain in undercover agents. In V.L. Allen and E. Van der Vliert (eds) *Role Transitions.* New York: Plenum.

Glasgow, M.R., Cartier, A.M. and Wilson, G.D. (1985) Conservatism, sensation-seeking and music preferences. *Personality and Individual Differences*, 3, 395–396.

Glover, E. (1990) Tragedy, myth and madness. *Bethlem-Maudsley Gazette*, 37, 43–46.

Gold, D.C. (1991) The theatre of human experience: an introduction to psychodrama. In G.D. Wilson (ed) *Psychology and Performing Arts*. Amsterdam: Swets and Zeitlinger.

Goldovski, B. (1968) *Bringing Opera to Life*. New York: Appleton, Century, Crofts.

Goldstein, A. (1980) Thrills in response to music and other stimuli. *Physiological Psychology*, 8, 126–129.

Goldstein, M.J., Kant, H.S., Judd, L.L., Rice, C.J. and Green, R. (1971) Exposure to pornography and sexual behaviour in deviant and normal groups. In *Technical Report of the Commission on Obscenity and Pornography*, Vol VII. Washington DC: US Government Printing Office.

Goodwin, D.W., Powell, B., Bremer, D., Hoine, H. and Stern, J. (1969) Alcohol and recall: State-dependent effects in man. *Science*, 163, 1358–1360.

Gordon, E. (1970) *Iowa Tests of Musical Literacy*. Iowa City: Bureau of Educational Research and Service.

Gordon, H.W. (1983) Music and the right hemisphere. In A. Young *Functions of the Right Cerebral Hemisphere*. London: Academic Press.

Gott, P.S. (1973) Language after dominant hemispherectomy. *Journal of Neurology, Neurosurgery and Psychiatry*, 36, 1082–1088.

Grainger, R. (1985) Using drama creatively in therapy: what are the advantages of a creative approach to therapy over other methods? *Dramatherapy*, 8, 33–46.

Grainger, R. (1990) *Drama and Healing: the roots of drama therapy*. London: Jessica Kingsley Publishers.

Grant, V.J. (1990) Maternal personality and sex of infant. *British Journal of Medical Psychology*, 63, 261–266.

Green, B. (1986) *The Inner Game of Music*. London: Pan.

Greenberg, J.A. (ed) (1974) *Psychodrama: theory and therapy*. New York: Behavioural Publications.

Groisman, A.L., Savostyanov, A.I. and Zhukov, I.G. (1990) Psychotherapeutic methods for optimizing an actor's capacity for creative work. *Soviet Journal of Psychology*, 11, 78–91.

Grumet, G.W. (1989) Laughter: nature's epileptoid catharsis. *Psychological Reports*, 65, 1059–1078.

Guinness, A. (1985) *Blessings in Disguise*. London: Hamish Hamilton.

Gunter, B. (1980) The cathartic potential of television drama. *Bulletin of the British Psychological Society*, 33, 448–450.

Guthrie, T. (1971) *On Acting*. New York: Viking.

Gutman, J. and Priest, R.F. (1969) When is aggression funny? *Journal of Personality and Social Psychology*, 12, 60–65.

Haider, V.M. and Groll-Knapp, E. (1981) Psychological investigation into the stress experiences by musicians in a symphony orchestra. In M. Piparek (ed) *Stress and Music*. Vienna: William Braumüller.

Haig, R.A. (1986) Therapeutic uses of humour. *American Journal of Psychotherapy*, 40, 543–552.

Hall, J.A. (1978) Gender effects in decoding non-verbal cues. *Psychological Bulletin*, 85, 845–857.

Hamann, D.L. (1982) An assessment of anxiety in instrumental and vocal performances. *Journal of Research in Musical Education*, 30, 77–90.

Hammond, J. and Edelman, R.J. (1991a) The act of being: personality characteristics of professional actors, amateur actors and non-actors. In G.D. Wilson (ed) *Psychology and Performing Arts*. Amsterdam: Swets and Zeitlinger.

Hammond, J. and Edelman, R.J. (1991b) Double identity: the effect of the acting process on the self-perception of professional actors – two case illustrations. In G.D. Wilson (ed) *Psychology and Performing Arts*. Amsterdam: Swets and Zeitlinger.

Hanna, J.L. (1988) *Dance, Sex and Gender: signs of identity, dominance, defiance and desire.* Chicago: University of Chicago Press.

Hanser, S.B. (1990) A music therapy strategy for depressed older adults in the community. *Journal of Applied Gerontology*, 9, 283–298.

Hardy, L. and Parfitt, G. (1991) A catastrophe model of anxiety and performance. *British Journal of Psychology*, 82, 163–178.

Hassler, M. (1990) Functional cerebral assymetries and cognitive abilities in musicians, painters and controls. *Brain and Cognition*, 13, 1–17.

Heal, M. and O'Hara, J. (1993) The music therapy of an anorectic mentally handicapped adult. *British Journal of Medical Psychology*, 66, 33–41.

Heal, M. and Wigram, T. (eds)(1993) *Music Therapy in Health and Education*. London: Jessica Kingsley Publishers.

Henderson, S.M. (1983) Effects of a music therapy programme upon awareness of mood in music, group cohesion and self-esteem. *Journal of Music Therapy, 20*, 14–20.

Henry, W.E. and Sims, J.H. (1970) Actors' search for self. *Transaction*, 7, 57–62.

Hevner, K. (1935) The affective character of major and minor modes in music. *American Journal of Psychology*, 47, 103–118.

Hokanson, J.E. (1970) Psychophysiological evaluation of the catharsis hypothesis. In E.I. Megargee and J.E. Hokanson (eds) *The Dynamics of Aggression: individual, group and international analyses.* New York: Harper and Row.

Holland, N.N. (1972) *Laughing: A psychology of humour.* Ithaca, NY: Cornell University Press.

Holmes, D.S. and McGilley, B.M. (1987) Influence of a brief aerobic training programme on heart rate and subjective response to a psychologic stressor. *Psychosomatic Medicine*, 49, 366–376.

Howat, R. (1984) *Debussy in Proportion.* Cambridge: Cambridge University Press.

Howe, M.J.A. (1991) *Fragments of Genius: the strange feats of idiots savants.* London: Routledge.

Hudak, D.A., Dale, J.A., Hudak, M.A. and De Good, D.E. (1991) Effects of humorous stimuli and sense of humour on discomfort. *Psychological Reports*, 69, 779–786.

Hurley, D. (1988) The end of celebrity. *Psychology Today*, 22, 50–55.

Intons-Peterson, M.J. and Smyth, M.M. (1987) The anatomy of repertory memory. *Journal of Experimental Psychology: Learning, Memory and Cognition*, 13, 490–500.

Jackendorff, R. and Lehrdahl, F. (1982) A grammatical parallel between music and language. In M. Clynes (ed) *Music, Mind and Brain*. New York: Plenum.

James, I.M., Griffith, D.N.W., Pearson, R.M. and Newbury, P. (1977) Effect of oxprenolol on stage-fright in musicians. *Lancet*, 2, 952–954.

James, I.M. and Savage, I.T. (1984) Beneficial effect of nadolol on anxiety-induced disturbances of performance in musicians: a comparison with diazepam and placebo. *American Heart Journal*, 108, 1150–1155.

James, W.T. (1932) A study of the expression of bodily posture. *Journal of General Psychology*, 7, 405–437.

Jamison, K. (1989) Mood disorders and seasonal patterns in British writers and artists. *Psychiatry*, 52, 125–134.

Janus, S.S. (1975) The great comedians: personality and other factors. *American Journal of Psychoanalysis*, 35, 169–174.

Janus, S.S., Janus, C. and Vincent, J. (1986) The psychosexuality of the stand-up comedian. *Journal of Psychohistory*, 14, 133–140.

Jennings, S. (1990) *Dramatherapy with Families, Groups and Individuals: Waiting in the wings*. London: Jessica Kingsley Publishers.

Johnson, M.A. (1990) A study of humour and the right hemisphere. *Perceptual and Motor Skills*, 70, 995–1002.

Johnson, M.A. (1992) Language ability and sex affect humour appreciation. *Perceptual and Motor Skills*, 75, 571–581.

Jones, E.E. and Berglas, S. (1978) Control of attributions about the self through self-handicapping strategies: the appeal of alcohol and the role of underachievement. *Personality and Social Psychology Bulletin*, 4, 200–206.

Kameoka, A. and Kuriyagawa, M. (1969) Consonance theory, Part II: consonance of complex tones and its calculation method. *Journal of the Acoustical Society of America*, 45, 1460–1469.

Kamien, R. (1980) *Music Appreciation*. New York: McGraw Hill.

Kemp, A. (1980) Personality differences between the players of string, woodwind, brass and keyboard instruments, and singers. Paper delivered at 8th International Seminar on Research in Musical Education. University of Reading School of Education.

Kemp, A. (1982) The personality structure of the musician: the significance of sex differences. *Psychology of Music*, 10, 48–58.

Kerr, W. (1967) *Tragedy and Comedy*. London: The Bodley Head.

Kelb, B. and Whishaw, I.Q. (1980) *Fundamentals of Human Neuropsychology*. San Francisco: Freeman.

Konečni, V.J. (1982) Social interaction and musical preference. In D. Deutsch (ed) *The Psychology of Music*. New York: Academic Press.

Konijn, E.A. (1991) What's on between the actor and his audience? Empirical analysis of emotion processes in the theatre. In G.D. Wilson (ed) *Psychology and Performing Arts*. Amsterdam: Swets and Zeitlinger.

Kubistant, T.M. (1986) *Performing Your Best*. Champaign, Ill: Life Enhancement Publications.

Labott, S.M., Ahleman, S., Wolever, M.E. and Martin, R.B. (1990) The psysiological and psychological effects of the expression and inhibition of emotion. *Behavioural Medicine*, 16, 182–189.

La France, M. (1982) Posture mirroring and rapport. In M. Davis (ed) *Interaction Rhythms: Periodicity in Communicative Behaviour*. New York: Human Sciences Press.

Lamb, W. and Watson, E. (1979) *Body Code*. London: Routledge and Kegan Paul.

Lane, R. (1959) *The Psychology of the Actor*. London: Secker and Warburg.

Lanone, D.J. and Schrott, P.R. (1989) Voters' reactions to televised presidential debates: measurement of the source and magnitude of opinion change. *Political Psychology*, 10, 275–285.

Lax, E. (1975) *On Being Funny: Woody Allen and comedy*. New York: Charterhouse.

Le Clair, J. (1986) An experiment to determine if music affects pulse rate. Unpublished research report, University of Nevada.

Lefcourt, H.M. Davidson-Katz, K. and Kueneman, K. (1990) Humour and immune system functioning. *Humour: International Journal of Humour Research*, 3, 305–321.

Leste, A. and Rust, J. (1984) Effects of dance on anxiety. *Perceptual and Motor Skills*, 58, 767–772.

Levine, J. (ed) (1969) *Motivation in Humour*. New York: Atherton.

Lindsay, S. (1991) Live music in hospitals. In G.D. Wilson (ed) *Psychology and Performing Arts*. Amsterdam: Swets and Zeitlinger.

Lipe, A.P. (1987) The use of music therapy as an individualized activity: music in nursing homes. *Activities, Adaption and Aging*, 10, 93–101.

Little, P. and Zuckerman, M. (1986) Sensation-seeking and music preferences. *Personality and Individual Differences*, 4, 575–577.

Lloyd-Elliot, M. (1991) Witches, demons and devils: the enemies of auditions and how performing artists make friends with these saboteurs. In G.D. Wilson (ed) *Psychology and Performing Arts*. Amsterdam: Swets and Zeitlinger.

Lockwood, A.H. (1989) Medical problems of musicians. *The New England Journal of Medicine*, 320, 221–227.

Love, A.M. and Deckers, L.H. (1989) Humour appreciation as a function of sexual, aggressive and sexist content. *Sex Roles*, 20, 649–654.

Lumsden, C.J. and Wilson, E.O. (1983) *Promethean Fire: reflections on the origin of mind*. Cambridge Ma: Harvard University Press.

Lyster, W. (1985) Deep and hairy. (Report by J Sweeney) *Sunday Times*, London, 7th April.

Mabie, C.B. (1952) The response of theatre audiences: experimental studies. *Special Monographs*, 19, 235–240.

McConnell, F. (1979) *Storytelling and Mythmaking: Images From Film and Literature.* New York: Oxford University Press.

MacDonald, D. (1969) *On Movies.* Englewood Cliffs, NJ: Prentice Hall.

MacDonald, S.T.S. (1991) Emotional costs of success in dance. In G.D. Wilson (ed) *Psychology and Performing Arts.* Amsterdam: Swets and Zeitlinger.

McGhee, P.E. (1979) *Humour: Its Origin and Development.* San Francisco: Freeman.

McGhee, P.E. and Goldstein, J.H. (eds)(1983) *Handbook of Humour Research (Vols 1 & 2).* New York: Springer Verlag.

McGuinness, D. (1972) Hearing: individual differences in perception. *Perception,* 1, 465–473.

McGuinness, D. (1976) Sex differences in the organization of perception and cognition. In B. Lloyd and J. Archer (eds) *Exploring Sex Differences.* London: Academic Press.

McHugo, G.J., Lanzetta, J.T., Sullivan, D.G., Masters, R.D. and Englis, B.G. (1985) Emotional reactions to a political leader's expressive displays. *Journal of Personality and Social Psychology* 49, 1513–1529.

Magee, B. (1969) *Aspects of Wagner.* New York: Stein and Day.

Malm, W.P. (1977) *Music Cultures of the Pacific, the Near East and Asia (2nd edition)* Englewood Cliffs, NJ: Prentice Hall.

Manturzewska, M. (1978) Psychology in the music school. *Psychology of Music,* 6, 36–47.

Marchant-Haycox, S.E. and Wilson, G.D. (1992) Personality and stress in performing artists. *Personality and Individual Differences,* 13, 1061–1068.

Margolis, J. (1992) *Cleese Encounters.* London: Chapman.

Marin, O.S.M. (1982) Neurological aspects of music perception and performance. In D. Deutsch (ed) *The Psychology of Music.* New York: Academic Press.

Marks, L.E. (1975) On coloured-hearing synesthesia: cross-modal translations of sensory dimensions. *Psychological Bulletin,* 82, 303–331.

Marsh, P. (1988) *Eye to Eye: How People Interact.* Topsfield, MA: Salem House.

Martin, R.A. and Dobbin, J.P. (1988) Sense of humour, hassles and immunoglobin A: evidence for a stress-moderating effect of humour. *International Journal of Psychiatry in Medicine,* 18, 93–105.

Masterson, J. (1984) The effects of erotica and pornography on attitudes and behaviour. *Bulletin of the British Psychological Society,* 37, 249–252.

Medicus, G. and Hopf, S. (1990) The phylogeny of male/female differences in sexual behaviour. In J.R. Feierman (ed) *Pedophilia: biosocial dimensions.* New York: Springer Verlag.

Mehrabian, A. (1969) Significance of posture and position in the communication of attitude and status relationships. *Psychological Bulletin*, 71, 359–372.

Meichenbaum, D. (1985) *Stress Inoculation Training*. New York: Pergamon Press.

Meuser, W. and Nieschlag, E. (1977) Sexualhormone und Stimmlage des Mannes. *Deutsch. Med. Wochensch.*, 102, 261.

Monti, C. (with Rice, C.) (1973) *W.C. Fields and Me*. New York: Warner Communications.

Moog, H. (1976) *The Musical Experience of the Pre-School Child* (trans C Clarke) London: Schott.

Moore, M.C., Skipper, J.K. and Willis, C.L. (1979) Rock and roll: arousal music or a reflection of changing mores? In M. Cook and G.D. Wilson (eds) *Love and Attraction: an international conference*. Oxford: Pergamon.

Moore, M.M. (1985) Nonverbal courtship patterns in women: context and consequences. *Ethology and Sociobiology*, 6, 237–247.

Moreno, J.L. (1964) *Psychodrama: First Volume (3rd edition)*. New York: Beacon House.

Moreno, J.L. (1959) *Psychodrama: Second Volume; Foundations of Psychotherapy*. New York: Beacon House.

Moreno, J.L. (1969) *Psychodrama: Third Volume; Action Therapy and Principles of Practice*. New York: Beacon House.

Morris, D. (1977) *Manwatching*. London: Cape.

Morris, D., Collett, P., Marsh, P. and O'Shaughnessy, M. (1979) *Gestures: their origin and distribution*. London: Cape.

Morrongiello, B.A. (1992) Effects of training on children's perception of music: a review. *Psychology of Music*, 20, 29–41.

Nadel, S. (1971) Origins of music. In D.P McAllester (ed) *Readings in Ethnomusicology*. New York: Johnson Reprint Corporation.

Neher, A. (1962) A physiological explanation of some unusual behaviour in ceremonies involving drums. *Human Biology*, 4, 151–160.

Neuringer, C. (1989) On the question of homosexuality in actors. *Archives of Sexual Behaviour*, 18, 523–529.

Nezu, A.M., Nezu, C.M. and Blisset, S.E. (1988) Sense of humour as a moderator of the relation between stressful events and psychological distress: a prospective analysis. *Journal of Personality and Social Psychology*, 54, 520–525.

Noack, A. (1992) On a Jungian approach to dance movement therapy. In H. Payne (ed) *Dance Movement Therapy: theory and practice*. London: Tavistock/Routledge.

Noller, P. (1986) Sex differences in nonverbal communication: advantage lost or supremacy regained. *Australian Journal of Psychology*, 38, 23–32.

Nordoff, P. and Robbins, C. (1977) *Creative Music Therapy*. New York: John Day.

Nottebohm, F. (1981) A brain for all seasons: clinical–anatomical changes in song control nuclei of the canary brain. *Science* 214, 1368–1370.

Olivier, L. (1982) *Confessions of an Actor*. London: Weidenfeld and Nicholson.

O'Neill, R.M., Greenberg, R.P. and Fisher, S. (1992) Humour and anality. *Humour: International Journal of Humour Research*, 5, 283–291.

Osborn, H.F. (1902) Rapid memorizing: 'Winging a part' as a lost faculty. *Psychological Review*, 9, 183–184.

O'Shea, J. (1990) *Music and Medicine.* London: Dent.

Overhulser, J.C. (1992) Sense of humour when coping with life stress. *Personality and Individual Differences*, 13, 799–804.

Paletz, D.L. (1990) Political humour and authority: from support to subversion. *International Political Science Review*, 11, 483–493.

Payne, H. (ed) (1992) *Dance Movement Therapy: theory and practice.* London: Tavistock/Routledge.

Pennebaker, J. (1980) Social coughs. *Basic and Applied Social Psychology*, 1, 83–91.

Phillips, D.P. (1980) The deterrent effect of capital punishment: new evidence on an old controversy. *American Journal of Sociology*, 86, 139–148.

Phillips, E.M. (1991) Acting as an insecure occupation: the flipside of stardom. In G.D. Wilson (ed) *Psychology and Performing Arts.* Amsterdam: Swets and Zeitlinger.

Piparek, M. (1981) Psychological stress and strain factors in the work of a symphony orchestra musician. In M. Piparek (ed) *Stress and Music.* Vienna: William Braumüller.

Pollio, H.R. and Talley, J.T. (1991) The concepts and language of comic art. *Humour International Journal of Humour Research*, 4, 1–22.

Pradier, J.M. (1990) Towards a biological theory of the body in performance. *New Theatre Quarterly*, 6, 86–98.

Prange, A.J. and Vitols, M.M. (1963) Jokes among Southern negroes. *Journal of Nervous and Mental Disease*, 136, 162–167.

Pusey, A. (1990) Mechanisms of inbreeding avoidance in nonhuman primates. In J.R. Feierman (ed) *Pedophilia: Biosocial Dimensions.* New York: Springer Verlag.

Rachman, S.J. and Wilson, G.T. (1980) *The Effects of Psychological Therapy.* Oxford: Pergamon Press.

Reciniello, S. (1991) Towards an understanding of the performing artist. In G.D. Wilson (ed) *Psychology and Performing Arts.* Amsterdam: Swets and Zeitlinger.

Reissland, N. (1988) Neonatal imitation in the first hour of life: observation in rural Nepal. *Developmental Psychology*, 24, 464–469.

Riggio, R.E., Salinas, C. and Tucker, J. (1988) Personality and deception ability. *Personality and Individual Differences*, 9, 188–191.

Rinn, W.E. (1984) The neurophysiology of facial expression: a review of neurological and psychological mechanisms for producing facial expression. *Psychological Bulletin*, 95, 52–77.

Roe, K. (1985) Swedish youth and music: listening patterns and motivations. *Communication Research*, 12, 353–362.

Rosenberg, G.B. and Langer, J. (1965) A study of postural-gestural communication. *Journal of Personality and Social Psychology*, 2, 593–597.

Rosner, B.S. and Meyer, L.B. (1982) Melodic processes and the perception of music. In D. Deutsch (ed) *The Psychology of Music.* New York: Academic Press.

Rothbart, M.L. (1973) Laughter in young children. *Psychological Bulletin,* 80, 247–256.

Rotton, J. (1992) Trait humour and longevity: do comics have the last laugh? *Health Psychology,* 11, 262–266.

Rouget, G. (1985) *Music and Trance: A Theory of the Relations Between Music and Possession.* Chicago: University of Chicago Press.

Rowe, A. (1989) Personality theory and behavioural genetics: contributions and issues. In D.M. Buss and N. Carter (eds) *Personality Psychology: recent trends and emerging directions.* New York: Springer Verlag.

Rowley, P.T. (1988) Identifying genetic factors affecting musical ability. *Psychomusicology,* 7, 195–200.

Rule, J. (1973) The actor's identity crisis: postanalytic reflections of an actress. *International Journal of Psychoanalytic Psychotherapy, 2,* 51–76.

Sackheim, H.A., Gur, R.C. and Saucy, M.C. (1978) Emotions are expressed more intensely on the left side of the face. *Science,* 202, 434–436.

Sagan, C. (1977) *The Dragons of Eden.* New York: Random House.

Salk, L.S. (1962) Mother's heartbeat as an imprinting stimulus. *Transactions of the New York Academy of Science,* 24, 753–763.

Salmon, P. (1991) Stress inoculation techniques and musical performance anxiety. In G.D. Wilson (ed) *Psychology and Performing Arts.* Amsterdam: Swets and Zeitlinger.

Salmon, P. and Newmark, J. (1989) Clinical applications of MIDI technology. *Medical Problems of Performing Artists,* March, 25–31.

Salmon, P., Schrodt, R. and Wright, J. (1989) Preperformance anxiety in novice and experienced musicians. *Medical Problems of Performing Artists,* 4, 77–80.

Sanders, T. (1978) *How to be a Compleat Clown.* New York: Stein and Day.

Saper, B. (1991) A cognitive–behavioural formulation of the relation between the Jewish joke and anti-Semitism. *Humour: International Journal of Humour Research,* 4, 41–59.

Schachter, S. (1959) *The Psychology of Affiliation.* Stanford: Stanford University Press.

Schachter, S. and Singer, J.E. (1962) Cognitive, social and physiological determinants of emotional state. *Psychological Review,* 69, 379–399.

Scheff, T.J. (1976) Audience awareness and catharsis in drama. *Psychoanalytic Review,* 63, 552–553.

Scheff, T.J. (1979) *Catharsis in Healing, Ritual and Drama.* Berkeley: University of California Press.

Schierman, M.J. and Rowland, G.L. (1985) Sensation-seeking and selection of entertainment. *Personality and Individual Differences,* 6, 599–603.

Schoenmakers, H. (1990) The spectator in the leading role. Developments in reception and audience research within theatre studies: theory and research. *Nordic Theatre Studies,* 3, 93–106.

Schopenhauer, A. (1819) *The World as Will and Representation.* Leipzig: F A Brockhaus.

Schreck, E.M. (1970) *Principles and Styles of Acting.* Reading, Ma: Addison-Wesley.

Schurcliff, A. (1968) Judged humour, arousal and the relief theory. *Journal of Personality and Social Psychology,* 8, 360–363.

Schuster, L. (1991) Effects of brief relaxation techniques and sedative music. In G.D. Wilson (ed) *Psychology and Performing Arts.* Amsterdam: Swets and Zeitlinger.

Schwartz, G.E., Brown, S.L. and Ahern, G.L. (1980) Facial muscle patterning and subjective experience during affective imagery: sex differences. *Psychophysiology,* 17, 75–2.

Seashore, C.E., Lewis, D. and Saetveit, J. (1960) *Manual of Instructions and Interpretations for the Seashore Measures of Musical Talents (2nd revision).* New York: The Psychological Corporation.

Seligman, M.E.P. (1989) *Learned Optimism.* New York: Knopf.

Sergeant, D.C. (1969) Experimental investigation of absolute pitch. *Journal of Research in Musical Education,* 17, 135–143.

Sher, A. (1985) *The Year of the King: an actor's diary and sketchbook.* London: Chatto.

Shields, J.R. (1991) Semantic–pragmatic disorder: a right hemisphere syndrome? *British Journal of Disorders of Communication,* 26, 383–392.

Shimoda, K. Argyle, M. and Ricci-Bitti, P. (1978) The intercultural recognition of emotional expressions by three national–racial groups. *European Journal of Social Psychology,* 8, 169–179.

Shuter-Dyson, R. and Gabriel, C. (1981) *The Psychology of Musical Ability (2nd edition).* London: Methuen.

Siegel, J.A. (1972) The nature of absolute pitch. *Experimental Research in the Psychology of Music,* 8, 54–89.

Simon, B. (1988) *Tragic Drama and the Family: psychoanalytic studies from Aeschylus to Becket.* New Haven, Conn: Yale University Press.

Skelly, C.G. and Haselrud, G.M. (1952) Music and the general activity of apathetic schizophrenics. *Journal of Abnormal and Social Psychology,* 47, 188–192.

Skinner, M. (1989) Face to face with assymetries in facial expression. *The Psychologist,* 10, 425–427.

Sloboda, J.A. (1990) Musical excellence – how does it develop? In M.J.A. Howe (ed) *Encouraging the Development of Exceptional Skills and Talents.* Leicester: British Psychological Society.

Sloboda, J.A. (1991) Music structure and emotional response: some empirical findings. *Psychology of Music,* 19, 110–120.

Sloboda, J.A. and Howe, M.J.A. (1991) Biographical precursors of musical excellence. *Psychology of Music,* 19, 3–21.

Smith, K.U. (1984) 'Facedness' and its relation to musical talent. *Journal of the Acoustical Society of America,* 75, 1907–1908.

Snow, S. (1991) Working creatively with the symbolic process of the schizophrenic patient in drama therapy. In G.D. Wilson (ed) *Psychology and Performing Arts.* Amsterdam: Swets and Zeitlinger.

Soibelman, D. (1948) *Therapeutic and Industrial Uses of Music.* New York: Columbia University Press.

Sommer, R. (1959) Studies in personal space. *Sociometry,* 22, 247–260.

Sosniak, L.A. (1990) The tortoise, the hare and the development of talent. In M.J.A. Howe (ed) *Encouraging the Development of Exceptional Abilities and Talents.* Leicester: British Psychological Society.

Spencer, H. (1885) *The Principles of Sociology.* London: Williams and Norgate.

Spencer, M.E. (1973) What is charisma? *British Journal of Sociology,* 24, 341–351.

Spender, N. (1983) The cognitive psychology of music. In J. Nicholson and B. Foss (eds) *Psychology Survey No. 4.* Leicester: British Psychological Society.

Stacey, C.L. and Goldberg, H.D. (1953) A personality study of professional and student actors. *Journal of Applied Psychology,* 17, 24–25.

Stafford, R.E. (1970) Estimation of the interactions between heredity and environment for musical aptitude in twins. *Human Heredity,* 20, 356–360.

Stanislavski, C. (1936) *An Actor Prepares* (trans. E R Hapgood). New York: Theatre Arts Books.

Starr, A. (1977) *Rehearsal for Living: Psychodrama.* Chicago: Nelson Hall.

Starr, A. (1979) *Psychodrama: Illustrated Therapeutic Techniques.* Chicago: Nelson Hall.

Steinberg, R. and Raith, L. (1985) Music psychopathology I: Musical tempo and psychiatric disease. *Psychopathology,* 18, 254–264.

Steptoe, A. and Fidler, H. (1987) Stage fright in orchestral musicians: a study of cognitive and behavioural strategies in performance anxiety. *British Journal of Psychology,* 78, 241–248.

Stevens, A. (1982) *Archetype: a natural history of the self.* London: Routledge and Kegan Paul.

Strasberg, L. (1988) *A Dream of Passion.* London: Bloomsbury.

Stumpf, K. (1898) *Die Anfänge der Musik.* Leipzig: Barth.

Styan, J.L. (1975) *The Dramatic Experience.* Cambridge: Cambridge University Press.

Suhor, C. (1986) Jazz improvisation and language performance. *Etc,* 43, 133–140.

Suter, S. (1986) *Health Psychophysiology: mind-body interactions in wellness and illness.* Hillsdale, NJ: Erlbaum Associates.

Thaut, M.H. (1989) The influence of music therapy interventions on self-rated changes in relaxation, affect and thought in psychiatric prisoner-patients. *Journal of Music Therapy,* 26, 155–166.

Thompson, W.B. (1987) Music sight reading skill in flute players. *Journal of General Psychology,* 114, 345–352.

Tiger, L. (1969) *Men in Groups.* New York: Random House.

Tomkins, S.S. (1991) *Affect, Imagery, Consciousness. Vol. III. The negative affects: anger and fear*. New York: Springer Publishing Co.

Toohey, J.V. (1982) Popular music and social values. *Journal of School Health*, 52, 582–585.

Tulloch, J.O., Brown, B.C., Jacobs, H.L., Prugh, D.G. and Green, W.A. (1964) Normal heartbeat sound and the behaviour of newborn infants: a replication study. *Psychosomatic Medicine*, 26, 661–670.

Valentine, E.R. (1991) Alexander technique for musicians: research to date. In G.D. Wilson (ed) *Psychology and Performing Arts*. Amsterdam: Swets and Zeitlinger.

Valentine, E.R. (1993) The effects of lessons in the Alexander technique on music performance in high and low stress situations. Paper presented at the *Second International Conference on Psychology and Performing Arts*, Institute of Psychiatry, London.

Varley, H. (ed)(1980) *Colour*. New York: Viking Press.

Vernon, P.E. (1977) Absolute pitch: a case study. *British Journal of Psychology*, 68, 485–489.

Wagner, R. (1851) A communication to my friends. In W.A. Ellis (trans) (1893) *Richard Wagner's Prose Works*. New York: Bronde Brothers.

Walk, R.D. and Samuel, J.M. (1988) Sex differences in motion perception of Adler's six great ideas and their opposites. *Bulletin of the Psychonomic Society*, 26, 232–235.

Ward, W.D. and Burns, E.M. (1982) Absolute Pitch. In D. Deutsch (ed) *The Psychology of Music*. New York: Academic Press.

Weaver, J.B. (1991) Exploring the links between personality and media preferences. *Personality and Individual Differences*, 12, 1293–1299.

Webster, J. (1991) The use of the movement metaphor in movement therapy. In G.D. Wilson (ed) *Psychology and Performing Arts*. Amsterdam: Swets and Zeitlinger.

Weick, K.E., Gilfillian, D.P. and Keith, T.A. (1973) The effect of composer credibility on orchestra performance. *Sociometry*, 36, 435–462.

Weidenfeller, J.W. and Zimny, G.H. (1962) Effects of music upon GSR of depressives and schizophrenics. *Journal of Abnormal and Social Psychology*, 64, 307–312.

Wertheim, N. and Botez, M. (1961) Receptive amusia: a clinical analysis. *Brain*, 84, 19–30.

Williams, K. (1985) *Just Williams*. London: Dent.

Wills, G. and Cooper, C.L. (1988) *Pressure sensitive: popular musicians under stress*. London: Sage.

Wilson, G.D. (1966) Arousal properties of red versus green. *Perceptual and Motor Skills*, 23, 947–949.

Wilson, G.D. (1973) Abnormalities of motivation. In H.J. Eysenck (ed) *Handbook of Abnormal Psychology*. London: Pitman Medical.

Wilson, G.D. (1978) *The Secrets of Sexual Fantasy*. London: Dent.

Wilson, G.D. (1981) *Love and Instinct*. New York: Morrow.

Wilson, G.D. (1982) Richard Wagner – psychoanalyst. *Bethlem and Maudsley Gazette* (Summer edition).

Wilson, G.D. (1984) The personality of opera singers. *Personality and Individual Differences*, 5, 195–201.

Wilson, G.D. (1989) *The Great Sex Divide*. London: Peter Owen.

Wilson, G.D. and Brazendale, A.H. (1973) Sexual attractiveness and response to risqué humour. *European Journal of Social Psychology*, 3, 95–96.

Wilson, P.R. (1968) Perceptual distortion of height as a function of ascribed social status. *Journal of Social Psychology*, 74, 97–102.

Winkleman, M. (1986) Trance states: a theoretical model and cross-cultural analysis. *Ethos*, 14, 174–203.

Wolverton, D.T. and Salmon, P. (1991) Attention allocation and motivation in music performance anxiety. In G.D. Wilson (ed) *Psychology and Performing Arts*. Amsterdam: Swets and Zeitlinger.

Wrightsman, L.S. (1977) *Social Psychology*. Monterey, CA: Brooks Cole.

Youngman, H. (1981) *Henny Youngman's 500 All-time Greatest One-liners*. New York: Pinnacle Books.

Zajonc, R.B. (1965) Social facilitation. *Science*, 149, 269–275.

Ziv, A. (1984) *Personality and Sense of Humour*. New York: Springer.

Zuckerman, M. (1991) *Psychobiology of Personality*. Cambridge: Cambridge University Press.

Subject Index

Author Index